EARLY AMERICAN ANTIQUE COUNTRY FURNISHINGS

Northeastern America, 1650–1800

George Neumann

AMERICAN LEGACY PRESS
New York

This 1988 edition is published by American Legacy Press, distributed by
Crown Publishers, Inc., 225 Park Avenue South, New York, New York 10003,
by arrangement with McGraw-Hill Book Company

Manufactured in the United States of America

Library of Congress Cataloging-in-Publication Data
Neumann, George C.
    Early American antique country furnishings.
    Reprint. Originally published: New York: McGraw-Hill,
c1984.
    Bibliography: p.
    Includes index.
    1. Country furniture—Northeastern States—History—
17th century.   2. Country furniture—Northeastern States
—History—18th century.   I. Title.
NK2408.5.N48   1988   749.214   87-33459
ISBN 0-517-66183-7

h g f e d c b a

❧ CONTENTS ☙

INTRODUCTION ● 7

VOLUME I.   COUNTRY FURNITURE ● 9

Beds ● 11
Chests ● 16
Cupboards ● 34
Desks and Boxes ● 45
Floor Coverings ● 53
Lighting ● 53-54
Looking Glasses ● 80
Seating ● 86
Tables, Stands ● 127
Timekeeping ● 151

VOLUME II.   COOKING AND EATING ● 155

Cooking ● 155
Woodenware ● 223
Ceramic Tableware ● 237
Pewter Tableware ● 276
Glassware ● 288

**VOLUME III.   PERSONAL CARE
AND INDULGENCES ● 301**

Art ● 302
Fabrics ● 304
Personal Articles ● 317
Smoking ● 328
Games and Playthings ● 332
Writing, Documents ● 333

GLOSSARY ● 343

BIBLIOGRAPHY ● 346

INDEX ● 350

With special appreciation to

Elaine Salls

*. . . who so generously shared her knowledge from
more than thirty years as a collector, dealer,
artisan, and historian in colonial furnishings to
make this book possible*

❦ INTRODUCTION ❦

The classification of colonial antiques is a tenuous state of the art that turns and twists according to the category, region, or individual. At one end of the scale we find the "high-style" forms of the wealthy class, and at the other, the "primitives"—typically viewed as crude products of the poor or newly settled families. Realistically, the overwhelming amount of furnishings in the colonies were used by those between these extremes. They comprised the middle ground that stretched from frugal farmers and rural squires, to artisans and small businessmen in the emerging urban centers.

When beginning this book, I was warned that most collectors are quick to say what *country* does *not* include, but are equally committed to evading a definition of their own. So let me begin by stating how I have used the term.

My objective is to describe and illustrate the home furnishings of that part of America's northeastern population that lived between the two social extremes. They are referred to today as the "broad middle class." They comprised the great bulk of the citizenry, and were the motivating force that made the colonies successful. They were neither the starving poor nor the merchant princes. They were hard-working and often crowded families who lived modestly but in tolerable comfort, with sufficient food for the table and effective shelter from the elements. It is their furnishings which I consider *country*.

Even by the mid-17th century, I believe, most established colonists in that agricultural economy were within this category. Moreover, many already owned singular possessions of comparative elegance, which were harbored for special occasions. As settlements spread inland during the 1700s, new villages appeared, and older centers expanded. Though still meager in outlying regions, life in most established communities grew increasingly easy and was more gently lived by these middling classes. Their steady progress toward affluence has been reflected here by the inclusion of more elegant forms toward the end of the 1700s.

Thus, my use of *country* might better be termed *broad country*—largely eliminating the *most primitive*, and the *most formal*—to present the *most typical*. The word, *furnishings*, in turn, has been limited to those common wares found in the living area of a middle-class colonial home. This definition led to the exclusion of such categories as farm implements, working tools, building hardware, and personal clothing.

Because country material covers so much of the breadth of early life, most publications describing it have been limited to individual categories such as furniture, lighting, treen, and ironware. In an effort to consolidate some of this dispersion, *Early American Antique Country Furnishings* has been prepared to provide a single source for the student to trace the variations of each country category through a series of dated illustrations. In this way, it is possible to go beyond the mere memorization of standard patterns and develop a sensitivity to the phases of a style's development. More than 1,500 photographs are included, showing in excess of 1,800 items.

To best organize this coverage, the book has been subdivided into three internal volumes: I. Furniture, II. Cooking and Eating, and III. Personal Care and Indulgences. They are comprised of a total of twenty-one categories, each of which is illustrated to best trace the subject's evolution from 1650 to 1800.

The dates were selected to cover the colonial era of America, extending from the mid-1600s, by which time the early colonists were established and producing more of their own furnishings, to the end of the 1700s, when precisely defined patterns from centralized production were beginning to flow into the marketplace.

Coverage has been restricted to the northeastern states in order to keep within the confines of a single book, and because the great majority of early country examples in today's market are attributed to this area. The geographic limitations also reflect: the establishment of New England, New York, New Jersey, and eastern Pennsylvania as the traditional center of colonial antique collecting; the fact that a great many of the northeastern styles were exported to other colonies; and, subsequently, that substantial numbers were transplanted westward by settlers moving across the country or around the Horn to California. Pennsylvania-German furnishings have been omitted in most cases because their distinctive form deserves a separate study.

European and oriental furnishings which would have been used in the colonies are also illustrated here. Household possessions accompanied many immigrating families. Moreover, contrary to the popular opinion that little more than English goods were imported under the restrictive Navigation Acts, such limitations were commonly evaded. Until the end of the Revolutionary War, smuggling from Continental Europe, Canada, Newfoundland, and the West Indies was among the most active occupations along the American seaboard. Even within the colonies, immigrating craftsmen tended to repeat the traditional styles of their homelands. In this way, the characteristics of England, Holland, France, Germany, Scandinavia, and Spain all contributed to our early country furnishings.

When a piece is not given a date, it is deemed to be typical of the period covered by this book. Despite efforts to verify all of the material shown, some incorrect identification is bound to occur, and for this I offer my apologies in advance. Further guidelines include decisions to allow for correct restoration work on unique pieces, to add an occasional example of development higher than country to illustrate a major style source or variation, and to combine all of the pictorial nomenclature for easier reference (pages 332–334). A handful of identified reproductions have also been illustrated to fill gaps in the reader's background. I hope that these judgments will prove helpful.

Pieces from my own collection are included and many are identified.

It is not possible to list all of those who generously gave their time and assistance to help produce this work. Many are noted with appreciation under illustrations from their collections, but special acknowledgment is also extended to these individuals:

To Elaine Salls, who so generously shared her extensive experience and knowledge of this field; to Frank Kravic for enthusiastic encouragement and access to his impressive collection; and to Marie Curtis who rescued my camera work with the endless photographic prints required.

To Horace Porter, Lillian Blankley Cogan, David Bland, Marvin Salls; Joan W. Friedland, Christopher P. Bickford, Anne F. Luders, and George M. Prattson of the Connecticut Historical Society; Patricia Ballard, Emery and Susan Fletcher, George C. Woodbridge, Leo Wilensky, Robert Nittolo; Kevin M. Sweeney at the Webb-Deane-Stevens Museum, Wethersfield, Conn.; Robert M. Sack of Israel Sack, Inc., New York City; David and Marjorie Schorsch, Inc., Greenwich, Conn.; Timothy C. Neumann, Deerfield Memorial Hall Museum of the Pocumtuck Valley Memorial Association, Deerfield, Mass.; Mrs. Dorothy Lunde for the Stanley-Whitman House, Farmington, Conn.; John Whitmore of the Thankful Arnold House, Haddam, Conn.; Naomi Johnson of the Museum of Fine Arts, Boston; Mrs. Dorothy Y. Armistead, Henry Whitfield House, Connecticut Historical Commission; Mrs. William S. Gaines from the Harrison House, Branford (Conn.) Historical Society; Richard Ryan, Nassau County Museum; the Metropolitan Museum of Art, New York City; Richard J. Koke at the New-York Historical Society; Mrs. Ward S. Becker, Jr., the Jonathan Dickerman House, Hamden (Conn.) Historical Society; William Cuffe, Yale University Art Gallery; James N. Haskett and Susan D. Hanna at the Colonial National Historical Park, Yorktown-Jamestown, Va.; Lorraine and Lennox Beach; William Markham; Ann Buckley, the Wadsworth Atheneum, Hartford, Conn.; Dr. and Mrs. Melvyn D. Wolf, Michelle Smith; Jean R. Butler at Robert W. Skinner, Inc., Bolton, Mass.; J. Paul Hudson, the Archeological Society of Virginia; Regina Blaszczyk, Alice McKinney, Wanda D. Peterson, and Joyce Gouliet of the Smithsonian Institution; Cindy Lawson, the Country Stencilers, Sandy Hook, Conn.

GEORGE C. NEUMANN

COUNTRY FURNITURE

"COUNTRY" DEFINED: In the absence of a precise meaning, the word *country* has been diffused through a multitude of applications—limited in some cases to the most primitive household wares, and in others to everything except the highest level of luxuries. In order to provide the most definitive coverage, I have chosen a liberal interpretation. It embraces the "broad middle class" that existed between the "primitive" and "high fashion" ends of the scale. Thus, the local farmer, small country squire, and urban artisan could all be included in this definition of country furnishings:

> . . . *Those pieces of furniture and in-home implements used by both the modest and more established middle-class families to satisfy their daily needs. This material was not necessarily crude, but utilitarian and sturdy—often incorporating design influences of the high styles found in wealthy homes.*

As described earlier, "my use of *country* might better be termed *broad country*—largely eliminating the *most primitive* and the *most formal*—to present the *most typical.*" The leveling of America's society toward this middle ground was well expressed by the wife of the Reverend Henry Smith (Wethersfield, Conn.) during the Revolutionary War: "A man of the best birth and breeding may yet be a mechanic or a tradesman by reason of the poverty of the land, and the fact that so many of our forefathers had been obliged to give up all their estates when for conscience sake they left the Mother Country."

SHIFT TO DOMESTIC PRODUCTION: Little has survived of the limited furnishings used in the initial settlements, but by the mid-1600s the colonists had begun to create more household wares. Restricted by space and sparse conditions, the furniture of the 17th century was essentially seats, tables, and storage chests. As the people prospered, however, new demands induced cabinetmakers, joiners, and country handymen to supply a wide range of material. Through our book's century-and-a-half period, the majority of America's manufactured goods were imported, but these local producers filled a steadily expanding share—particularly furniture. In the process, they created simpler and less ornate styles which were often unique variations of the familiar European patterns.

INDIVIDUAL INTERPRETATIONS: Instead of designing their furniture from models or style books of the period, the country craftsmen usually created forms from memory, incorporating their own interpretations of contemporary high styling they might have been exposed to in such centers as Boston, Newport, New York, Philadelphia, or Charleston. Moreover, this work was usually modified to fit a specific space and use, usually from materials at hand. To cope with the trying demands of active colonial life, their work was functional, sturdy, and surprisingly innovative—but seldom shoddy.

VARIETIES OF WOOD: Living near the great forests of North America, the makers had an almost unlimited choice of woods to draw upon. Following the English practice, oak was the principal selection of the 1600s, but a broad variety soon came into play. Pine (initially the "hard yellow" pine which predominated in the Northeast at the time) and maple were widely employed, as were walnut, cherry, butternut, hickory, ash, and the fruitwoods. "Whitewood" (usually tulip, poplar, or basswood) was commonly used as a secondary wood for the parts of an object normally out of sight.

It was not unusual to choose several varieties for a single piece of furniture. The selection would take into account the wood's availability, how it behaved when green or dry, plus personal preferences toward texture, color, and finishing. For example, a chair seat of green wood with well-dried legs inserted into it would shrink to form an extremely tight bind. To cope with the various stresses and properties of a Windsor armchair, you might find a hickory back bow, ash spindles, maple arms, a pine or chestnut seat, and maple legs. Nails were used sparingly as the wood-on-wood interlocking dovetails, pinned mortise-and-tenon joints, et cetera were found to be stronger and more durable. It should also be remembered that most of the furniture was painted.

EUROPEAN STYLING INFLUENCE: During the 17th and 18th centuries, a succession of fashions from Europe were adopted here (although lagging several years behind the Old World). As might be expected, they became incorporated into our local country pieces, whose characteristics commonly overlapped during periods of change or in regions which were slow to abandon established forms. Thus, the majority of items were transitional, and combined more than one pattern. The periods during which these designs were most accepted by Americans are considered in this work to be circa

Pilgrim	1650–1720
William & Mary	1700–1725
Queen Anne	1725–1770
Chippendale	1750–1790
Hepplewhite	1780–1800

Variations of specific types of furniture such as the Windsor and Pembroke forms were also important and are illustrated. Against this background, it should be kept in mind that some individual makers continued to produce these styles well into the 1800s—thus the broad dating for some items shown.

Further distortions were introduced as many of the prospering middle-class families retained their earlier simple furniture for servants, handymen, or visitors long after it was out of fashion—and, conversely, lesser colonists frequently obtained elegant furnishings of an earlier era at auctions or as castoffs by the well-to-do.

The periods can be briefly described as:

PILGRIM (1650–1720): *Characteristics*—heavy, bold turnings; massive proportions; shallow incised carvings; applied moldings; wooden knob handles; *woods favored*—oak, pine, maple.

WILLIAM & MARY (1700–1725): *Characteristics*—lighter turnings; large ball, "bun," and turnip feet; trumpet, cup, or block-and-turned legs; flat or turned stretchers; wooden knob handles, teardrop brasses or cotter-pin bail handles; *woods favored*—pine, maple, walnut.

QUEEN ANNE (1725–1770): *Characteristics*—more delicate proportions; cabriole legs with pad feet; shell and sunrise carvings; the scrolled skirt; scrolled bracket feet; chair yoke-type crest rails and vase-shaped splats; large turned stretchers; both flat and broken pediments on case pieces; bat wing or early willow brass plates with bails; *woods favored*—pine, maple, cherry, walnut.

CHIPPENDALE (1750–1790): Originally recorded in Thomas Chippendale's *The Gentleman and Cabinet-Maker's Director* (London, 1754); *Characteristics*—more formal designs; straight fluted, reeded, or beaded square-sectioned legs; bracket-type chest bases; pierced chair splats; simple inlays; cabriole legs with claw and ball feet on the more formal pieces; willow brass, or loop handles mounted on small circular or oval rosettes; *woods favored*—maple, walnut, cherry, mahogany (imported).

HEPPLEWHITE (1780–1800): Summarized in George Hepplewhite's posthumous *The Cabinet-Maker and Upholsterer's Guide* (London, 1788); *Characteristics*—formal but more slender forms; square-sectioned tapering legs (often with spade feet); shield-shaped open chair backs; inlays of contrasting woods; brass handles with rosettes, or stamped oval brass plates and bails; *woods favored*—maple, walnut, cherry, mahogany.

Beds

During the 17th and 18th centuries, the term *bedstead* was used to identify the wooden frame on which bedding was placed. *Bed*, in turn, usually referred to the bedding itself, i.e., the mattress and hangings.

At the time of the first American settlements, the tradition of a high 4-post bedstead covered with heavy cloth curtains and trappings (to keep out the night cold) had already been well established in Europe. It was usually limited to the master and mistress of the home, however, and left the rest of the household to less pretentious arrangements. Surprisingly, this practice was continued here in many country dwellings, but with a lighter frame than the Old World's heavily turned form. Thus the lesser members of the early family often fared as did the newest settlers, by sleeping on top of storage chests, on the floor, or under the eaves—with little more than a bed of straw or a lumpy tick.

These early improvised situations were soon improved by elementary bedsteads of low posts and rails, often incorporating simple headboards. Rope was used to crisscross the center of the frame as a support for the mattress ("bed") stuffed with a wide range of materials at hand such as feathers, straw, corn husks, wool, or horsehair.

The high-post bedstead persisted through the 18th century for the master and mistress (see **#5**), with lighter cloth hangings reflecting the advent of smaller rooms and relatively warmer homes. It also appears that the European practice of sleeping in a half-sitting position by using a long bolster under the pillows was continued in America for much of this period.

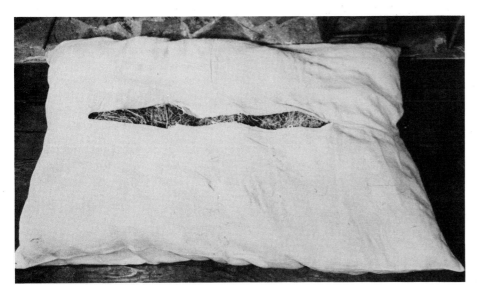

(Left) **1. TICK (or BED):** A tow linen bag stuffed with straw or soft fillers usually served as bedding on the roped bedstead or the floor. (Lower left) **2. UTILITY BEDSTEAD, c.1690–1820:** A simple bedstead form that fitted into a crowded chamber, attic, or back room; the pinned butternut frame has mortise & tenon joints; 17$^{1}/_{2}$" H, 74$^{1}/_{2}$" L, 25$^{3}/_{4}$" W. (Below) **3. LOW-POST BEDSTEAD, c.1740–1800:** This more finished 18th-century bedstead adds a double-arched headboard of pine to its chestnut frame; 22$^{1}/_{2}$" H, 78$^{1}/_{2}$" L, 55" W (Author).

(Above) **4. BED HANGINGS, c.1750–1760:** Hangings were used throughout the colonial period—usually including an upper valance and four side curtains ranging from a plain or check design (*above*) to the more formal crewelwork (see **#1375**); they concealed most of the bedstead, which encouraged simple frames until shorter hangings, c.1790, increased their visibility enough to spur the ornamental post turnings of the 1800s.

(Upper left) **5. HIGH-POST BEDSTEAD, c.1740–1800:** Such tall thin-posted frames persisted throughout the 18th century; "testers" join the posts' upper ends to create the flat canopy from which the hangings were draped. These tapering faceted posts are now known as the "pencil-post" form; curly maple, 86″ H, 77″ L, 53$\frac{1}{2}$″ W (Conn. Historical Society).

(Left) **6. LOW-POST BEDSTEAD, c.1720–1740:** A rare New England bedstead that incorporates a pair of Queen Anne cabriole legs with pad feet, as well as more typical turned legs under the headboard; maple, 28$\frac{1}{2}$″ H, 74$\frac{1}{2}$″ L, 51″ W (Israel Sack, Inc., N.Y.C.).

(Lower left) **7. TRUNDLE (TRUCKLE) BEDSTEAD, c.1750:** A low-post applewood New England bedstead with a space-saving "trundle" bed that could roll on wooden casters under the higher frame during the day; it was used mostly for children, servants, or visitors (see **#12**); 76″, 60$\frac{1}{4}$″ Lengths (Israel Sack, Inc., N.Y.C.).

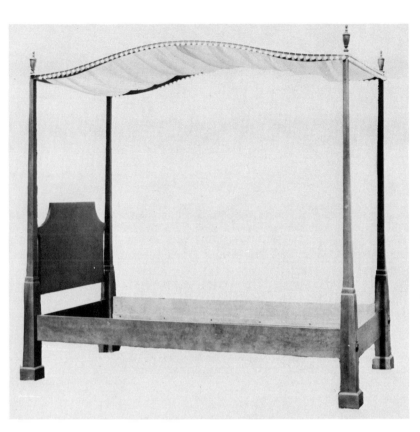

(Left) **8. FIELD (TENT) BEDSTEAD, c.1780–1800:** About 1780 a new frame with an arched canopy was introduced in Philadelphia and rapidly gained popularity in the Northeast. It was originally designed for easy dismantling when not in use—in a manner similar to the military camp bedstead; this curly maple New England version includes Hepplewhite-style urn finials and squared Marlborough legs; 73″ H, 78″ L, 53½″ W (Conn. Historical Society).

(Below) **9. FOLDING (PRESS, SLAW) BEDSTEAD** (two views), **c.1740–1760:** To save space, some bedsteads were hinged to raise the lower section of their frame during the day, as shown in the two positions (*below*); the partial "crane" canopy with its diagonal braces supported two wide curtains which normally concealed the raised section; the frame is maple and still bears the original red paint. It was found in Mass. Note, too, the exposed bulbous turned posts at the foot vs. the more mundane squared legs of the usually covered headboard; 89″ H, 77½″ L, 53″ W (Israel Sack, Inc., N.Y.C.).

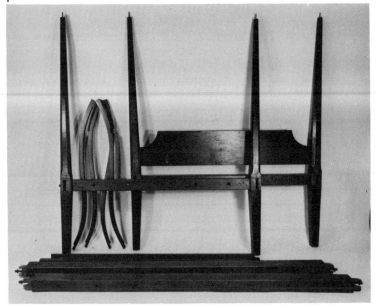

(Upper left) **10. FIELD BEDSTEAD, c.1780–1800:** A field bedstead ("pencil-post" form) disassembled to illustrate its convenience for storage between periods of use; note the hinged arched-canopy frame and mortises in the posts to receive the side-rail tenons, which were often marked with Roman numerals for matching; 51″ W (Private Coll.).

(Upper right) **11. COT (CAMP) BEDSTEAD, c.1750–1800:** This simple country form folds lengthwise where the legs cross; the two pine headboards are removable (their pivoting wooden pins penetrate holes in the side rails), and heavy tow canvas is nailed along the sides of its chestnut frame; the chamfered legs secure mortised side stretchers; 24″ H, 72″ L (Author).

(Left) **12. TRUNDLE BEDSTEAD, c.1740–1800:** Wooden wheels for rolling under a larger bedstead or into a corner are set into each of the turned maple posts (see **#7**); its chestnut rails secure a roped linen canvas that supported the bedding—a variant (mostly after 1730) to the more common crisscrossed cords (see **#2**); 16″ H, 66″ L.

(Lower right) **13. IRON BEDKEY, c.1780:** A handwrought iron key used to tighten those bedsteads that were held together with iron bolts; 6½″ H.

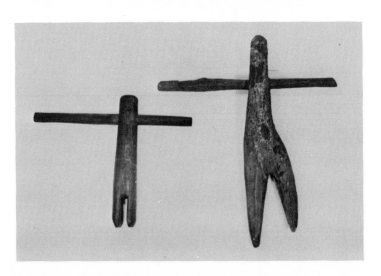

(Lower left) **14. WOODEN BEDKEYS (WINDERS, WRENCHES), c.1700–1850:** These forked implements helped to tighten the cord laced through holes in the frame; the rope was hooked through the forked end outside of the rail, and the handle turned to take up the slack; 11½″, 19″ H.

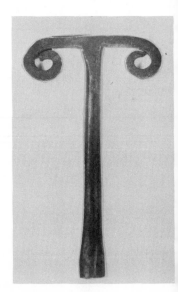

(Upper left) **15. CRADLE, c.1660–1690:** Cradles were important not only as a baby's sleeping and resting place, but also as protection from chilling drafts in the house; this early oak example employs the pegged frame construction of the Pilgrim period (see page 21) and includes a "hood" (or "bonnet"); 36″ L (Museum of Fine Arts, Boston).

(Upper right) **16. CRADLE, c.1720–1740:** By the 1700s, some cradles omitted the hood (the homes were warmer); note, too, these board sides vs. the 17th-century paneled form (see #15), although the earlier knob finials on its posts remain; Queen Anne influence appears in both of the double-scrolled ends; 36³/4″ L (Henry Whitfield House, Guilford, Conn.; Conn. Historical Commission).

(Center left) **17. CRADLE, c.1750–1850:** A further variation of the hoodless cradle evolved later in the 1700s by omitting the footboard; these corners are dovetailed, and the bottom is attached by heavy rosehead nails. (Above) **18.** This underside view illustrates the common use of a stretcher to strengthen the rockers; 40″ L.

(Below) **19. BED SMOOTHER, c.1700–1820:** A heavy form that was drawn over the bedding to smooth it; the top of this example has chamfered edges; 24″ L.

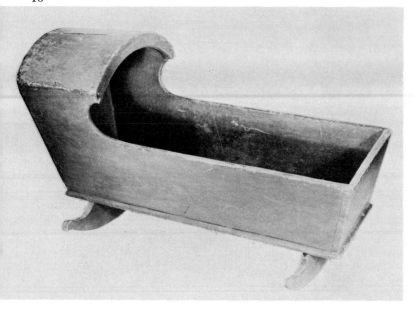

Chests

The American settlers used chests primarily to hold clothing, household linens, and bedding. In the 1600s, they were essentially large wooden boxes with a hinged lid. Most consisted of plain ''6-board'' construction (four sides, top, and bottom), although the better 17th-century chests were of the framed-panel form and even bore carving in the tradition of the Old World (see **#42**). English-made examples were invariably of oak. The early colonists continued this precedent initially, but often substituted pine for the lid and back.

As the 1600s ended, one or more drawers were often being added at the bottom. Their number increased during the early 18th century, forcing the box area higher and higher—creating in many cases a combination of the chest-of-drawers form supporting a top-lidded blanket chest, on which were mounted false drawer fronts that imitated the real ones below.

About 1700, a further European innovation made inroads among the more worldly Americans as the ''highboy'' appeared on the scene (see **#91**). This concept of a chest mounted on a long-legged base was, in turn, fading by 1780 as the Chippendale and Hepplewhite traditions restored preference for the lower chest-of-drawers (**#74**), or the more capacious chest-on-chest (**#97**).

In the course of this evolution, the successive styles continually overlapped in use, while the ever practical 6-board chest remained the principal storage vehicle. Although many of these finer 18th-century American ''case pieces'' utilized chestnut, walnut, and mahogany (plus interior whitewoods), the less pretentious country chests generally clung to the traditional pine, cherry, or maple.

HOODED CRADLES: (Upper left) **20. c.1700–1760:** The rounded hood was popular during the earlier 1700s; 39″ L. (Upper right) **21. c.1730–1760:** Note the Queen Anne scrollwork on this footboard, as well as the sidewalls of its flattened hood; side handholds have also been added; pine; 41½″ L (Branford [Conn.] Historical Society; on loan from Mr. & Mrs. Frank H. Reichert).

(Lower right) **22. BOARD CHEST, c.1620–1680:** This English ''Pilgrim'' chest includes early broad dovetails, an applied scalloped apron, incised front-edge molding in the lid, plus projecting ''shoe feet''; oak; 18″ H, 44″ W (Author).

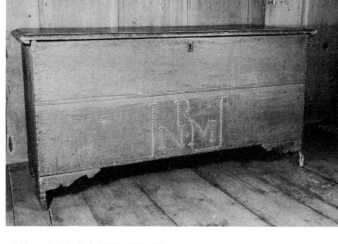

(Upper left) **23. BOARD CHEST, c.1650–1680:** An early long, narrow form in hard pine, plus whitewood (secondary) for the back, bottom, and till; its lower front molding is applied, and the bottom follows the English practice of boards from front to back; butt joints; the lid includes a thumb-molded edge and end cleats to prevent warping; 20$\frac{1}{2}$″ H, 46″ W (Private Coll.).

(Above) **24. BOARD CHEST, c.1680–1700:** This heavy pine chest has applied scalloped brackets at the base corners, and a center punchwork design forming family initials (Middletown, Conn.); notice the deep shadow molding across its front; cotter-pin hinges; old brownish-red paint; 26$\frac{1}{2}$″ H, 53″ W (Lillian Blankley Cogan).

(Right) **25. BOARD CHEST, c.1690–1700:** An oak 6-board chest with incised carving and lower scalloped brackets; the sideboards are extended and notched in typical fashion to create the legs; nailed butt joints; 24″ H, 40$\frac{1}{2}$″ W (Private Coll.).

(Below) **26. BOARD CHEST, c.1700–1710:** This hard pine single board chest front includes a scrolled lower profile, while the lid adds two incised decorative channels along its leading edge; wooden pintle hinges; nailed butted joints; 24$\frac{3}{4}$″ H, 40$\frac{1}{2}$″ W (Author).

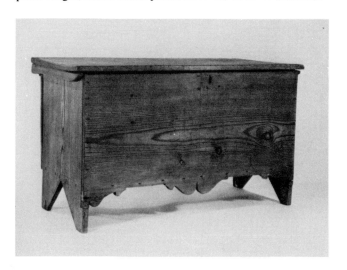

(Below) **27. PINTLE HINGE:** Because of the scarcity of iron, many early chests used a "pintle" or wooden hinge; it was normally an extended dowel penetrating the cleat of a lid as shown.

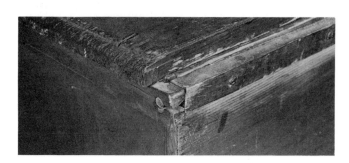

18

(Upper left) **28. BOARD CHEST, c.1680–1700:** Rows were often cut into the front and sides by a "creasing" plane to create "shadow" or "linenfold" molding (17th-century decoration); 24″ H, 53¹/₂″ W (Private Coll.). (Below) **29. BOARD CHEST, c.1720–1760:** This raised paneling was carved into the chest face; pine, painted red; 23″ H (Conn. Historical Society).

(Upper right) **30. BOARD CHEST, c.1720–1760:** Lower base molding was often applied to balance an extended lid; these sides are rabbeted and nailed; pine; 25″ H. (Below) **31. COTTER-PIN (STAPLE, SNIPE) HINGES:** This rear of a thumb-molded lid shows the interlocked loops of a cotter-pin hinge, and the spread of its emerging ends at the top.

(Lower left) **32. BOARD CHEST, c.1750–1780:** A "shoe foot" chest (i.e., projecting feet) with applied moldings; Mohawk Valley; 19¹/₂″ H. (Lower right) **33. TILL:** A small interior compartment (normally with a dowel-hinged lid); this open pair is unusual.

BOARD CHESTS: (Upper left) **34. c.1750:** A plain chest (Mohawk Valley, N.Y.) with a single strip of molding nailed across the front; its plank sides are scroll-cut to create the common leg form; pine; nailed rabbeted joints; 20″ H, base 33¼″ W, 14¼″ D. (Upper right) **35. c.1770–1820:** Furniture was often made for a specific space—per this narrow chest; flat molding is applied to three sides of the lid, and the butted joints are nailed; pine, red paint; 25″ H, 22¼″ W, 17⅛″ D.

BOARD CHESTS: (Left) **36. c.1750–1800:** A simple pine storage form with nailed joints, cotter-pin hinges, and blue paint; 25″ H, 44″ W, 17″ D. (Lower left) **37. c.1780–1800:** The molded bracket base continued until c.1820, but this pine chest in red includes 18th-century features, i.e., the lid's molded edge, its nailed end cleats, an inside till, and a dovetailed base (*close-up below*); 19½″ H, 31 W, 15″ D (Author).

BOARD CHESTS: (Upper left) **38. c.1690–1720:** Many chests omitted feet; note the early broad dovetails, reinforcing iron straps (arrowhead finials) and oval lock plate; hard pine; 11″ H, 28¹/₂″ W, 14¹/₂″ D. (Above) **39. c.1740–1760:** A base molding has been applied here to complement the extended thumb-molded lid; dovetailed body; pine; 13″ H, 37″ W, 16¹/₂″ D.

(Above) **40. BOARD CHEST, c.1750–1820:** Chests with an applied bracket on each end that held a looped handle ("becket") are usually attributed to shipboard use, but they also saw service in the home; strap hinges; covered till (usual wooden dowel hinge); 15¹/₂″ H, 40³/₄″ W, 14³/₄″ D.

(Above) **41. BOARD CHEST, c.1790–1820:** False graining was a decorative practice that became fashionable in the late 1700s; it enhanced simple furniture and covered marginal woods; the paint was often applied by corncobs, sponges, feathers, combs, cloth, brushes, and even potatoes; this is an early effort; 19″ H, 47″ W, 17″ D.

(Left) **42. JOINED (FRAMED, WAINSCOT) CHEST, c.1667–1700:** Formal 17th-century English chests were usually "joined," i.e., a basic frame of pinned horizontal "rails" and vertical "stiles" enclosing panels; this oak example, attributed to Thomas Dennis (1638–1706, Ipswich, Mass.), includes face and side panels with carving in the shallow manner of the 1600s; 30¹/₈″ H, 49¹/₈″ W, 21¹/₄″ D (Metropolitan Museum of Art).

JOINED CHESTS: (Left) **43. c.1660–1700:** An American chest with four face panels, plus three on each end; "palm" carving appears in the front panels, "lunettes" on the upper rails, and "rosette" forms in the front drawer; it has a white oak body and pine lid; 36″ H, 53¾″ W, 21″ D (Wadsworth Atheneum). (Center Left) **44. c.1650–1680:** A foliate frieze outlines the three front raised panels; the side panels are also carved; its lid lifts out (never hinged), and the bottom boards are from front to back in the English tradition; pinned oak frame; 21″ H, 35½″ W, 17″ D. (Below) **45. c.1680–1700:** Dutch and William & Mary influence are apparent in this applied geometric molding and indented panel pattern; American (New England); the hard pine is painted red and black; its 2-piece lid has reeded edges; 25½″ H, 39¾″ W, 20¾″ D (Private Coll.).

(Below) **46. JOINED CHEST, c.1680–1700:** A chest made low enough for normal seating (19″ H); notice, too, the two raised panels, lift-off lid (two cleats fit back into the rear wall), the shallow drawer, and teardrop pulls (Author).

(Below) **47. JOINED CHEST, Marked 1648:** Only a single lunette frieze, initials, and the date 1648 are carved into this less-ornate framed chest; oak; 25½″ H, 50½″ W, 22″ D.

(Left) **48. JOINED CHEST, c.1670–1700:** Some chests added turned black spindles and applied panel moldings; red and black paint traces remain here; oak; 24″ H, 42″ W, 15″ D (Conn. Historical Society). (Center left) **49. "SUNFLOWER" CHEST, c.1680–1710:** A form too elaborate for most country homes, but popular in central Conn.; note its characteristic sunflower and tulip carving, plus applied spindles and egg-shaped "bosses"; pegged oak frame; 39¾″ H, 48″ W, 21″ D (Conn. Historical Society). (Below) **50. "HADLEY" CHEST** (two views), **c.1670–1710:** A style found in the Hadley, Mass., area having flat shallow-carved tulip and foliage designs (*see close-up*); these chests were commonly given in the dowry (note the initials); 30″ H, 43″ W, 18″ D (Stanley-Whitman House, Farmington, Conn.).

(Lower left) **51. JOINED CHEST, c.1700:** A "Hadley"-style chest holding three drawers (notice the period's turned wooden drawer pulls); flat foliate carving covers the entire front—painted for contrast in black and red; its body is oak with a pine lid; 45¾″ H (Deerfield Memorial Hall Museum, PVMA).

JOINED CHESTS: (Upper left) **52.** Dated **"1705/6":** About 1700, painting began to replace carving; this black-painted Guilford (Conn.) area chest bears "tulip" panels and colored "speckles"; 32″ H (Conn. Historical Society). (Right) **53. c.1695–1720** (two views) A "Deerfield" variation of the "Hadley" form uses painted designs (not carved) in black, orange, mustard, brown, and white; 44″ H (Deerfield Memorial Hall Museum, PVMA).

(Below) **54. JOINED CHEST, c.1700–1710:** This "Hatfield" (Mass.) area type is an uncarved 3-panel chest with unusual turned legs; its pinned hard pine frame is painted in red and black; the single-board top is held by cotter-pin hinges; 43¼″ H, 38″ W, 18″ D (Author).

(Above) **55. DRAWER CONSTRUCTION** (*From top*): (*1*) **c.1650–1700**, grooved for a side runner; the nailed sides include a single dovetail; (*2*) **c.1700–1750**, the drawer now sits on its runners and includes broad dovetails; (*3*) **c.1730–1810**, note the smaller dovetails; bottoms were now chamfered and held in side grooves (nailed at the back).

BLANKET CHESTS: (Upper left) **56. c.1690–1720:** A board chest with a bottom drawer added to create a "blanket chest"; it omits drawer pulls, and has a rabbeted, nailed body; 29″ H. (Upper right) **57. c.1700–1720:** By now plank chests with drawers were popular; this one mounts the early ball feet, brass "cotter-pin" handles (*right close-up*), plus applied base molding; 35″ H.

(Above) **58. BLANKET CHEST, c.1700–1720:** This top-hinged chest has two real bottom drawers with two false fronts above to simulate a chest-of-drawers; notice the typical William & Mary ball feet, teardrop brass pulls, single arch molding outlining the front, and applied base moldings; 41″ H (Author).

(Above) **59. BLANKET CHEST, c.1720–1750:** A lift-top chest that includes two real drawers (*bottom*) and two false panels; this period has added overlapping drawer edges, and "bat's-wing" pulls (only on the working drawers); 40¼″ H.

(Above) **61. BLANKET CHEST, c.1700–1730:** Country "case" furniture was often decorated in paint copying earlier carved patterns; this hinged-lid chest (Branford-Guilford, Conn., area) has one real drawer (two false), applied moldings, and painted designs in red and white on black; whitewood; 34″ H, 42″ W, 17½″ D (Conn. Historical Society).

(Above) **60. BLANKET CHEST, c.1720–1750:** A hinged-top pine chest above four actual drawers; its bracket base has dovetails, while the upper case is rabbeted; 56″ H (Stanley-Whitman House, Farmington, Conn.).

(Below) **64.** To dress a board, cabinet makers employed a jack ("fore," "jointer") plane which had a convex cutting edge. Its concave marks can still be seen in out-of-sight areas or felt by drawing your hand across a surface.

(Above) **62. CHEST BACKBOARD:** Wide boards were nailed to the rear and often beveled to reduce their visibility from the sides. (Center right) **63.** One way to lock a lidded chest's drawers was to cut a hole in line through their bottoms and pass a stick down from the top (lid had a lock).

BLANKET CHESTS: (Above) **65. c.1780–1800:** This chest's bracket base and simple bail handles with rosettes reflect the Chippendale influence; since most chests were painted, different woods were often used—per these contrasting upper false fronts and base; 37$\frac{1}{2}$″ H. (Upper right) **66. c.1780–1790:** A lift-top pine chest with double-arched front molding; 34″ H.

(Below) **67. BLANKET CHEST,** Dated **"1786":** A Pennsylvania "dower" (dowry) chest typically in paint-decorated softwood (poplar in this case); hinged lid; note the three drawers above its molded base (Metropolitan Museum of Art).

BLANKET CHESTS: (Above) **68. c.1780–1820:** Molded bracket bases sometimes became heavier in the late 1700s per this lidded chest; 44$\frac{3}{4}$″ H. (Right) **69. c.1785–1810:** These narrowed bracket base lines reflect the "French feet" (which curved slightly outward) used on finer Hepplewhite case pieces; 39$\frac{3}{4}$″ H.

(Above) **70. CHILD'S BLANKET CHEST, c.1790–1810:** Children's furniture was popular throughout our period; this black and red paint pattern and simple bracket base are typical of the late 1700s; its lift-top has leather hinges; 21½″ H.

(Above) **71. JOINED CHEST-OF-DRAWERS,** Marked **1701:** A William & Mary chest-of-drawers form with the usual molded panels and base, teardrop handles, and elaborate escutcheons; similar larger chests were often in two horizontal sections (center molding hid the joint); these front legs are flattened ball ("bun") feet; its back legs are rectangular extensions of the rear stiles; 30½″ H (Private Coll.).

CHESTS-OF-DRAWERS: (Above) **72. c.1700:** A pine 4-tier chest painted in a pastoral motif; notice the pierced escutcheons, teardrop pulls, and turned feet of this William & Mary era (Metropolitan Museum of Art). (Right) **73. c.1770–1800:** A rural example that mounts the typical Chippendale applied cornice and bracket base; five diminishing drawers; pine, painted red; 61″ H (Au.).

CHESTS-OF-DRAWERS:

(Left) **74. c.1750:** A midcentury form in cherry; note its molded drawer edges, willow brasses, and bracket base. (Right) **75. c.1780–1800:** As highboys lost appeal at this time, many had bracket bases added to their upper case to make a chest-of-drawers (see **#90**); walnut; 38³/₄″ H.

CHESTS-OF-DRAWERS:

(Middle left) **76. c.1720–1780:** A miniature chest for valuables that includes incised designs and inlays on the drawers; turned feet; pine; 13³/₄″ H. (Lower left) **77. c.1780–1810:** A rural form (Mass.) made of maple with straight plank legs and willow brasses; it was never painted; 37¹/₄″ H. (Lower right) **78. c.1785–1810:** Notice the late-century influence in these plain handles (round rosettes), oval escutcheons, and simplified scrolled feet; 35″ H (Author).

(Below) **79.** The upper case of a highboy re-mounted as a chest-of-drawers (see **#75**); it now shows the exposed ends of the top dovetails, normally left visible only on tops above eye level.

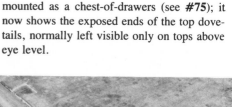

CHESTS-OF-DRAWERS: (Upper left) **80. c.1780–1800:** Note the period "serpentine" front, rosette handles, overlapping molded top, and scrolled bracket feet; its raised drawer molding is also Hepplewhite styling; 32³/₄″ H. (Upper right) **81. c.1780–1810:** A broad cornice, fan carving, willow brasses, and ogee bracket feet; 33¹/₂″ H. (Right) **82. c.1780–1810:** A N.H. pine chest; the initials "PB" are painted under a drawer (typical impromptu marking); 35″ H. (Lower left) **83. c.1790–1810:** Hepplewhite ogee bracket feet, oval brasses, curving "oxbow" front (the reverse of #80), and reeded corner columns; 38″ H (Conn. Historical Society). (Lower right) **84. CHEST-ON-FRAME, c.1690–1710:** Chests were sometimes raised on stands; this one has a hinged top and a single drawer; oak, pine, and maple; 34¹/₄″ H (Metropolitan Museum of Art).

CHESTS-ON-FRAME: (Upper left) **85. c.1720–1730:** A lift-top Conn. chest (top two drawer tiers are false fronts) on a frame with a scalloped apron and turned legs; pine, painted red; 57″ H (Conn. Historical Society). (Upper right) **86. "HIGH DADDY," c.1740–1760:** A Queen Anne scrolled apron and cabriole legs with cushioned pad feet; curly maple; made in Penn.; 55¹/₂″ H. **LOWBOYS (DRESSING TABLES):** (Below) **87. c.1700–1720:** The English William & Mary trumpet/inverted cup legs plus ball feet are braced by flat X-stretchers; scalloped apron and raised front molding; oak; 28³/₄″ H (Private Coll.). (Lower right) **88. c.1740–1760:** Note these Queen Anne cabriole legs plus scrolled apron and a thumb-molded top; sycamore; 27¹/₂″ H (Conn. Historical Society).

(Above) **89. DRAWER INTERIOR:** These recesses for the handle's screw extensions minimized damage to the drawer's contents; the nuts are cut from sheet brass.

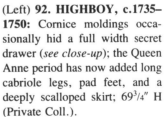

(Above) **90. CONVERTED LOWBOY, c.1780–1800:** As highboys lost favor, some were split into a chest-of-drawers (see **#75**) and a lowboy; this walnut base (c.1740) added a birch top to create an oversized lowboy—yet it retains the original "drops" (acornlike extensions under the apron); 36⅝″ H.

(Upper right) **91. HIGHBOY (HIGH CHEST), c.1700:** Highboys (chests on a low frame with drawers) appeared c.1700 in this William & Mary form that included a flat top, arched apron, and six ball-footed trumpet/inverted cup legs (often "trumpet & vase"); note the period teardrop pulls, pierced escutcheons, and double-arched outline molding; painted red; 60″ H (Conn. Historical Society).

(Left) **92. HIGHBOY, c.1735–1750:** Cornice moldings occasionally hid a full width secret drawer (*see close-up*); the Queen Anne period has now added long cabriole legs, pad feet, and a deeply scalloped skirt; 69¾″ H (Private Coll.).

(Right) **93. HIGHBOY, c.1740–1760:** An English form (American made) anticipates the Chippendale shorter legs; white oak; 59″ H.

(Left) **94. HIGHBOY, c.1750–1770:** As the Chippendale period develops, the cabriole legs are becoming shorter (and some added claw & ball feet); the heavy cornice continues, but the scrolled apron is less flamboyant (see **#92**); note, too, the graduated drawer heights and upper case's reeded corners; cherry; from Conn.; 71¼″ H (Private Coll.).

(Upper right) **95. HIGHBOY, c.1750–1770:** The straighter Chippendale lines appear in this classic country highboy from Portsmouth, N.H., (attributed to Dunlap); note the subdued apron, short cabriole legs, broad cornice (with dentil frieze), and fan carving on the bottom drawer (see **#96**); 75½″ H (Private Coll.).

(Right) **97. CHEST-ON-CHEST, c.1780–1800:** The highboy's decline at this time emphasized the more spacious "chest-on-chest" (i.e., double chests-of-drawers); this cherry example includes the period's wide cornice, broad ogee bracket feet, "roped" corner carving, and a fan-carved top drawer; 75¼″ H (Jonathan Dickerman House, Hamden [Conn.] Historical Society).

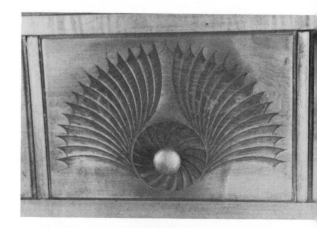

(Above) **96. HIGHBOY:** A close-up of the unique fan carving on the lower drawer of **#95**; note its interesting swirled technique vs. the normal straight radiating lines.

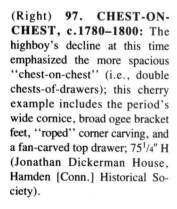

TRUNKS: (Upper left corner) **98. c.1690–1740:** Most personal shipping containers were 6-board chests (screw and nail holes are often found in lids); this alternate "trunk" has a staved dome lid, broad dovetails, and cotter-pin hinges; 13½" H. (Upper right corner) **99. c.1740–1800:** A Germanic style from Penn. mounting iron serpentine straps, end handles ("bails"), and a lock; pine; **inside till; 23″ H.**

TRUNKS: (Center left) **100. c.1770–1810:** Many were now covered by calfskin, deer hide, or canvas; this hide retained its fur (a "hair" trunk); most are lined by newspapers, wallpaper, or cloth; 13″ H. (Center right) **101. c.1770–1810:** A flat-top hair trunk; 17″ H. (Lower left) **102. c.1750–1800:** The cylindrical "round" hair trunk; 11½″ H. (Lower right) **103. c.1790–1830:** This heavy leather covering and elaborate tack design remained popular into the 1800s; its expandable lid is accessible through an inside trapdoor; 12″ H.

Cupboards

Cup boards was the early name for a series of open shelves that held cups and other eating utensils. About the third quarter of the 17th century, a supporting frame with doors began to be added. Two basic forms evolved from this: 1) a triangular shape made to fit into the corner as a self-contained unit, or built into the room's woodwork; and 2) the rectangular cupboard made to hang on a wall or stand against it. Large freestanding versions appeared in the 1600s as heavy "court" and "press" cupboards (which are too ornate for our country category), or as the large "kas" (see **#106**), a traditional form among Dutch and German settlers.

By 1700, the court and press styles had lost most of their appeal, while the kas continued in favor through midcentury. Their successors were more elementary storage enclosures—often with open shelves for displaying tableware above a closetlike base (see **#109**).

(Above) **104. CUPBOARD, c.1710–1750:** A country version of the 17th-century press cupboard; note its baluster-turned columns, scroll-cut sideboards, and raised door panels; pine and maple; 48¹/₂″ H (Metropolitan Museum of Art). (Below) **105. KAS, c.1740:** An unusual lighter form; pine and gumwood; from the Hudson River Valley (David & Marjorie Schorsch, Inc.).

(Below) **106. KAS (SCHRANK), c.1720–1740:** A large type of cupboard used to store clothes primarily by Dutch settlers ("kas"), and Penn. Germans ("schrank"); many were painted in this Old World fashion; notice the typical heavy cornice, broad doors, and ball feet; pine and oak; many had bottom drawers (Metropolitan Museum of Art).

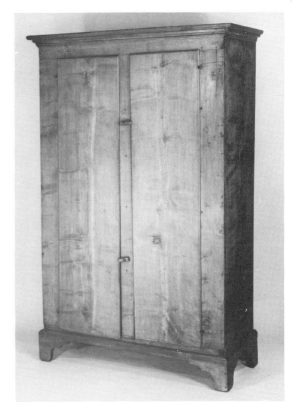

(Left) **107. CLOSED CUP-BOARD, c.1750:** A "stepback" pine cupboard from the Hudson Valley with four raised-panel doors on H hinges—which include typical inside latches (*lower right, opposite page*); 79″ H. (Center left) An outside latch shows a common leather washer under the nailhead.

(Lower left corner) **108. OPEN CUPBOARD (DRESSER), c.1730–1760:** This Penn. form mounts a heavy cornice (with a dentil frieze), raised-panel side drawers, shoe feet, and a spoon rack on the second shelf; walnut (Metropolitan Museum of Art).

(Lower right) **109. OPEN CUP-BOARD, c.1750–1780:** A New England dresser (open to display tableware and cooking vessels) includes scalloped sides, shelf grooves for standing plates, and protective rails; 71″ H (Author).

(Above) **110. CLOSED CUPBOARD, c.1760–1790:** Two plain doors on cotter-pin hinges, plus an applied cornice and a bracket base; blue paint traces remain; maple; four shelves inside; 69″ H.

CUPBOARDS: (Upper left) **111. OPEN, c.1750–1780:** A free-standing cupboard in green paint with an applied dentil-frieze cornice, beaded front corners, and a double-paneled door; 74″ H (Thankful Arnold House, Haddam, Conn.). (Upper center) **112. OPEN CORNER, c.1750–1770:** This barrel-back (i.e., rounded) cupboard includes typical open shelving (center oval projection) and a blue case—outlined by raised molding; 86″ H. (Upper right) **113. CLOSED CORNER, c.1740–1760:** It was permanently built into this corner; the butterfly hinges above and H-type below suggest that the top was originally open; a cornice usually repeated the room's molding; 88 1/2″ H (Author).

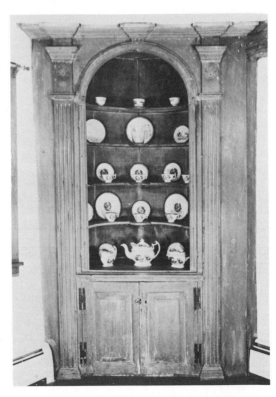

CORNER CUPBOARDS: (Far left) **114. BARREL-FRONT, c.1750–1770:** This rural pine New England cupboard has a flat cornice above a bowed molded front; the two doors are held by H hinges; four inside shelves; 73″ H (Roger Bacon; Robert W. Skinner, Inc.). (Near left) **115. OPEN, c.1740–1790:** A more refined example that bears classic flat columns at the sides, plus a rounded back and shelving; note the H hinges on its lower raised-panel doors; 88 1/2″ H (Harrison House, Branford [Conn.] Historical Society).

WALL CUPBOARDS: (Upper left) **116. c.1740–1760:** The back of this hanging cupboard is scrolled in the Queen Anne style, and iron strap hinges support the plank door; butt joints; two interior shelves; 30½" H. (Upper center) **117. c.1720–1750:** Note the three graduated drawers under a raised-panel door with butterfly hinges; applied moldings appear at each end; 47" H (Wadsworth Atheneum). (Upper right) **118. CORNER, c.1750–1770:** A pinned mortise & tenon frame holds this wide-paneled pine door on H hinges; New England; 32" H.

WALL CORNER CUPBOARDS: (Lower left) **119. c.1740–1760:** A black and red Penn. form with applied flat panels resembling the turned spindles and bosses of the 1600s (see #49); notice, too, the drawer in its upper frieze; 30" H (Ballard Coll.). (Lower center) **120. c.1740–1760:** A Penn. pine cupboard that includes a scalloped extension; applied molding; rare rattail hinges; 40½" H (Israel Sack, Inc., N.Y.C.). (Lower right) **121. SUNKEN WALL CUPBOARD, c.1780–1810:** A later flat frame (beaded edge) and plank door that cover a cupboard extending into the wall; from Maine; 18¾" H x 13½" W (Merle E. Bouchard).

WALL BOXES: (Above left) **122. c.1650–1660:** This early English oak box displays the common sloping lid (leather hinges) and bottom drawer (nailed); its early carving includes the "tree of life"; the sides taper toward the rear; 20″ H (Private Coll.). (Center) **123. c.1740–1780:** A later uncarved version retains the sloping lid and single drawer; it normally held salt or other kitchen needs; the joints are pegged; 14³/₄″ H. (Above right) **124. c.1760–1790:** A multi-unit form that contains an open box, lidded compartment, and a small base cupboard with a plank door (wire cotter-pin hinges); pine; corner beading; 22¹/₄″ H (Author).

WALL BOXES: (Above left) **125. c.1750:** A Penn. box for salt crystals; the scrolled sides reflect Queen Anne influence; yellow pine, painted in red (Metropolitan Museum of Art). (Above center) **126. c.1750–1800:** A common form for candles; its lid has a wooden dowel hinge; the corners are dovetailed—while the base is nailed; red painted pine; (*above right*) the arch includes a rear shim inset to retard warping; 12¹/₄″ H.

WALL BOXES: (Upper left) **127. c.1720–1750:** A salt box with a body and back carved from a single block of wood; its lid (cotter-pin hinges) and face bear chip and geometric carving; there are two internal compartments; 6⁵/₈″ H. (Below) **128. c.1750–1800:** A typical open candle box using butt joints; 12¹/₄″ H (Private Coll.). (Lower left corner) **129. c.1770–1780:** This later candle box has lowered the back and extended the base; 6¹/₂″ H.

(Above) **130. WALL BOX, c.1730–1780:** A compartmented box with a small drawer; it probably had a lid originally; note the front dovetailing (the rear is nailed); red paint over a mustard color; 11¹/₂″ H.

(Upper right) **131. WALL BOX, c.1750–1800:** A utility pine box made with narrow-headed nails and a framed back; 12³/₈″ H.

WALL BOXES: (Lower center) **132. c.1700–1740:** An early oak form using a vertical sliding cover; note the wide dovetailing; 12¹/₄″ H. (Lower right) **133. c.1730–1750:** This later English channeled cover omits the handle; a molded front; nailed joints; 20¹/₂″ H (Private Coll.).

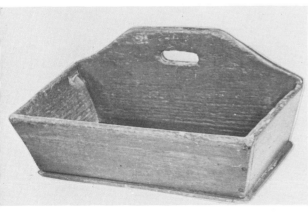

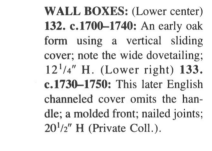

TABLE BOXES: (Near right)
134. c.1720–1750: A common
type for candles; the body is carved
from a single piece of wood, with
a sliding convex cover; blue-gray
paint; 3³/₈″ H. (Far right) **135.
c.1760–1780:** This is made in pine
using nailed sides and a wood-
pinned bottom (not to scratch the
table); note its raised panel on the
sliding cover; 4¹/₂″ H.

(Center left) **136. WALL BOX,
c.1750–1850:** A popular tinned
iron candle box incorporating
punched designs and a hinged oval
cover; 13″ L. (Center right) **137.
TABLE BOX, c.1750–1800:** The
body and handle are from one
piece of wood; 2″ H (Private
Coll.). (Left) **138. PIPE BOXES,
c.1740–1800:** Hanging boxes for
long clay pipes; their drawers held
accessories; 18″–23″ H (Wadsworth Atheneum). (Right) **139.
SPOON RACK, c.1690–1720:**
An early carved maple spoon rack
from New England; 15″ H (Private Coll.).

SPOON RACKS: (Upper left) **140. c.1700–1750:** (*Left to right*) (*1*) a New England carved form, dated "1745"; 24″ H; (*2*) a Dutch style, 24¹/₂″ H; (*3*) a Penn.-German type; 23¹/₂″ H (Wadsworth Atheneum). (Left) **141. c.1690–1730:** A rack shaped and carved from one piece of hard pine; 6¹/₄″ H. (Above) **142. c.1700–1750:** 2-tiered frame construction; note the scrolled Queen Anne top with scalloped valance and apron; green paint; 20³/₈″ H (Author).

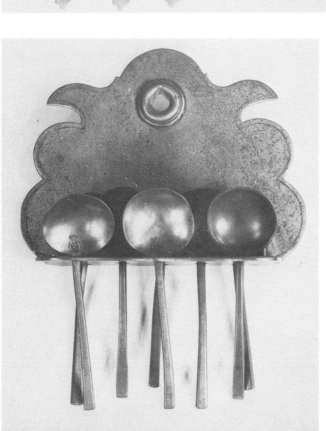

(Left) **143. SPOON RACK, c.1700–1750:** A William & Mary pewter form bent at a right angle to contain the spoons; note, too, the incised outline of its lobed silhouette; 7³/₄″ H (Joan W. Friedland).

(Right) **144. SPOON RACK, c.1730:** This tiered wooden form includes an inverted heart cutout at the top; 20″ H (Lillian Blankley Cogan).

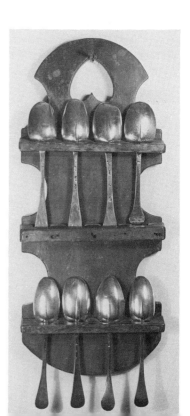

(Left) **145. WALL SHELF, c.1725–1800:** An elementary scalloped pine rack with plate rails and a covered top; nailed joints; 28³/₄″ H (Private Coll.). (Right) **146. OPEN FLOOR RACK (PEWTER STAND), c.1720–1760:** These shelves are mortised and tenoned; the stand also includes scrolled shoe feet, cutout forms at the top, rosehead nails, and rear plate rails; 33³/₄″ H (Au.).

(Right) **147. WALL SHELF, c.1730–1760:** A popular form having scrolled sides in the Queen Anne tradition; the shelves are mortised, and in this case, contain slots to hold spoons; 18¹/₂″ H.

(Lower left) **148. TABLE CHEST, c.1660–1690:** Such small chests held personal valuables, records, and papers; note its 17th-century characteristics, e.g., a heavy iron lock and escutcheon, broad dovetails, and a wide-channeled X decoration; its lid has cotter-pin hinges; the turned feet are restored; hard pine; crude nails; 8³/₄″ H. (Lower right) **149. TABLE BOX, c.1650–1720:** A primitive form having nailed butt joints and wire cotter-pin hinges; in dark oak; 2⁵/₈″ H.

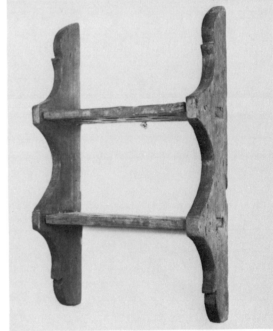

TABLE CHESTS: (Left) **150. c.1700–1730:** A miniature copy of a larger form—with applied base molding, simulated drawers, and ball feet; pine; 12″ H (Conn. Historical Society). (Right) **151. c.1740–1760:** An embossed leather-covered European chest outlined in brass petal brads—for the more affluent homes; 4³/₄″ H.

TABLE CHESTS: (Right) **152. c.1700–1750** (two views): A popular domed style covered in tooled brown leather; note the usual squared iron bail and lock plate; many such chests were lined with newspaper or book pages (*inside view*, dated "1677"); 4″ H. (Below) **153. c.1720–1750:** A miniature chest that includes applied lid and body molding, plus plank sides; 10³/₄″ H (Author).

TABLE CHESTS: (Below) **154. c.1750–1800:** A Mohawk Valley (N.Y.) domed box in green paint; it has a wire latch, cotter-pin hinges, nailed butt joints, and wallpaper lining; 3¹/₈″ H. (Right) **155. Marked "1780":** A box covered by painted scenes of trees, hills, and houses; its base is pegged and the corners rabbeted.

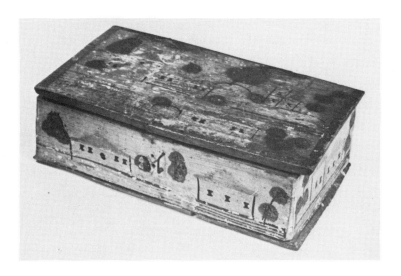

TABLE CHESTS: (Upper left) **156. c.1750–1780:** This plain pine box includes a projecting base, molded lid, and a reused brass escutcheon; 4³/4″ H. (Upper right) **157. c.1770–1820:** A small version of a hair chest (see **#100**); note its brass brads, and reuse of a willow drawer pull; "JP" were an owner's initials; 6³/4″ H. (Right) **158. c.1780–1800:** A leather-covered chest with decorative brass tacks, lock plate, and end handles; 5¹/2″ H.

(Above) **159. TABLE CHEST, c.1780–1800:** A Chippendale mahogany veneered chest with bracket feet; 7¹/2″ H. (Right) **160. TABLE CHEST, c.1790–1810:** An "oilcloth" box, using tow linen coated by tar and red-painted decoration; 4¹/2″ H. (Lower left) **161. KNIFE TRAY, c.1750–1780:** A green scrolled pine cutlery tray; 4³/4″ H. (Lower right) **162. TEA CHESTS (CADDIES), c.1770–1790:** They usually had two interior foil-lined compartments (for black and green teas); 5¹/2″, 6¹/4″ H.

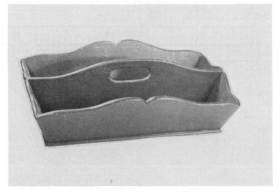

(Left) **163. KNIFE CASE, c.1750–1780:** An English formal form (vs. the common knife tray, #161); it includes gold-stamped leather, and interior table knife slots; 10³/₈″ H. (Right) **164. BANDBOX (BONNET BOX), c.1785–1830:** A clothing box for storage and travel; this early form has splint-wood sides and a wall-paper covering (cardboard typical in the 1800s); 10³/₄″ H.

Desks and Boxes

During the 1600s, the word *desk* meant a box for holding personal papers, writing materials, or valuable items such as the family Bible (thus today's term, *Bible box*). It normally sat on a table when in use and had a hinged lid which was either flat or slanted to serve as a writing and reading surface (see **#167–#183**). Many of the early versions continued the English practice of incised carving on the front, and often on both sides. By 1700, a number of desk boxes were being mounted on stands—subsequently known as "desks-on-frame" (see **#184–#186**).

The "slant-top" (or "front-fall") desk which was to dominate the 18th century, evolved just after 1700 (see **#187**). This design consisted of a writing compartment above a solid base that resembled a chest-of-drawers. The slant top swung out from the top to rest horizontally on a pair of retractable "pulls" at the sides. This provided a writing surface, and exposed a series of interior pigeonholes and small drawers. Its legs successively reflected the styles of the 1700s, from ball feet and cabriole legs to the later bracket bases of the Chippendale and Hepplewhite periods. The form finally lost its broad appeal by 1800.

A further development in the 18th century was the mounting of a bookcase or closed cabinet on the top of a front-fall desk to create the "secretary." Although most of them were too sophisticated to be considered country, some less formal examples do survive with a simple dignity (see **#193–#195**).

DESK BOXES: (Above) **165. c.1550–1650:** A peaked ("gabled") carved document box form brought by the earliest settlers; the center hinged lid is on this side only; iron straps and period carving; no compartments; 12″ H. (Below) **166. c.1580–1650:** The later flat-top box also has a hinged lid that extends to the center; turned feet; exterior iron hinges; 7³/₄″ H (Author).

DESK (DOCUMENT) BOXES: (Upper left) **167.** Marked **"1649"**: An early English box carved in the "Friesian" style (after the Dutch province); 9″ H (Conn. Historical Society). (Upper right) **168. c.1660–1690:** The typical English flat-top form of the late 1600s; its broad lid has wooden dowel hinges; carved lunette designs appear on three sides; pegged rabbeted corners; oak; 9″ H (Author).

DESK BOXES: (Upper left) **169. c.1675–1700:** English; the front carving includes pineapples (symbolizing "hospitality"); cotter-pin hinges; oak; 8¹/₂″ H (Private Coll.). (Upper right) **170. c.1680–1700:** This lid bears a fluted front edge and a pivoting support at the far side to hold it in a raised position; tulip-vine carving; chamfered base; rabbeted and nailed corners; oak; 6³/₄″ H.

DESK BOXES: (Above) **171. c.1700:** This flat carving resembles the Hadley chests (see **#50**); the "A B" was Abigail Ball of Springfield, Mass., 1683–1760 (probably part of her dowry); made of beech, oak, and pine; 9″ H. (Right) **172. c.1680–1710:** Early shadow molding (see **#28**) was employed here; hand-painted red wavy lines added decoration to a black base; nailed; 9″ H (both, Conn. Historical Society).

(Upper left) **173. DESK BOX, c.1690–1710:** A burl veneered box of the William & Mary period that is not typically country, but appears for the reader's information; burl veneer was common on finer furniture at this time; notice also the curving brass inlays; its original leather hinges were replaced by brass; 5″ H.

(Upper right) **174. DESK BOX, c.1700–1720:** Another William & Mary form mounting the popular raised geometric molding on its overhanging lid; hard pine, painted brown and green; iron strap hinges; dovetailed corners; it was used by Dutch settlers in the Hudson Valley; 7″ H (Private Coll.).

(Center left) **175. DESK BOX, Marked "1725":** This is the simplified New England overhanging lid style (c.1700–1730) that superseded the elaborate Pilgrim types (*opposite page*); nailed rabbeted corners; "M 1725 R" is painted on the front of its red base; an interior till includes a molded lid; 8½″ H (Author).

(Upper left) **176. DESK BOX, c.1780–1800:** A Conn. pine box (never painted) with applied moldings on the cover and base (see **#39**); note the narrow dovetails of the late 1700s; strap hinges; 6½″ H. (*Right*) The interior of **#176** shows its common iron box lock (c.1750–1850) set into a mortise cut behind the front; turning the key extends a notched catch to engage a slot in the lid; finer pieces usually had brass locks.

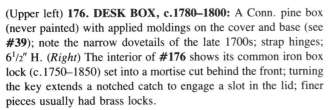

48

(Upper left) **177. DESK BOX, c.1750–1770:** A Penn. box with incised carving of a bell ringer and barnyard fowl; chip carving appears on the dovetailed corners—the top and bottom are pegged: 10¼″ H.

(Upper right) **178. DESK BOX, c.1740–1790:** Desk boxes became simpler and usually omitted carving after 1735; this blue-painted pine example from Maine retains rabbeted joints (large rosehead nails), and the overhanging lid (which includes side cleats and chamfered edges), but reduces its base flush with the sides; 10″ H.

(Left & below) **179. DESK BOX (three views), c.1690:** A companion to the flat desk boxes was the "slant-top" form; the English oak version here displays butterfly hinges, carved rosettes, tulips, and the S pattern of the late 1600s—as well as the initials "IH" and date "1690"; the close-up (*below*) shows its shallow 17th-century carving with a typical stippled background; (*lower left*) interior reveals shelves and double-faced drawer; 13″ H (Author).

(Right) **180. DESK BOX, c.1690–1720:** An early European slant top that omits the flat rear surface but has strap hinges, broad dovetails (bottom is nailed), and squared iron side handles; 6³/₄″ H. (Below) **181. PORTABLE DESK** (two views), **c.1750–1790:** A tapered chest from N.J. that includes an interior hinged writing board, storage compartments, and a covered till; exterior tinned-iron straps; pine, painted blue; a practical design for travel or a crowded home (see **#1494**); 11³/₄″ H.

(Above) **182. DESK BOX, c.1720–1740:** This oak "Bible box" has a reduced base and early rectangular iron hinges (early screw slots off-center); three inside drawers; 10¹/₂″ H.

(Right) **183. DESK BOX, c.1740–1760:** An American example using an extended chamfered base and a thumb-molded lid held by exterior butterfly hinges (notice the jack-plane marks on its surface; see **#64**); it includes a single internal shelf; pine, painted red; nailed; pointed keyhole escutcheon; 14″ H (Author).

DESKS-ON-FRAME: (Upper left) **184. c.1690–1710:** As house space increased, desk boxes acquired tablelike bases; this William & Mary walnut version sits on "vase & ring" turned legs, and ball (bun) feet—joined by period flat stretchers; 38″ W (Wadsworth Atheneum). (Above) **185. c.1680–1695:** An early oak table desk that was mounted on a later chestnut country base (c.1710–1730); note its scrolled apron and pad feet; 28″ W. (Left) **186. c.1720–1730:** A pine slant-top desk box (molded bookrest on lid) above a single drawer and turned legs; maple H-stretcher; 29″ W (Wadsworth Atheneum).

SLANT-TOP (FRONT-FALL) DESKS: (Left) **187. c.1700–1710:** The lid is hinged to open forward as a horizontal writing surface; this early walnut example mounts ball feet and outline arched molding on the front (Metropolitan Museum of Art). (Right) **188. c.1730–1750:** A Mass. Queen Anne base that includes drawers, a cyma-curved apron, and cabriole legs; maple (Smithsonian Institution).

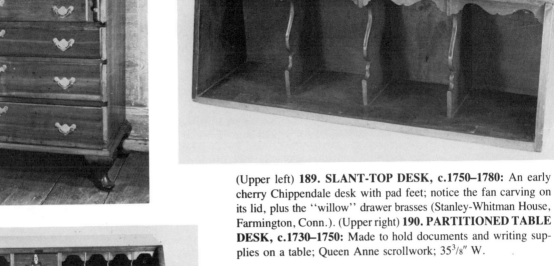

(Upper left) **189. SLANT-TOP DESK, c.1750–1780:** An early cherry Chippendale desk with pad feet; notice the fan carving on its lid, plus the ''willow'' drawer brasses (Stanley-Whitman House, Farmington, Conn.). (Upper right) **190. PARTITIONED TABLE DESK, c.1730–1750:** Made to hold documents and writing supplies on a table; Queen Anne scrollwork; 35^{3}/$_{8}$″ W.

(Above & right) **191. SLANT-TOP DESK** (two views), Marked **''1783'':** Mahogany; on the drawer bottom is written, ''. . . built at Newport, R.I., for Joseph Congdon . . . 1783'' (a common dating practice); (*above*) the ''blockfront'' interior is typical of Newport; molded base and ogee bracket feet; 37″ W (Author).

(Left) **192. SLANT-TOP DESK** (two views), **c.1790–1820:** This late-century desk has a simple bracket base and willow brasses; (*below*) most desks included a secret compartment; 35^{1}/$_{2}$″ W (Author).

(Left) **193. SECRETARY, c.1700:** Secretaries were slant-top desks with a cabinet mounted on top; they appeared about 1700 in this William & Mary form, i.e., ball feet, teardrop brass pulls, and single-arch outline molding (see **#187**); the detachable upper section here may have been added later (re the Queen Anne arched door panels); 34″ W (Wadsworth Atheneum).

(Right) **194. SECRETARY** (two views), **c.1771–1780:** A bonnet-top Chippendale cherry secretary attributed to Eliphalet Chapin (Conn.); note the top's three finials, scrolled cornice (with dentil frieze), and carved rosettes (*close-up below*); two pull-out candlestick slides are just above the work area; 37″ W (Private Coll.).

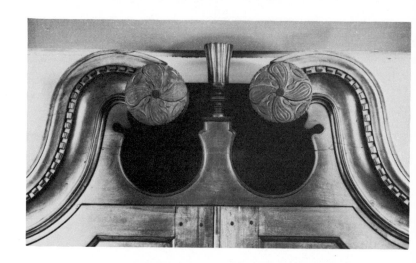

(Left) **195. SECRETARY, c.1780–1800:** Secretaries became most popular during the 18th century's last quarter; country versions were usually this flat-top Chippendale form; later Hepplewhite secretaries often had windows (i.e., "glazed"); notice these late-century flat door panels and plain bracket base; the shelves are adjustable (slotted sides); walnut and cherry, plus pine as a secondary wood; eastern Conn.; 40″ W (Private Coll.).

Floor Coverings

Floor coverings were the exception rather than the rule in colonial America. Oriental-style carpets (called "Turkey carpets") were owned only by the wealthy, and are usually pictured draped over furniture instead of underfoot. Most early home floors were packed earth or plank flooring that remained bare, except for occasional small plaited or woven mats of grass or rushes—or a daily sprinkling with sand.

By the mid-18th century, however, a number of the more well-to-do middle class began using imported or domestic "canvas carpets" (or "floorcloths") to cover heavily trafficked areas. These were pieces of canvas covered with coats of paint or varnish, usually in or-

namental designs (see **#196**). They wore well and were easily repaired. Some households even painted floors of less active rooms in geometric patterns.

Toward the late 1700s, striped carpets were sometimes created locally from heavy homespun woolen yarn in broad lengthwise stripes. Despite these limited innovations, the professional carpets being produced in England and Scotland at the time made little penetration in America, as the traditional bare floors predominated well into the 19th century. (Note: Prior to 1800, the word *carpet* designated floor and table coverings; *rug* referred to covers for the bed, e.g., **#1379**).

(Left) **196. CANVAS FLOORCLOTH,** A reproduction of a c.1750–1810 painted floorcloth; it was normally a canvas or sailcloth covered with several coats of paint; squares, cubes, diamonds, or marblelike designs were typical (Reproduced by Country Stencilers, Sandy Hook, Conn.).

(Right) **197. WOVEN FLOOR COVERING, c.1770–1810:** A section (21″ W; several were sewn together for full size) of a wool and linen floor covering; its colors are black, brown, red, white, and three shades of green; from northern N.Y. (Private Coll.).

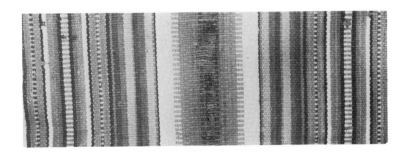

(Below) **198. NAILS:** These handwrought nails include the common rosehead forms (*left*), produced by five hammered strokes at an angle, plus the narrow L-headed nails (*right*) for trim and flooring. Machine-made cut nails with hammered heads appeared in the late 1700s (identifiable by their even and uniform shank).

Lighting

Lighting the home during our colonial era was at best inadequate. The most effective illumination after dark remained the ever-present fire on the hearth until oil lamps became popular around 1820. In the meantime, such sources as grease, oil, rushes, splints, pine knots, and candles were all burned to produce small flames, which did little beyond bringing a suggestion of light to a darkened room. Yet, in the pursuit of these alternatives, lamps and holders were produced in a great variety of shapes from numerous materials.

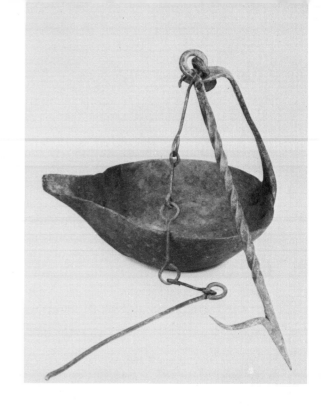

GREASE (CRUSIE, SLOT) LAMPS: (Right) **199. c.1680–1780:** This earliest supplementary lighting form began in the ancient world and was common in Europe and America; the pan was filled with grease, fat scraps, fish oil, vegetable oil, and (after c.1760) whale oil; a simple wick or rag in the nose slot fed from the fuel; this early sheet-iron open pan has a chain-attached pick to remove or adjust the wick, and a hanging spike; 7^1/$_2$″ W. (Left) **200. c.1700–1800:** A single open pan with a long handle for carrying or attaching it to the wall; 7^1/$_2$″ H.

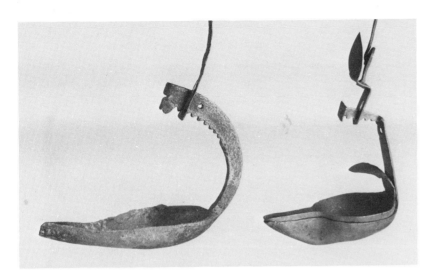

GREASE LAMPS: (Above) **203. c.1700–1800:** This "canting" crusie style with its notched arm allowed a forward tip to feed oil into the wick. (Right) **204. c.1700–1730:** A Dutch brass "pan" (or "sad") lamp which permitted wicks along its edge; 5″ L (Au.).

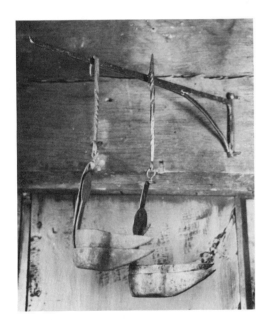

(Opposite page, two, far left) **201. DOUBLE GREASE LAMPS, c.1700–1820:** These nested crusie lamps doubled the light potential and caught dripping grease from the top lamp—which was also removable as a portable light; 4³/₄″–5³/₄″ W. (Two, near left) **202. 4-SPOUT GREASE LAMPS, c.1680–1780:** These squared crusie lamps could burn up to four wicks; 5″–6″ H.

GREASE LAMPS: (Center left) **205.** Double crusie lamps are hanging from a pivoting iron wall crane. (Above) **206. c.1785–1820:** This variation, called the "Betty" lamp, was a late 1700s improvement; its slot now mounted a V-shaped or tubular wick support and a hinged cover; 4⁷/₈″, 3³/₄″ W. (Left) **207. c.1700–1800:** A glazed earthenware single crusie, plus a turned wooden stand (to raise the lamp for greater light and cleanliness).

(Upper left, two rows) **208. LAMP HOLDERS, c.1690–1760:** European-made wrought-iron hooks that supported grease lamps; (upper right) their rear spikes were driven into a wall or post. (Left) **209. GREASE LAMP, c.1680–1700:** An English Lambeth Delft lamp with a saucer base to catch the overflow; 4″ H (Private Coll.). (Lower left & below) **210, 211.** **GREASE LAMPS, c.1725–1825:** Redware lamps on columns with saucer bases (called "fat lamps" in Penn.); 9½″, 10½″ H. (Lower right) **212. OIL LAMP, c.1700–1800:** The brass "lucerna" lamp popular in Mediterranean areas; the wicks in its three spouts fed from a central oil reservoir; the handle was also for hanging; 12⅞″ H.

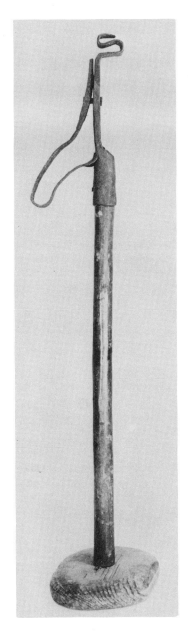

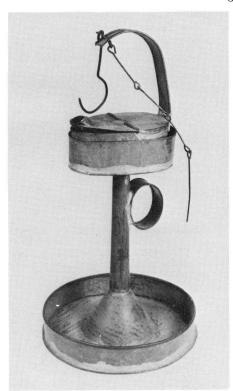

The other primitive lighting method (vs. the grease lamp) was to coat wooden splints or the center (''pith'') of rushes with fat for burning. (Left) **213. SPLINT HOLDER, c.1660–1750:** This S-shaped iron head held splints (horizontally), and its spring handle formed rushlight jaws; the wooden base is restored; 30″ H. (Below) **214. RUSHLIGHT HOLDERS, c.1680–1750:** Typical wrought-iron holders that used plierslike pincers to secure a burning rush (or splint); (*right*) a candle socket has been added (c.1720); 9″–10½″ H (Author).

(Above center) **215. GREASE LAMP, c.1750–1840:** A cast-iron form that includes a post and 3-legged saucer base; 6¼″ H. (Above right) **216. ''IPSWICH'' GREASE LAMP, c.1790–1820:** A hinged-top Betty lamp sits in this tinned-iron columnar stand (a ''tidy''); note the hanging hook and wick pick; 11½″ H.

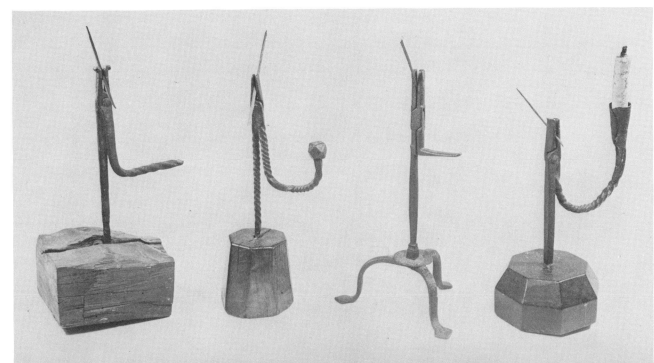

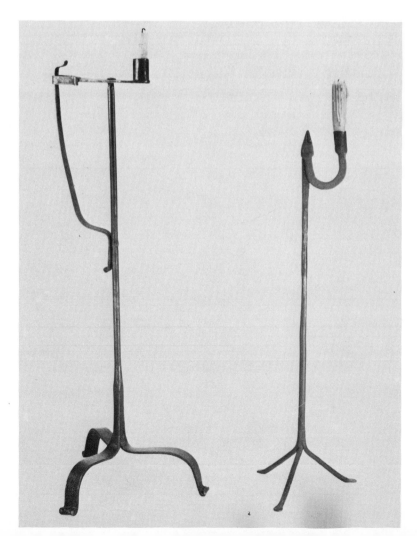

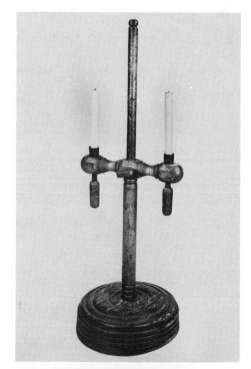

 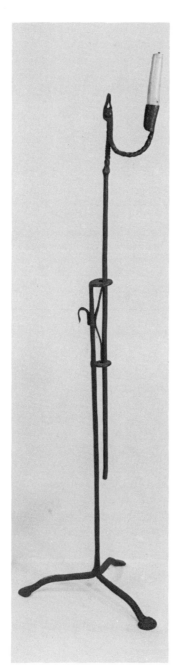 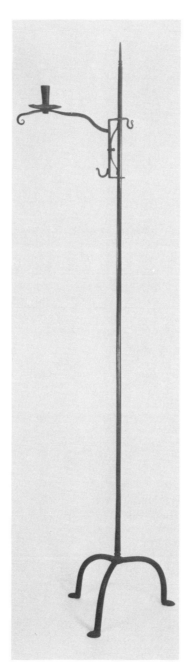 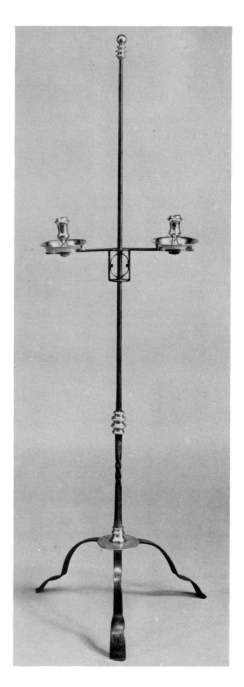

CANDLESTANDS: (Opposite page) **217. c.1690–1740:***(upper left)* This iron stand has a cup on trunnions with a candle socket; its side ring originally attached a snuffer; 13″ H; *(upper center)* a turned wooden base; the iron extension holds a rushlight and candle; 13³/4″ H. (Lower left and center) **218. c.1700–1750:** Note these convenient heights for either the floor or table (28¹/2″, 24¹/4″); both were designed to secure a rushlight and candle. (Upper right) **219. c.1700–1725:** This wooden step-up and baluster column support an open scrolled candle shield; red paint; the pole is 50¹/2″ H (Lillian Blankley Cogan). (Lower right) **220. c.1720:** A turned wooden 2-light stand with an adjustable height thumbscrew; the threaded extensions push up their candles; red paint; 33¹/4″ H (Lillian Blankley Cogan).

WROUGHT-IRON FLOOR CANDLESTANDS: (Above, left to right) (*1*) **221. c.1700–1740:** An adjustable height tray (springs underneath) that holds four different-size candle sockets (used according to the light needed); found in Cape Cod, Mass.; 41¹/2″ H (Private Coll.). (*2*) **222. c.1680–1700:** A double-sectioned (spring-adjusted height) rushlight and candle holder; 37¹/2″ H (Lillian Blankley Cogan). (*3*) **223. c.1750:** This single arm was designed to swing 360°, and move vertically; 60″ H (Conn. Historical Society). (*4*) **224.** Marked "**l736**": An adjustable double-light wrought-iron and brass stand; it is signed, "B GERRISH/1736" (Boston area); 49¹/4″ H (Museum of Fine Arts, Boston).

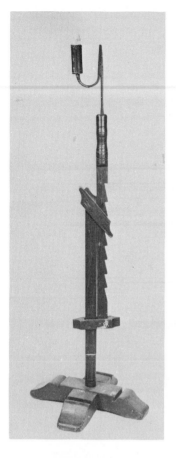
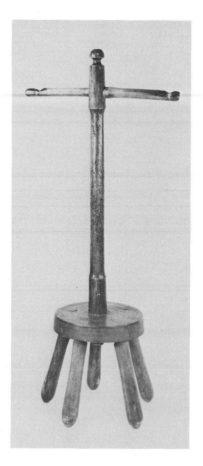
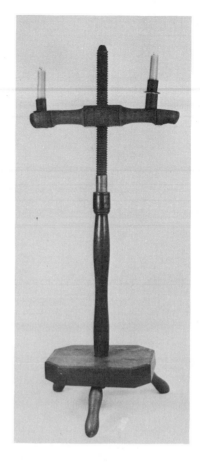

CANDLESTANDS: (Above, left to right) (*1*) **225. c.1700–1750:** A wooden adjustable ratchet form with a scrolled X base; the iron cap supports rushlight pincers and a candle socket; 29″–38″ H. (*2*) **226. c.1720–1750:** A 5-legged platform base; maple, ash, and chestnut; 38″ H (Private Coll.). (*3*) **227. c.1740–1780:** This pole is threaded for height adjustment; the crosspiece's tinned iron socket inserts are weighted with sand; 39″ H (Private Coll.). (*4*) **228. c.1770:** A single socket on an adjustable center upright; 22″ H (David & Marjorie Schorsch, Inc.).

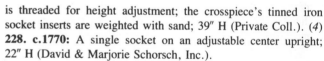
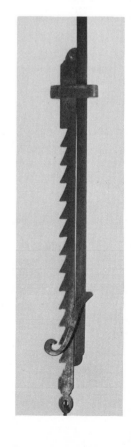

(Far left) **229. CANDLESTAND, c.1740–1760:** The threaded post holds a movable 2-light arm and drip tray; its extensions force up the candles; N.H.; 29$^{1}/_{2}$″ H (Wadsworth Atheneum). (Near left) **230. RATCHET HANGING LIGHT, c.1700–1750:** The wrought-iron "sawtooth" ratchet extends to a rush holder and candle socket; 31″–43$^{1}/_{2}$″ H. (Right) **231. RATCHET HANGER, c.1690–1720:** A graceful wooden sawtooth lamp suspension; 36″ H as shown (Anthony T. Wehman).

(Upper left) **232. GERMAN "PRICKET" CANDLESTICK:** Among the earliest candlestick forms was the "pricket" type which impaled its candle on a large spike; most of them were used in churches, but some have been excavated on American homesites; brass and iron (Museum of Fine Arts, Boston).

(Upper center) **233. ENGLISH EARTHENWARE CANDLE-STICK, c.1650–1700:** A sgraffito slipware candlestick produced in North Devon—with a mid-drip pan and restored handle (Colonial National Historical Park, Yorktown-Jamestown, Va.).

(Upper right) **234. WOODEN CANDLESTICKS, c.1680–1800:** (front) A simple turned wooden stem is socketed into the squared base; a single-piece round stick appears at the rear; 8½″, 8″ H.

(Lower right) **235. PEWTER CANDLESTICKS, c.1680–1700:** An early form of Low Country styling that combined a distinctive bulbous domed base with a baluster stem; they were usually cast in one piece; 5½″ H (Roger Bacon; Robert W. Skinner, Inc.).

(Above) **236. BRASS (CAPSTAN) CANDLESTICKS:** (Pair at left) **c.1650–1660,** this form employed a broad base, mid-drip pan, and early squared "push-out" hole (to pry out the old candle stub); 3⅝″ H; (*Right*) **c.1650–1680;** a more developed, broader profile; continental European origin (the English did not include push-out holes in the socket); 4¾″ H (Author).

BRASS CANDLESTICKS: (Upper left) **237. c.1650:** This continental European style includes a wide drip pan and domed base; note the stem's typical raised rings of the 1600s; 5¼″ H (Private Coll.) (Upper center) **238. ENGLISH, c.1650–1680:** Note the narrow capstan foot under a broad drip pan; its bulbous stem supports a period ringed socket; 6″ H. (Upper right) **239. DUTCH, c.1660–1690:** A 3-legged design with a baluster stem resembling contemporary furniture turnings; the drip pan is now elevated from the base; small punch-out hole (Author).

BRASS CANDLESTICKS: (Upper left) **240. ENGLISH, c.1680:** A period British form using a trumpet base, ribbed column, and mid-drip pan; 6¼″ H (Lillian Blankley Cogan). (Upper center) **241. DUTCH, c.1680:** A deeply turned column on a ball-foot platform—now dished to replace the drip pan; 5″ H (Lillian Blankley Cogan). (Upper right) **242. DUTCH OR SPANISH, c.1690:** As the earlier drip pan disappeared, new base forms evolved; this trumpet shape has added a lip to contain candle drippings; 3⅝″ H.

CANDLESTICKS: (Above) **243. FRENCH, c.1660–1690:** Notice the deep turnings and extended rings of the 17th century; flattened dome base; 6¹/₂″ H. (Right) **244. FRENCH, c.1670–1700:** The base continues to flatten, and turnings are becoming less strident; its early brass column casting is still a single piece (i.e., not yet halved); 8¹/₂″ H.

BRASS CANDLESTICKS: (Above) **245. SPANISH, c.1690:** These squared bases include raised edges to contain the drippings; (*from the left*) stud legs, a flat bottom, and paw feet; their column turnings are typical; 5″–6¹/₄″ H. (Right) **246. SPANISH, c.1690–1700:** Squared variations using a sunken center or raised ring; 5³/₈″, 6¹/₂″ H.

CANDLESTICKS: (Upper left) **247. SPANISH, c.1690:** A popular Spanish brass style using an octagonal base, faceted column, and ringed socket; 5³/₄″ H. (Upper center) **248. DUTCH OR SPANISH, c.1690–1700:** A brass saucer base form; 5¹/₂″ H. (Upper right) **249. FRENCH, c.1710:** The new century's baluster stem and square molded base with clipped corners is now evolving; 6¹/₂″ H. (Lower left) **250. FRENCH, c.1710:** The English and continental Europeans used similar styling, but often at different times; note the emerging shouldered stem and scalloped base form; French sockets and stems were commonly faceted; pewter; 6⁵/₈″ H. (Lower center) **251. FRENCH, c.1700–1710:** The shouldered stem continues to grow, and its molded base has a bolder outline; 6¹/₂″ H. (Lower right) **252. FRENCH, c.1710–1720:** Higher and more distinct shoulders are now apparent; 7⁵/₈″ H.

(Left) **253. ENGLISH CANDLESTICK, c.1700–1710:** During this decade, the new Dutch-inspired Queen Anne baluster stem grew, as did the squared base with clipped corners; brass; 6⅛″ H (Author).

(Right) **254. ENGLISH CANDLESTICKS, c.1715–1720:** French influence is seen here (see **#252**) as these upper stems acquire a vase profile, the sockets adopt a faceted surface, and the cut-corner molded base strengthens; brass; 7⅞″ H.

CANDLESTICKS: (Upper left) **255. ENGLISH, c.1720–1730:** The sockets are now expanding; also note their more pronounced column shoulders and new notched base corners (Queen Anne bases assumed round, square, or lobed shapes); 6½″ H. (Upper center) **256. ENGLISH, c.1720–1730:** The socket has added an integral drip pan at the top and a raised middle ring; a more slender stem profile is also evolving; brass; 7¼″ H. (Upper right) **257. ENGLISH, c.1740:** A more mature pair in bell metal (near bronze) display wider drip pans (scalloped edges), faceted stems, and stronger molded bases; 8½″ H.

258. ENGLISH, c.1720–1730: A more slender baluster stem with an integral socket drip pan (''bobeche'') is now appearing—mounted here on a squared base having lobed corners that anticipate the developing petal form (see **#260**); brass; 8³/8″ H.

259. ENGLISH, c.1735–1750: Evolution toward the post–1750 rounded base is evident here as earlier notched corners interrupt the curving sides. The established heavy baluster stem and long socket with a mid-ring plus wide drip pan remain; brass; 6¹/4″ H.

260. ENGLISH, c.1740–1755: Here the petal base is finally formed. Note the concave and convex petals which are reinforced in the stem's faceted shoulders and scalloped drip pan; it is cast in brass (base plus two vertical sections); 7³/4″ H (Author).

(Left) **261. ENGLISH, c.1750–1760:** This pair's late petal-base variation joins rounded lobes with scalloped junctions. The stem's narrower shoulder turnings and drip pan are also in keeping with this later dating; brass; 8⁷/8″ H.

(Right) **262. ENGLISH, c.1750:** The base shows apparent influence from the petal shape. Note, too, the disappearance of its mid-socket ring at this date, and the modified shoulders in the stem; brass; 7³/8″ H.

(Above) **265. FRENCH, c.1750:** A continental pewter candlestick that shows the close style relationships in Europe. Its base repeats the English form of **#263**, but includes a depressed well around the stem, and retains the early mid-ring socket without a drip pan; 7¹/₄″ H.

(Above) **266. GERMANIC,** Dated "1777–78": This rounded base reflects **#263**, yet mounts a baluster stem c.1700 (see **#243**); pewter; 6¹/₄″ H. (Lower right) **267. AMERICAN, c.1710–1750:** A unique pair combining early "bell" bases with modified stems and removable drip pans; pewter; 10″ H (Private Coll.).

(Upper left) **263. ENGLISH, c.1735–1750:** Double scallops between sloping straight-edged panels help to round off this modified petal base (see **#260**). Its stem and socket were cast in hollow halves, and brazed together along a vertical seam (typical from c.1670 to 1780); brass; 9³/₄″ H (Author).

(Below) **264. BASE UNDERSIDES:** The sand marks on brass castings were often left unfinished in the base's bottom. The soldered center and copper disk mask openings where the stem was attached—usually by a threaded tang or peened extension.

(Left) **268. ENGLISH CANDLESTICKS, c.1750–1760:** These hollow stems have a push rod from the bottom to help eject the old candle; note the round decorated bases of this period, plus the narrowing baluster stems; brass; 9 1/8″ H.

(Right) **269. CANDLESTICKS, c.1760–1770:** A cheaply cast pair (probably French) that now have a vaselike faceted stem which supersedes the baluster profile; the molded octagonal base, however, persists; 7 1/2″ H.

(Left) **270. DUTCH CANDLESTICKS, c.1770–1790:** A heavy brass pair with a round raised-edge base that supports a pinched column form of the late 1700s (see #274); 4 1/2″ H.

(Left) **271. DUTCH CANDLESTICK, c.1770:** A cast brass stick that exhibits the new slender stem on a round base—although the earlier ringed socket and integral drip pan have not yet been abandoned by this maker; 9″ H.

(Right) **272. EUROPEAN CANDLESTICKS, c.1790–1810:** A distinctive plain column style popular at the turn of the century; note the raised edges on both its round base and socket drip pan; brass; 7 3/8″ H.

BRASS CANDLESTICKS: (Upper left) **273. ENGLISH, c.1780–1800:** A late-century urn-shaped socket, tapering stem, and trumpet base; internal push-up rod; cast in two vertical halves; 8⅝″ H. (Upper center) **274. AMERICAN, c.1790–1800:** Side push-up levers were now gaining acceptance; note its similarity to the later "hog-scraper" form; 7½″ H. (Upper right) **275. ENGLISH, c.1780–1820:** The new neo-classical styling is evident in these popular ringed columns and sloping squared bases; 6″ H.

CANDLESTICKS: (Left) **276. EUROPEAN, c.1750–1800:** Unadorned brass saucer types of the later 1700s; 4″, 5″ H. (Lower left) **277. ENGLISH, c.1780–1790:** An example of the emerging Federal-period elegance; this reeded tulip-socket pair is "Sheffield plated" (thin silver sheets attached by fusion over a copper center); 11¼″ H. (Lower right) **278. c.1730–1800:** Such coarse earthenware "chamber-sticks" were produced in great volume by local potters; 4½″, 5″ Dia (Author).

(Upper left) **279. CANDLESTICKS, c.1740–1770:** These are light portable candlesticks with sockets that easily unscrew from the base (for travel, storage); 3″, 2⁷/₈″ H.

(Upper right) **280. CHAMBERSTICK, c.1720–1740:** The chamberstick normally had a broad base and handle—to help light the way to one's chamber; this round-edged base supports a ringed candle socket with straight sides per the contemporary style; note the handle designed for finger and thumb; brass; 3″ H.

(Above) **281. CHAMBERSTICK, c.1750:** Broken candle holders often had their sockets remounted on a wooden base—per this case as a chamberstick; the early round punch-out hole was favored by continental Europeans (not the English), and saw little use after 1740; 6⁷/₈″ L.

(Right) **282. CHAMBERSTICKS, c.1750–1790:** This popular form during the later 1700s includes the period's socket styles attached to rimmed trumpet bases and flat pierced handles; brass; 4⁵/₈″–5″ Dia (Author).

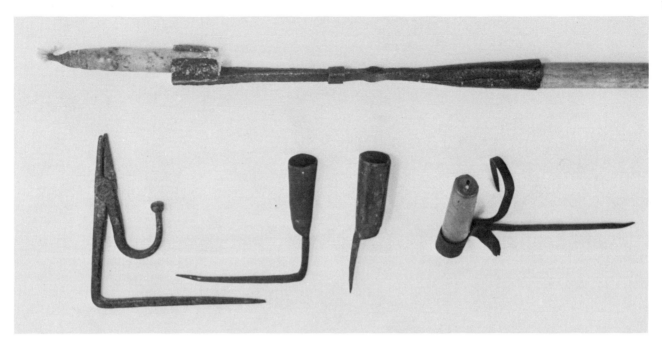

(Above) **283. IRON CANDLEHOLDERS, c.1700–1800:** These forms of wrought-iron candleholders include (*top*) a pole attachment using split arms that tighten on the candle as the ring is advanced; 10³/₄″ H; (*lower row, left to right*) a spike (driven into a post or wall) with pincers for a rushlight, 5³/₄″ H; two crude spiked sockets, 4¹/₄″, 4³/₄″ H; and a spike plus hook for a chair's back (similar to a contemporary miner's lamp); 6⁵/₈″ L (Author).

(Lower right) **284. SPIRAL (HELIX) CANDLESTICKS, c.1740–1820:** Two adjustable spiral-type holders that employ a simple handle (or chair-back hook) at the top, and a lower knob that slides along the spiraled opening to raise or lower the candle; 7⁷/₈″, 7¹/₈″ H.

(Above) **285. SPIRAL CANDLESTICK, c.1740–1820:** A spiraled iron variation that was mounted on a round platform with three cabriole-type legs; the original sliding knob is missing; 7¹/₂″ H.

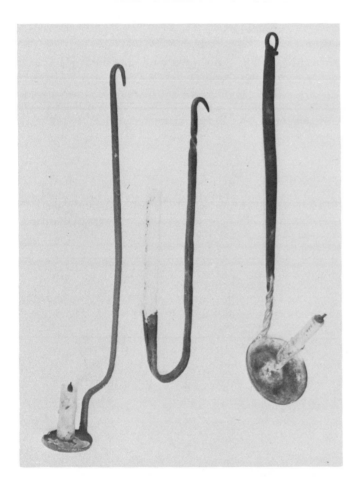

(Above) **286. CANDLEHOLDERS/TINDERBOXES, c.1770–1820:** Three variations of this popular tinned-iron form that mounted a candle socket on the round cover of a drum-shaped tinderbox; the box usually held a flint, "steel" (see **#738**), and tinder (charred linen, dried grass, etc. to catch the sparks)—plus a tin disk (damper) to extinguish the tinder after transferring the flame; $4^1/4''$–$4^1/2''$ Dia (Author).

(Left) **287. WORK (LOOM) LIGHTS, c.1700–1800:** Made of hand-forged iron; the two at left have hooks for hanging (e.g., loom, hearth); the other is a crude chamberstick (see **#282**); $16^3/8''$, $18^1/2''$ L.

(Below) **288. EXTENSION CANDLEHOLDER, c.1740–1800:** A flexible arrangement of pivoting iron arms riveted together to expand or retract the socket from a wall or post as required; it was held by the spike at left; from N.J.; $9^1/2''$ to $30^1/2''$ L (Author).

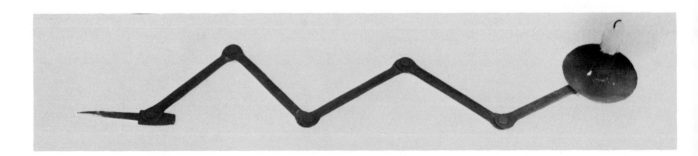

(Left) **289. GLASS OIL LAMPS:** Early hand-blown glass versions of the whale oil lamps that became established by 1820; the tinned iron wick holders are typical; (*left*) c.1780–1800; (*right*) c.1790–1820; they were initially accepted near the seacoast—using fish and whale oils; 3³/₈″, 3⁷/₈″ H. (Below left) **290. SCONCES:** Tinned iron sconces hung on the wall to support candles and reflect their light; (*left*) c.1780, a rounded fenced base and embossed arrow decoration; (*right*) c.1750, a punched-dot chicken design; 9¹/₂″, 11″ H. (Below right) **291. SCONCES, c.1770–1810:** (*left*) a diamond-shaped back with a crimped border and ribbonlike socket extension; (*right*) a truncated reflector on a triple candle platform; 11″, 6³/₈″ H (Conn. Historical Society).

(Below) **292. SCONCES, c.1700–1800:** A crude pair folded from sheet iron; their sockets are riveted to the base; 3⁷/₈″ H.

(Below) **293. SCONCES, c.1780–1810:** A crimped round top and line-embossed back—bent to create the flat socket base; 9⁵/₈″ H (Private Coll.).

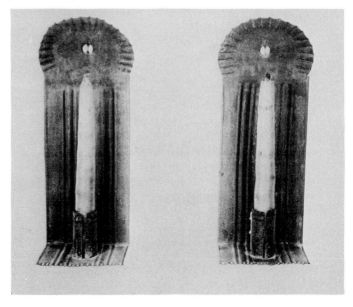

74

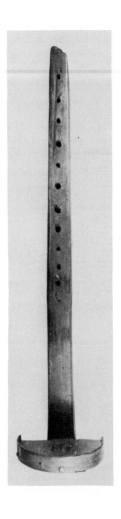

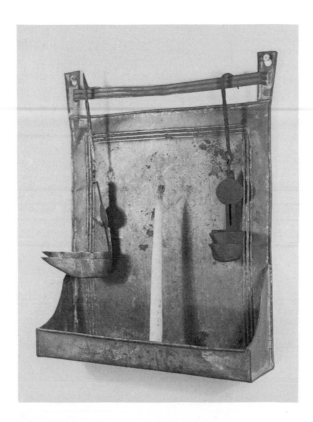

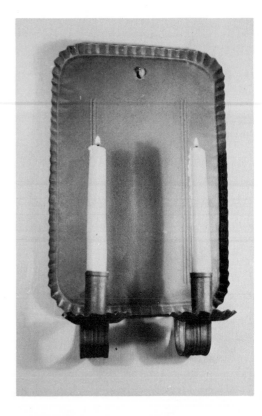

(Left) 294. HANGING CANDLEHOLDER, c.1700–1800: A simple wooden form with a fenced base that held the candlestick; the back's holes allowed various heights on the wall; painted red; 24½″ H.

(Upper center) 295. SCONCE/LAMP HOLDER, c.1720–1760: This large European-made tinned iron sconce adds a top bar to hold grease lamps; the fenced base also provides storage space for accessories; 17½″ H.

(Upper right) 296. DOUBLE SCONCE, c.1780–1820: An attractive rectangular tinned iron sconce with a raised crimped edge; its straps support two candles and drip pans; 12″ H.

(Left) 297. MIRRORED SCONCES, c.1780–1820: To increase candlepower, the better homes often used this design that attached segments of mirrored glass to a dished tin backing; similar faceted tinned forms lacking the glass were also employed; 9″ Dia (Merle E. Bouchard).

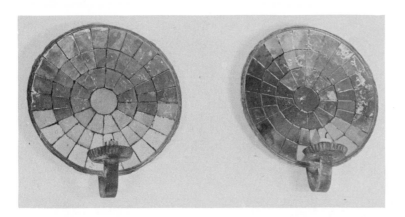

(Right) 298. EXTENDED SCONCES, c.1730–1750: This more elegant wall style mounted pivoting arms (note their Queen Anne cyma-curve form) that supported sockets and drip pans; brass; bases 4⅝″ H (Author).

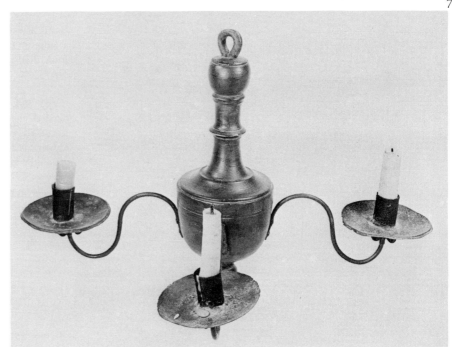

CHANDELIERS: Because of the expense of burning many candles, chandeliers were rare in country homes; they usually hung in churches, meeting rooms, and public taverns. Some of the better families did have them for special occasions, and two basic forms are shown. (Right) **299. c.1780–1800:** A turned wooden center (using the urn shape of that neoclassical period), which supports four wrought-iron arms for the candleholders; from Berlin, Conn.; 17¹/₂″ Dia (Lillian Blankley Cogan).

(Left) **300. CHANDELIER, c.1790–1820:** A tinned iron style that won broad acceptance in the early 1800s; note the characteristic crimped "reflectors" on the double tapered center—opposite its ribbonlike arms leading to six sockets and pans; 28¹/₂″ Dia (Author).

(Right) **301, 302. CRESSETS, c.1700–1800:** When extra light was needed on the hearth or out of doors, knots from the pitch pine or other resinous woods would be burned—usually in these wrought-iron frames ("cressets"); (*near right*) the "bracket" form with a spike for driving into a wall or timber; 9¹/₈″ H; (*far right*) a ribbed cylindrical type to set on a hearthstone or the ground (Mercer Museum, Bucks County Historical Society).

 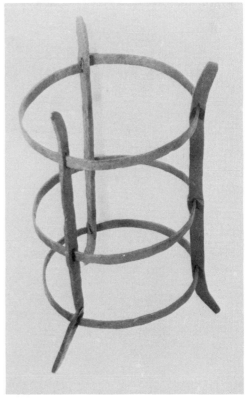

(Left) **303. DOUTER, c.1750–1820:** These scissorslike tongs are a more utilitarian version of the elegant bulbous-tipped "douter" form used to extinguish candles by pinching their lighted wick; 5¼ L.

(Left) **304. CANDLESNUFFER, c.1670–1700:** Today's candlewick that is consumed by the flame was not developed until the 1800s; earlier versions accumulated charred remains which had to be constantly removed. These scissorslike snuffers trimmed the candle by cutting the old wick with the blades and pushing it into the boxlike attachment in one motion; note this early ringed cast brass form with scrolled finger loops (Colonial National Historical Park, Yorktown-Jamestown, Va.).

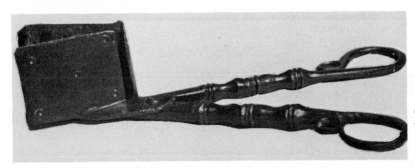

(Below left) **305. CANDLESNUFFERS:** *(Top)* c.1760, notice the oval receptacle and pointed tips favored during much of the 1700s; 6⅜" L; *(bottom)* c.1740, an earlier crude form; both are iron and did not have legs; 5⅝" L.

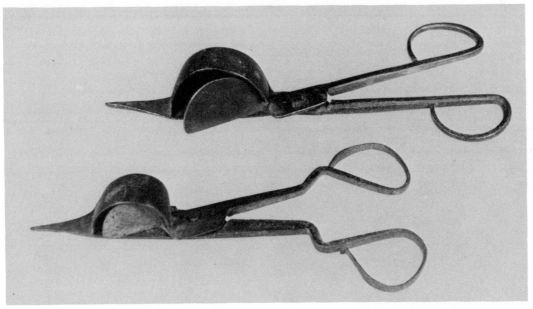

(Lower right) **306. CANDLESNUFFER, c.1750–1770:** This more pretentious snuffer (6¼" L) has acquired three legs to sit on its lobe-shaped tray (7⅜" L), and mounts a hollow muffinlike wick receptacle (Author).

(Lower left corner) **307. CANDLE EXTINGUISHERS, c.1750–1810:** These cones capped the flame to extinguish it; they were held by a ring handle, as shown, or a straight side arm (Lillian Blankley Cogan).

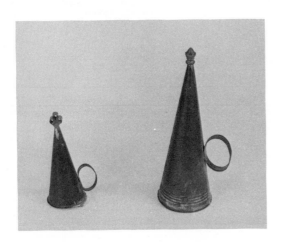

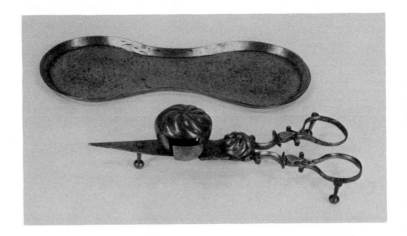

77

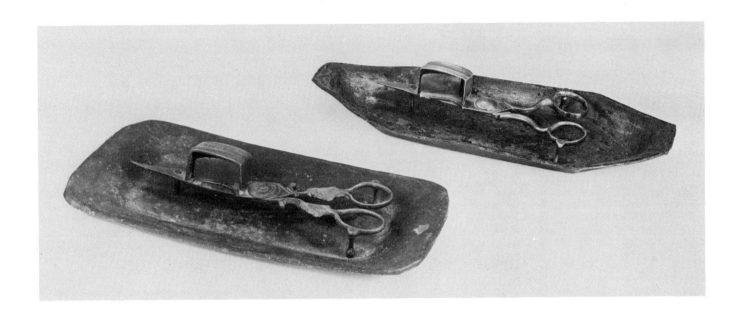

LANTERNS: Most lanterns provided lighting both inside and outside the house; (Below, left to right) *(1)* **309. c.1780–1840:** A pierced tinned iron lantern; the punched holes limited the light, but shielded the candle from wind and drafts, and were safer in a hay-strewn barn; 15⅝″ H; *(2)* **310. c.1780–1840:** A similar pierced lantern; note the candle socket on its roof for indoor use, plus the typical flat-ring handle; 15″ H; *(3)* **311. c.1760–1780:** A 6-sided glass window form that adds three gabled roof vents; 14¼″ H (Conn. Historical Society); *(4)* **312. c.1780–1810:** A later squared lantern mounting a conical top vent and protective rings for the windows (''lights''); 17¼″ H.

(Above) **308. CANDLESNUFFERS, c.1785–1825:** Such cast snuffers on legs with slightly arched wick boxes became accepted near the end of the 1700s and continued well into the 19th century; their trays (brass or tinned iron) were often painted; 8¾″, 6½″ L.

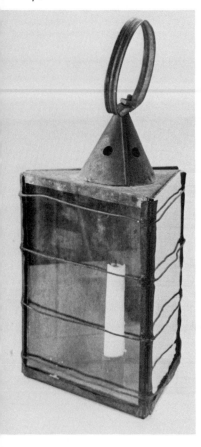
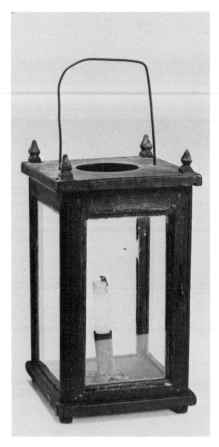

LANTERNS: (Above, left to right) *(1)* **313. c.1740–1800:** A triangular form with a tinned iron back and two angled glass windows (protective iron wires); 16¼″ H; *(2)* **314. c.1760–1790:** A popular rectangular wooden lantern design (the "bowet") having four glassed sides (one a hinged door); the corner posts extend to form legs and top finials; note also the typical wire handle and ventilating hole (some had an arched tin cover); *(3)* **315. c.1750–1820:** A cylindrical ("barrel") lantern with shaved horn "lights" (mica was sometimes used); both top and side handles are attached; 18½″ H; *(4)* **316. c.1750–1820:** A barrel lantern (tinned iron) also using horn lights—which transmitted subdued illumination without resolution; 15¼″ H (Author).

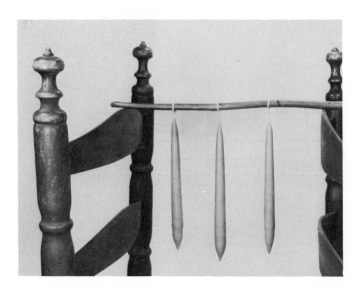

(Left) **317. CANDLE DIPPING:** The earliest candlemaking was done by repeatedly dipping a long wick into heated tallow to build layers to the desired thickness; this primitive arrangement simply looped wicks over a stick. (Above) **318. CANDLE DIPPING RACK, c.1750–1800:** A grid-type frame that allowed more candles per dipping; 23″ x 10¾″.

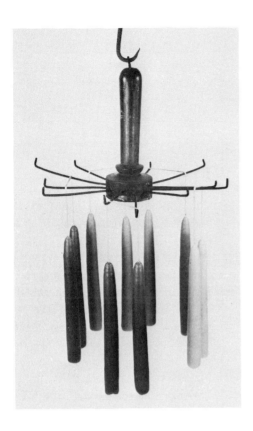

(Above) **319. CANDLES:** Most rural candles were of tallow (animal fat); the better ones employed beeswax and bayberries. They were made by two methods: (*top*) repeated dipping; notice its tapered uneven appearance; (*bottom*) pouring into molds to create this cylindrical body and conical top; the wicks were of twisted tow, hemp, or cotton. (Left) **320. DIPPER, c.1750–1820:** A handle with arms for dipping (Private Coll.).

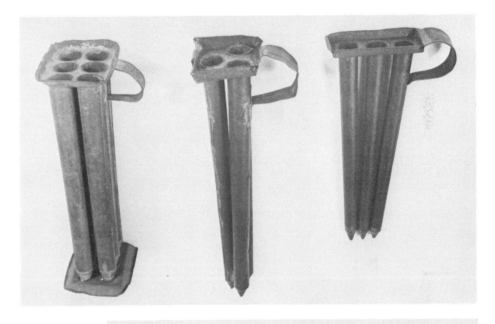

(Right) **321. CANDLE MOLDS, c.1750–1850:** The knotted wick passed upward through a bottom hole; melted tallow was then poured to fill the tube; because of the odor and bother, candles were usually made only once or twice a year and stored against rodents and heat. (Below) **CANDLE-MOLD FRAMES, c.1750–1810.** (Lower left) **322.** Rods along the top secure the wick ends; its frame is wood, the molds are pewter; 18¼″ H (Hamden [Conn.] Historical Society); (Lower right) **323.** Similar frame with "bootjack" ends; 17¾″ H (Au.).

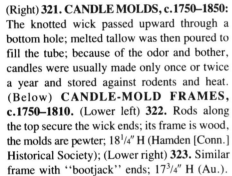

(Above) **325. LOOKING GLASS, c.1680–1710:** A William & Mary–period example from a Dutch source in N.Y.'s Hudson Valley; notice the straight-sided sloping frame with its raised decorative molding; made of pine with wooden pegged mortise & tenon joints; 10$\frac{1}{2}$" H, 9$\frac{1}{2}$" W (Private Coll.).

(Above) **324. LOOKING GLASS, c.1650–1700:** A 17th-century form with gothic carving; its side rails admitted sliding wooden cover to protect glass; 13$\frac{1}{4}$" H, 5$\frac{1}{2}$" W (Au.).

Looking Glasses

The "looking glass" (mirror) was a luxury limited largely to the affluent during the 17th century. Even until after the Revolutionary War, virtually all of the reflecting glass and the majority of mirrors were imported. Yet, by the beginning of the 1700s, some frames were already being fashioned by the colonists to combine the foreign glass with their own unpretentious efforts in pine, cherry, and walnut.

During the second half of the 1700s, American makers began to produce large numbers of the popular Chippendale "scrolled" ("silhouette," "fretwork") looking glasses to grace even the more modest middle-class homes (see **#333**). In some instances, this led to duplicating the more sophisticated European practices of veneered surfaces, gilded inner frames, and decorative cresting.

(Far left) **326. LOOKING GLASS, c.1710–1725:** An early New England mirror retaining the straight-sided heavily molded Pilgrim influence—but adding a scrolled-top carving (cresting) with a crude heart in the developing Queen Anne tradition; 13$\frac{3}{8}$" H, 8$\frac{1}{2}$" W (Lillian Blankley Cogan).

(Near left) **327. LOOKING GLASS,** Marked **"1713":** Reflecting glass was so limited that broken pieces ("fractures") were remounted for continued use, as shown; this American improvised frame includes a scrolled cresting, plus a carved heart above "1713" on the reverse side; painted green; 8$\frac{3}{8}$" H, 4$\frac{1}{4}$" W (Henry Whitfield House, Conn. Historical Commission).

(Left) **328. LOOKING GLASS, c.1700–1730:** This Dutch style (Hudson Valley) displays the indented William & Mary–period outline with raised molding; pegged mortise & tenon corners; painted black; note the later "courting-mirror" shape on the inside frame bordering the glass (see **#344**); 26½″ H, 21″ W (Private Coll.).

(Above) **329. LOOKING GLASS, c.1720–1740:** The rectangular molded frame with a solid scrolled crest is typical of the early Queen Anne period; old mirrors were "silvered" by a thick tin amalgam which acquires dark areas and spots with age; 14¾″ H.

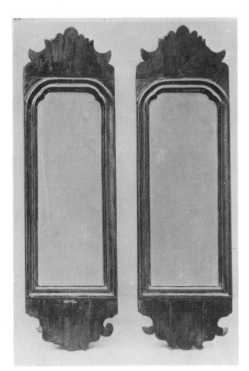

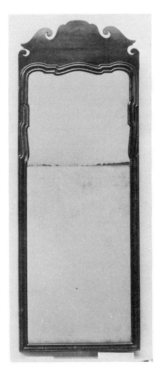

(Above left) **330. LOOKING GLASSES, c.1740:** Examples with skirts to balance the top cresting; note the Queen Anne scrolled upper corners of the frame surrounding the glass; this style often mounted sconces or was placed to reflect candles. (Above right) **331. LOOKING GLASS, c.1755–1760:** Another Queen Anne form; since glass was limited in size, long mirrors often used two sections (the top overlapped) (both, Metropolitan Museum of Art).

(Above) **332. LOOKING GLASS, c.1740–1750:** An attractive English Queen Anne style; its wooden base added molded designs in plasterlike "gesso," which were then gilded with sheets of gold leaf (not brushed on); 15″ H, 9½″ W.

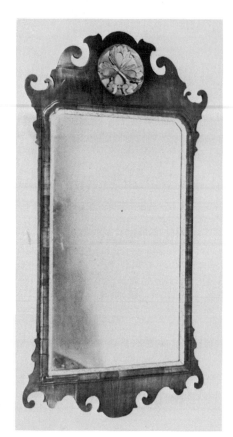

FRETWORK (SILHOUETTE) LOOKING GLASSES: (Upper left) **333. c.1740–1760:** Scrolled ''fretwork'' mirrors appeared in the late Queen Anne years, and became very popular by the Chippendale period; this early version includes the Queen Anne curved upper corners on the inner frame; 36³/₈″ H, 19¹/₂″ W. (Upper center) **334. c.1740–1760:** An early fretwork variation that adds a pierced gilded design in the cresting; many were veneered in walnut or mahogany; 40″ H, 21″ W. (Upper right) **335. c.1750–1770:** A transitional form toward the Chippendale styling; a molded and gilded composition figure is applied to the cresting, and the inner frame is now squared; walnut veneer; 26³/₄″ H (Private Coll.).

(Left) **336. FRETWORK LOOKING GLASS, c.1760–1800:** This is typical of the Chippendale era when fretwork mirrors were extremely popular in America; note its scrolled extensions on all sides, and the rectangular gilded molding adjacent to the glass; wooden blocks were often glued to the rear to retard warping; 21″ H, 12¹/₄″ W.

(Right) **337. FRETWORK LOOKING GLASS, c.1760–1800:** A unique variation of the fretwork style was this incised openwork pattern; pine; 22″ H, 13³/₄″ W (Private Coll.).

(Left) **338. FRETWORK LOOKING GLASS, c.1780–1800:** Carved and gilded bird figures were a common decorative addition in the later 1700s. This removable eagle slides into a socket behind the crest; mahogany (solid and veneered); 32$^1/2$″ H, 16$^3/4$″ W (Author).

(Right) **339. LOOKING GLASS, c.1760–1780:** Such European latticelike forms that added gilded gesso molding to a wooden frame were used in America, and are known today as "Cape Cod" mirrors; they reflect the Chippendale penchant for rococo design; 23$^1/2$″ H.

(Near right) **340. FRETWORK LOOKING GLASS, c.1780–1820:** A transitional-period mirror that exhibits the new inner flat frame, which bears a thin straight inlay; the trend to less elaborate scrollwork omits the upper corner frets.

(Far right) **341. LOOKING GLASS, c.1785–1820:** This evolution is now apparent, as the new flat frame eliminates all fretwork except the scrolled cresting at the top—in the manner of the early Queen Anne era (see **#329**); walnut crest, and a veneered frame; 17$^1/4$″ H.

(Left) **342. LOOKING GLASS, c.1750–1760:** An American looking glass with molding applied to the frame's outer edge and around the glass; red paint; 17″ H, 14″ W (Author).

(Right) **343. LOOKING GLASS, c.1740–1760:** A more costly mirror from England that bears an outward beveled frame having panels of reflecting glass set into it; gilded molding; 12″ H, 9¼″ W.

(Lower left) **344. COURTING MIRROR, c.1740–1760:** A courting mirror was supposedly given to a young woman by her suitor; its unique form mounted an angular crest enclosing a painted glass insert; this early example having an arched frame (veneered), displays a flower design (reverse painted in blue, orange, green, and white); 15½″ H, 10″ W (Private Coll.).

(Lower right) **345. COURTING MIRROR, c.1760–1800:** Most were imported from Holland (see **#328**), and arrived in a wooden box, as shown; with the cover removed, the mirror was often hung on a wall in the box; note this later form that inserted painted glass strips throughout the frame; 16″ H, 11″ W (Smithsonian Institution).

DRESSING GLASSES: (Upper left) **346. c.1740–1750:** Appearing c.1740, dressing glasses stood on a table or chest; this English example displays Queen Anne rounded frame corners and the common use of beveled glass; scrolled feet; 22″ H. (Upper center) **347. c.1740:** A more formal English example in walnut veneer, mahogany, and pine; the Queen Anne period crest includes a gilded concave shell; 17¹/₂″ H (Webb-Deane-Stevens Museum, Wethersfield, Conn.). (Upper right) **348. c.1770–1800:** This adds drawers and bracket feet of the Hepplewhite years; mahogany and oak; 21″ H (Conn. Historical Society). **LOOKING GLASSES:** (Lower left) **349.** Two small rural American forms; 8″, 4⁷/₈″ H (Private Coll.). (Lower right) **350. c.1750–1850:** Elementary hand mirrors; 9¹/₈″, 6⁵/₈″ L.

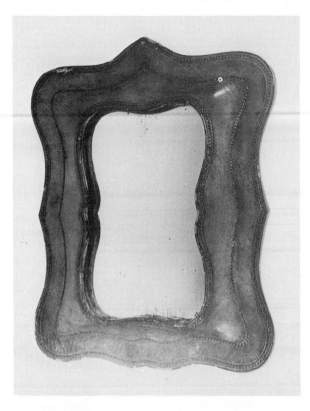

(Left) **351. LOOKING GLASS, c.1760–1780:** A leather-framed (cowhide) looking glass, probably for home and travel; it uses a thicker glass for strength; note, too, the subdued but graceful scrolled outline; $10^3/4''$ H, 8'' W (Private Coll.).

(Above) **352. LOOKING GLASS, c.1780–1810:** Another portable mirror; mounted in birch, it is protected by a pivoting cover; $5^1/2''$ H, $3^1/4''$ W.

(Above) **353. SPINDLE CHAIR, c.1640–1680:** A rare early American turned chair with spindles that resemble the Carver and Brewster forms (see **#354, #355**); note its massive Pilgrim posts; the canted back is set into a horizontal turned rail; oak and ash; $41^1/2''$ H (Conn. Historical Society).

Seating

The early 17th-century chair was a rare piece of furniture. Ordinary people sat on long benches ("forms"; see **#514**), "joint stools" (see **#520**), or simple chests. The heavy thronelike chairs of the middle 1600s were normally reserved for the head of the family or persons of importance. Both imported and locally made, they varied from the sturdy "wainscot" type of framed construction (see **#397**) to the heavily turned "Brewster" (see **#354**) and "Carver" styles (see **#355**)—as well as the enduring "slat back" (see **#360**). Although such "great" chairs were not commonplace, they still functioned as domestic forms in that agrarian society, and illustrate characteristics carried into the 18th century. As such, the principal "Pilgrim" styles are included in this coverage of country furnishings.

During the 1700s, most settlers were better established, and chairs proliferated in the household for use by the entire family. Yet, in the tradition of country furniture, these forms reflected the European fashions—while varying in myriad details according to the local maker and region.

(Far left) **354. SPINDLE ("BREWSTER") ARM-CHAIR, c.1650:** This multispindled design—with double-banked spindles in the back, sides, and under the seat—is known as the "Brewster" form (one was owned by Elder Brewster in Plymouth, Mass.); the wooden seat typically has a cushion; hickory, and oak; 44³/₄″ H (Metropolitan Museum of Art).

(Near left) **355. SPINDLE ("CARVER") ARMCHAIR, c.1660–1680:** Such heavily turned chairs—including single or double rows of back spindles (but not under the seat)—are considered the "Carver" style (named for Gov. John Carver of Plymouth); note the Carver's usual rush seat and ball handholds; ash; Mass.; 42″ H (Conn. Historical Society).

(Left) **356. SPINDLE ARM-CHAIR, c.1670–1700:** These early tapered back spindles are socketed into the crossrails; also characteristic are the single upper rung, bulbous post finials, high armrests, and maturing (flatter) mushroom handholds; ash; eastern Mass.; 48″ H (Private Coll.).

(Right) **357. SPINDLE ARM-CHAIR, c.1690–1720:** By the later 1600s, lighter spindle chairs had appeared; this more delicate Carver style has smaller turnings and a shallower seat—possibly for the lady of the home; ash; New England; feet restored; 40³/₄″ H.

(Right) **358. SPINDLE ARM-CHAIR, c.1720–1740:** Vertical back spindles continued in modified variations during the 1700s; these dowel forms appear between posts turned like contemporary banister-back chairs; the mushroom handles are now flatter, and an early set of rockers was added at one time; splint seat; blue paint.

(Above) **359. SPINDLE SIDE CHAIRS, c.1780–1810:** Even at the end of the 18th century, the Carver tradition is still evident in this pair; notice, however, the lack of turnings in the narrower posts, legs, and spindles; maple; ash stretchers; brown paint; 35½″ H.

(Left) **360. SLAT-BACK (LADDER-BACK) ARM-CHAIR, c. 1650–1665:** Such Pilgrim chairs are also called "turned great chairs"; the heavy posts include period turnings, plus "urn & flame" finials; midcentury ball handholds; the second slat is an early replacement; 41″ H (Private Coll.).

(Right) **361. SLAT-BACK ARMCHAIR, c.1670–1700:** This 5-slat chair has the early deeply turned posts (2½″ Dia), yet displays the evolving vase outline in its arm support; note, too, the sloping arms and flatter handholds; ash; Long Island; 48″ H (Private Coll.).

SLAT-BACK ARMCHAIRS: (Upper left) **362. c.1690–1730:** Note the new century's trends to "sausage & ring" posts, sloping arms, and thinner "mushrooms" (always turned as part of the post); 44$\frac{1}{2}$" H (Private Coll.). (Upper center) **363. c.1730–1760:** Further evolution shows in these plainer turnings, and arms closer to the seat; 45$\frac{3}{4}$" H. (Upper right) **364. c.1750–1780:** By now, there are fewer turnings, less slats, and narrower handholds; 42" H. (Near right) **365. c.1690–1720:** An attractive form with extended arms and incised ring decorations; 40$\frac{1}{2}$" H (Private Coll.). (Far right) **366. c.1700–1720:** Note the angled arms that resemble earlier wainscot chairs (see **#397**); 47$\frac{1}{2}$" H (Author).

SLAT-BACK ARMCHAIRS: (Upper left) **367. c.1720–1740:** This includes both the tall "vase" and "sausage & ring" post turnings—as well as "baluster & ring" front stretchers; 46½" H. (Upper center) **368. c.1745–1760:** A marriage of the earlier spindle form (i.e., rungs above slats and under the arms) with slat-back styling; its posts, stretchers, and mushrooms are also trending thinner; maple; ash stretchers; 46½" H. (Upper right) **369. c.1720–1750:** Note this period's overhanging arms, and sausage turnings on the front stretchers—plus its secondary arms; maple, ash; 46" H. (Lower left) **370. c.1740–1760:** A broad midcentury chair with active turnings and graduated slats; the arms continue to lower; 44" H (Author).

(Above) **371. WOVEN CHAIR SEATS:** (*Left to right*) (*1*) Splint—woven strips of hickory, oak, or ash inner bark; (*2*) Rush—from strands of rush twisted into "ropes"; (*3*) Cane—interlaced outer strips of imported rattan.

SLAT-BACK ARMCHAIRS: (Upper left) **372. c.1750–1780:** An English style that employs shaped slats, stubby finials, and flat arms; 42¹/₂″ H. (Upper center) **373. c.1720–1740:** This Penn.–N.J. (i.e., Delaware Valley) form includes five arched slats, vase-shaped arm supports, massive ridged cabriole legs, plus a ball & ring stretcher; 46¹/₂″ H. (Upper right) **374. c.1740–1800:** A later Delaware Valley chair that uses straight legs and subdued turnings; maple; 48³/₄″ H (Metropolitan Museum of Art).

(Left) **375. SLAT-BACK ARM-CHAIR, c.1740–1750:** The posts and front stretchers have become further muted; note, too, the usual socketed armrests and interesting peaked slats; a rush seat; 42¹/₂″ H.

(Right) **376. SLAT-BACK ARMCHAIR, c.1780–1820:** By this late date, most turnings are shallow contours, the armrests sit lower, stretchers have become dowels, and the finials lack crisp definition; maple; painted black; 44³/₄″ H.

SLAT-BACK ARMCHAIRS: (Left) **377. c.1790–1830:** By the century's end, many turned chairs had acquired a functional plainness little resembling the deep bold contours of the early 1700s; 45$\frac{1}{2}$" H. (Right) **378. c.1750–1830:** A "stepback" form that mounts flat stubby arms; its arm supports, in turn, penetrate to the stretcher to reinforce the drilled seat rung; New York; 43$\frac{3}{4}$" H (Private Coll.). (Lower left) **379. c.1775–1840:** Rocking ("crooked-foot") chairs developed by the mid 1700s; most were regular chairs with rockers added later, but these broad legs suggest original construction as a rocker; 40$\frac{1}{2}$" H (Branford [Conn.] Historical Society; on loan, Mr. & Mrs. Shaun R. Shattuck).

(Above center) **380. CHILD'S TABLE CHAIR, c.1690–1720:** Note these thick turned posts of the Pilgrim period; 34$\frac{1}{2}$" H, seat 19$\frac{1}{2}$" H (Author).

(Above right) **381. CHILD'S TABLE CHAIR, c.1720–1740:** Painted red, with widely splayed legs, bell-shaped finials, and turned (socketed) arms; 39" H, seat 22" H.

(Left) **382. CHILD'S ROCKER, c.1690–1730:** A child's slat-back chair with the early heavy posts, and rockers added by slotting the legs (pinned); note these rockers' balanced profile vs. the long-tailed 19th-century form; the top of its upper slat is broken off (common—from constant lifting); red paint; 25¼″ H.

(Right) **383. CHILD'S CHAIR, c.1760–1790:** A child's armchair using doweled stretchers and arms that penetrate through the legs (a practice in rural Britain; see **#396**); great wear is often found on the face of front legs from a child pushing the tipped-over chair while learning to walk; 23½″ H.

(Left) **384. SLAT-BACK CHAIR, c.1690–1720:** This transitional chair retains the back's early top rung (re the Carver form) and Pilgrim finials; the "sausage" turned front stretchers arrived c.1710–1720; 17th-century rungs for woven seats were round—but by the early 1700s most were shaped like an airplane wing in section (leading edge outward); Mass.; 39″ (Private Coll.).

(Right) **385. SLAT-BACK CHAIRS, c.1720–1740:** An early 18th-century pair display typical sausage & ring posts, bulbous finials, vase-turned front legs, and a "blocked" seat front (i.e., a socketed piece set on the legs—vs. **#384**); 43½″ H (Author).

(Above left) **387.** Scribe marks on posts were normally guides for cutting the mortise slots or sockets. (Above right) **388.** Most slat-backs pinned the top slat (mortised) to keep the frame tight; original hardwood pins are usually found projecting slightly (from the softer post's greater shrinkage). (Below) **389, 390.** These chairs from the same period (c.1770–1790) reflect regional differences (turnings, slats, seats), i.e., (*lower left*) one of a pair from central Conn.; 39″ H; (*lower right*) similar Maine chairs; 38¹/₂″ H (Au.).

(Above left) **386. SLAT-BACK SIDE CHAIRS, c.1750–1780:** A later pair vs. **#385**; (their post & finial turnings are less defined); notice, too, that substantial wear shows on the front stretchers and that their legs have worn shorter; most chair seats were originally 16″ to 18″ high; 40¹/₂″ H.

391. SLAT-BACK SIDE CHAIR, c.1780–1820: A form associated with Bergen County, N.J., i.e., the low-back, urn-style finials, sausage & ring posts, and arched slats; 36″ H.

392. SLAT-BACK SIDE CHAIR, c.1770–1810: A Delaware Valley style (N.J., Penn.) with a tall back, arched slats, and ball feet (see #374); 41¹⁄₂″ H (Ballard Coll.).

393. SLAT-BACK SIDE CHAIR, c.1790–1820: Another Delaware Valley form displays scroll-like ''salamander'' slats, stubby finials, and ringed feet; 34³⁄₄″ H.

(Left) **394. SLAT-BACK ''HEARTH'' CHAIR, c.1780–1800:** Some chairs were made low (seat here is 13″ H) for working at the hearth—or even sitting inside one end of a large fireplace on cold nights; N.J.; cherry and ash; 31″ H.

(Right) **395. TREE-TRUNK CHAIR, c.1750–1850:** A primitive type known in rural England and repeated here; a hollow tree trunk was cut to form, and a circular seat inserted; applewood; 29¹⁄₂″ H (Private Coll.).

(Left) **396. SQUARED-POST SLAT-BACK CHAIRS, c.1650–1820:** Such child-size squared-back forms are dated from the mid-1600s in New England to the 1800s in Canada; they are an early rural slat-back style of the British Isles and Central Europe—including the hewn rungs and stretchers penetrating the posts; possibly tied to the Old World practice of making rough chairs and benches out of marginal lumber; $20^{3}/_{4}''$–$32^{1}/_{4}''$ H.

(Lower left) **397. WAINSCOT CHAIR, c.1640–1660:** The other primary early form (vs. the turned chair) was the English wainscot style, having a rigid pinned frame with panels, a plank seat, and downcurving arms; the rear posts were squared, and their front legs often turned; traditionally in oak. Note this usual low-relief carving, arched cresting, and modest seat apron scalloping; heavy box stretchers; white oak; found in N.H.; 43" H (Private Coll.).

(Lower right) **398. WAINSCOT CHAIR, c.1660–1710:** A New England joined "great chair" bearing impressive floral carving on its back and cresting, as well as channeled molding, pegged joints, and sloping arms; oak (David & Marjorie Schorsch, Inc.).

(Left) **399. "CROMWELLIAN" CHAIR, c.1650–1675:** This was a popular low-backed English style; note the ball turnings on its legs and stretchers; the upholstery is tacked "Turkey work" covering (usually loom woven and hand knotted), plus marsh grass stuffing; from Conn.; maple, oak; 37″ H (Metropolitan Museum of Art).

(Right) **400. SPINDLE SIDE CHAIR, c.1690–1710:** A Dutch form also used in Britain; it combines framed with spindle characteristics, as well as the developing block & vase front legs (see **#402**); 31″ H.

401. WAINSCOT CHAIR, c.1650–1690: This English child's wainscot chair employs the period's back panel and cresting, "ringed" front legs, sloping arms, plank seat, and squared rear posts; 45″ H (Author).

402. WAINSCOT CHAIR, c.1680–1690: The framed construction is now evolving to block & vase legs and stretcher, plus the isolation of its back panel from the side posts; 44¹/₂″ H.

403. CANE (RESTORATION, FLEMISH) CHAIR, c.1690–1700: A Low Country/English form bearing a caned seat and back; notice its usual open carved cresting, front stretcher, and block & turned posts; .50³/₄″ H.

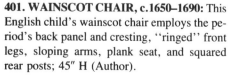

(Upper left) **404. "BOSTON" SIDE CHAIR, c.1700–1725:** A leather-covered "back-paneled" chair variation associated with the Boston area; maple; canted back; 49″ H (Wadsworth Atheneum). (Upper center) **405. BANISTER-BACK CHAIR, c.1710–1730:** Carved cresting persists here (see #403), but the back now adds vertical turned banisters (split in half); 43¼″ H (David Bland).

(Upper right) **406. BANISTER-BACK CHAIR, c.1720-1750:** By the 1720s a solid crest was replacing the carved form—while the block & vase posts and the canted back continue; 46¼″ H.

407. TURNED BASE, c.1680–1850: A form with all posts and stretchers turned; it continued, even as the back changed for each succeeding style, into the mid-1800s.

408. BLOCK & VASE, c.1690–1820: This combination of block & turned front legs, squared rear legs, and baluster stretchers also survived well past our period.

BANISTER-BACK ARMCHAIRS: (Upper left) **409. c.1740–1760:** These serpentine arms end in the "elephant trunk" form found mostly in N.H.–north Mass.; note, too, that the double arch in its seat rail is repeated in the crest; maple, with ash stretchers; 47$\frac{1}{2}$" H. (Upper center) **410. c.1750–1775:** Similar arms, but now combined with the "staghorn" or "fishtail" crest rail, plus later modified turnings; the feet were slotted for added rockers; 43" H (David Bland).

(Upper right) **411. BANISTER-BACK SIDE CHAIR, c.1720–1750:** The "Deerfield" style from the Conn. River Valley that reversed its banisters, i.e., not the flat, but the round side faced forward; the legs include Spanish feet; 45$\frac{1}{4}$" H.

(Left) **412. BANISTER-BACK SIDE CHAIR, c.1750–1780:** Basically a New England form, the banister-back chair used from three to six banisters—often with a shaped lower seat rail that reflected the crest rail; red paint; 44$\frac{1}{8}$" H.

(Right) **413. BANISTER-BACK ARM-CHAIR, c.1730–1750:** Notice these earlier crisp post turnings and finials, plus the heart-pierced crest; the banisters' outline usually matched the side posts; they were split first and rejoined for turning—then mounted with the flat face forward (more comfortable); 43$\frac{3}{4}$" H (Author).

BANISTER-BACK CHAIRS: (Upper left) **414. c.1750–1775:** A Conn. chair with arched serpentine arms & rosette-carved crest; 53¼″ H (Au.). (Upper center) **415. c.1760–1775:** A rural extended "yoke" crest rail; 38½″ H. (Upper right) **416. c.1740–1760:** An alternate form with flat reeded banisters; 42½″ H.

(Near right) **417. c.1740–1760:** The popular arched cresting plus sausage & ring legs are combined with the flat banister form; 43″ H. (Far right) **418. c.1740–1760:** A high-backed chair that includes the earlier block & turned rear posts; notice, too, its arched crest and Queen Anne cyma-scrolled seat rail; 48¾″ H.

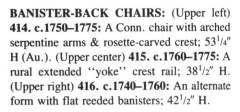

(Left) **419. HEART & CROWN (HEART) CHAIR, c.1745–1765:** A southern Conn. scrolled and pierced "heart & crown" form (this one from the Milford area); the style normally included straight reeded banisters, secondary spindle arms, and crisply turned posts; $46^{3}/_{4}''$ H (Conn. Historical Society). (Right) **420. HEART & CROWN CHAIR, c.1720–1740:** An alternate heart-pierced crest that adds flanking cutouts; sausage-turned stretchers appear on three sides; Conn.; $46^{1}/_{2}''$ H (Lillian Blankley Cogan).

BANISTER-BACK CHAIRS: (Lower left) **421. c.1740–1760:** A New England flat-reeded banister armchair with the common "saddle" crest rail; 48″ H. (Lower center) **422. c.1760–1800:** These later turnings are now less distinct; 41″ H. (Lower right) **423. c.1780–1820:** The active turnings continue to fade as the new century begins; 39″ H.

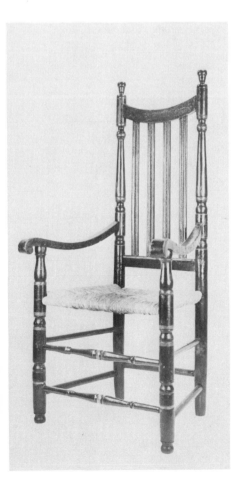

(Upper left) **424. BANISTER-BACK SIDE CHAIR, c.1770–1800:** A reeded banister-back variation that adds a yoke crest rail with extended Chippendale "ears" (see **#452**); 39¾" H.

(Upper center) **425. BANISTER-BACK CHAIR, c.1720–1730:** A banister-style "great chair" using strong block & vase front legs, and flat beaded banisters; 56" H (Conn. Historical Society).

(Upper right) **426. SPINDLE-BACK CHAIR, c.1760–1820:** A similar, but later example joining spindles with squared posts and legs; 42¾" H.

(Left) **427. SIDE CHAIR, c.1760–1800:** In this case, the Queen Anne influence has modified the banister-back form by inserting a curved-yoke crest rail (see **#438**) and a single vase-shaped splat (or "fiddleback") between the usual turned posts; 40¼" H.

(Right) **428. SIDE CHAIR, c.1770–1810:** Another version of this combined period uses a saddle-type crest rail with a center splat; only one "baluster & ring" front stretcher was included; 39¼" H.

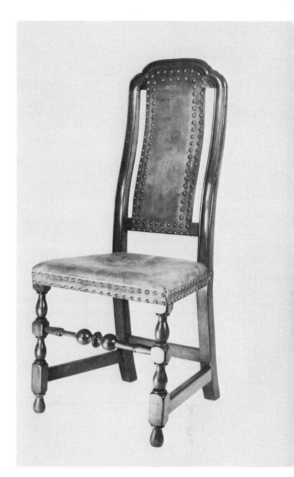

(Upper left) **429. SIDE CHAIR, c.1760:** This variation includes a pierced heart and molded crest over a vase splat; birch and oak; 42″ H (Webb-Deane-Stevens Museum, Wethersfield, Conn.). (Upper center) **430. SIDE CHAIR, c.1700–1720:** The carved front stretcher and block & vase legs of the Flemish cane chairs (see #403) appear here—while the back evolves the yoke crest rail, solid panel, and spoon-back curve of the emerging Queen Anne style; probably central European; 41¹/₂″ H (Henry Whitfield House, Conn. Historical Commission).

(Upper right) **431. SIDE CHAIR, c.1720–1740:** A leather-covered form popular in the Boston area (see **#404**); maple; 42³/₄″ H (Conn. Historical Society).

QUEEN ANNE SIDE CHAIRS: (Left) **432. c.1740–1770:** This includes the usual Queen Anne solid vase splat, a yoke crest rail, spoon-shaped back, cabriole legs (pad feet), squared rear legs, and scrolled seat apron; 41″ H (Conn. Historical Society). (Right) **433. c.1740–1760:** The more elegant chair shown here is better formed, and adds block & turned stretchers; a removable slip seat was probably placed over the rush base originally; 39¹/₄″ H (Webb-Deane-Stevens Museum).

(Left) **434. c.1730–1750:** This is typical of the carving found on early Queen Anne–period yoke crest rails; note, too, the outline molding on its rail and posts.

(Upper right) **435. QUEEN ANNE COUNTRY SIDE CHAIR, c.1730–1740:** The Queen Anne chair usually had cabriole legs in formal surroundings (see **#433**), but kept the established block & vase or turned base in rural areas. This back includes a carved crest and molded posts, as well as block & vase legs with turned feet; 41¼″ H (Author).

(Lower left) **436. QUEEN ANNE SIDE CHAIR, c.1730–1750:** A more sophisticated use of cabriole legs—attached to the seat by baluster turnings; Colchester, Conn. area; original black finish; 43″ H (Conn. Historical Society).

(Lower center) **437. QUEEN ANNE SIDE CHAIR, c.1740–1760:** A rural New England interpretation that includes a recessed center crest and a large ball & disc front stretcher; striped maple; 39″ H.

(Lower right) **438. QUEEN ANNE SIDE CHAIR, c.1740–1760:** A plain crest was used here, but the lower seat rail has added molding; these front legs project up above the seat (vs. the block front, **#439**); 42¼″ H.

439. QUEEN ANNE SIDE CHAIR, c.1740–1760: A popular uncarved yoke chair with Spanish feet and the common woven rush seat; 40³/₈″ H.

440. QUEEN ANNE SIDE CHAIR, c.1740–1760: These chairs used mixed woods and were normally painted; note the "slipper" (spooned) feet and baluster stretchers; 41¹/₂″ H.

441. QUEEN ANNE SIDE CHAIR, c.1750–1780: A later regional variation that employs round rear posts, combined with "vase-sausage-ring" front legs; 41″ H.

QUEEN ANNE ARMCHAIRS: (Above left) **442. c.1730–1750:** Note the carved back, ram's-horn handholds, and Spanish feet (David Bland). (Above center) **443. c.1730–1750:** A less for-mal armchair form; 43¹/₂″ H (Author). (Right) **444. SIDE CHAIR, c.1760–1800:** The square (beaded outer corner) Chippendale legs were also used with this style; 41¹/₄″ H.

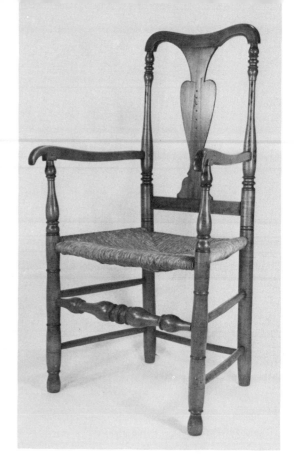

(Left) **445. QUEEN ANNE ARMCHAIR, c.1720-1730:** This more rustic Queen Anne style mounted a flat-faced yoke crest rail (socketed and pinned) on a baluster-turned frame; note the early sloping scroll-ended arms, vase splat, and stepped seat rail (one piece of wood); maple; 46″ H (Author).

(Right) **446. QUEEN ANNE ARMCHAIR, c.1750-1770:** A later version of **#445** that demonstrates more conservative turnings and straighter arms; nail holes in the splat are from later upholstery; maple; 41″ H.

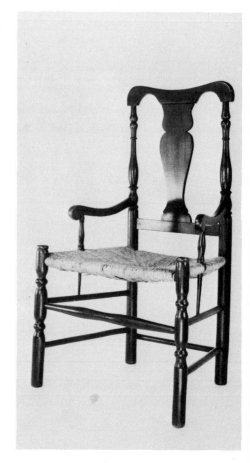

447. QUEEN ANNE SIDE CHAIR, c.1760–1800: A rural form made with spindlelike posts, a flat crest rail, and a turned base; 39$\frac{1}{2}$″ H.

448. QUEEN ANNE SIDE CHAIR, c.1780–1800: Now near the century's end, the turnings have been simplified and are less distinct; 38$\frac{1}{2}$″ H.

449. QUEEN ANNE STEPBACK CHAIR, c.1770–1790: Such half-length arms were convenient for a woman's full skirts or when used at the table.

(Near right) **450. QUEEN ANNE CHAIR, c.1750–1810:** A version of the plain yoke Queen Anne style using straight trumpet-shaped front legs that end in pad feet; it was most popular among Dutch settlers, i.e., in the Hudson Valley, Long Island, and New Jersey (also some in New England); note, too, the typical bulbous front stretcher and broad rush seat; 40$\frac{1}{2}$″ H (Author).

(Far right) **451. QUEEN ANNE CHAIR, c.1760–1810:** A similar form mounts a flatter crest rail with projecting ears (the new Chippendale influence—see **#452, #454**); 39$\frac{1}{2}$″ H.

(Lower left) **452. CHIPPENDALE CHAIR, c.1760–1790:** Chippendale-period country chairs often kept the earlier block & turned front legs and squared posts, but introduced a curving crest rail with projecting ears; 39$\frac{1}{2}$″ H.

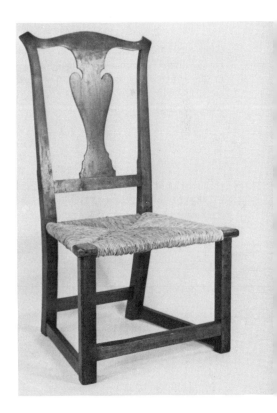

450. QUEEN ANNE CHAIR, c.1750–1810

CHIPPENDALE CHAIRS: (Above) **453. c.1770–1800:** The version shown here uses channeled ears, chamfered rear legs, Spanish feet, and a broader splat; maple, ash; 38$\frac{5}{8}$″ H. (Upper right) **454. c.1780–1810:** A chair that adopts the later squared beaded legs and stretchers (these legs were shortened in use).

(Above) **458. CHIPPENDALE SIDE CHAIR, c.1770–1790:** An alternate version adds a distinctive arched-center crest rail and broader splat; also included are squared rear posts, block & turned legs, and Spanish feet; maple; 37″ H.

(Above) **459. CHIPPENDALE SIDE CHAIR, c.1775–1800:** Note the variations by craftsmen and region vs. **#458**; both are from Conn. in the same period and style, but vary by size, shape, and turnings; 41¼″ H.

(Upper left) **455. SIDE CHAIR, c.1770–1830:** A transitional form that combines turned posts in the banister-back tradition, a Chippendale crest rail (with reeded ears), plus a late-turned base; 41½″ H.

(Near right) **456. ENGLISH SIDE CHAIR, c.1750–1760:** Chippendale styling also led to the pierced-splat design; this English oak chair (typically predating American acceptance) includes a concave yoke center and Spanish feet limited within the leg's parameter; 40¼″ H.

(Far right) **457. CHIPPENDALE SIDE CHAIR, c.1760–1790:** An American combination of the pierced splat, altered vase outline, and lobed ears; painted black; 40″ H.

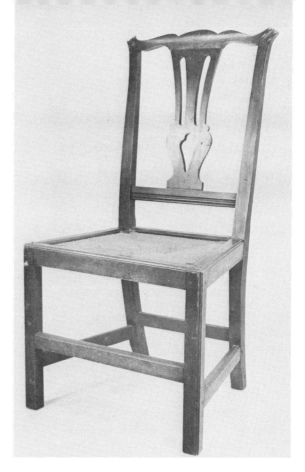

(Left) **460. SIDE CHAIR, c.1780–1800:** Another Chippendale form uses the period's alternate squared legs (with outside corners beaded), but injects earlier ladder-back slats under the prevailing eared crest rail; upholstered slip seat (removable); typical mortised and pinned construction; 37½″ H (Conn. Historical Society).

(Right) **461. SIDE CHAIR, c.1780–1810:** This chair combines a crest and an arched center with a pierced, long-necked splat—plus the common squared legs; its slip seat is removed (rush base is visible); 38½″ H.

CORNER (ROUNDABOUT) CHAIRS: These square-seated chairs were angled in design, and although odd appearing, are surprisingly comfortable; the low back (cut out in two pieces and joined at the rear—not steam bent) circled two sides of the seat; their turnings and forms followed period styles; mostly used in New England.

(Above) **462. SIDE CHAIR, c.1780–1810:** A long-necked pierced splat joins a shell-carved crest rail on this chair; its posts are chamfered at the rear for a thinner impression, and the legs have been shortened about 2″; 38¼″ H.

CORNER CHAIRS: (Above) **463. c.1740–1760:** Notice these typical flat arms with an applied crest, the rush seats, plus turned legs and stretchers; red paint; 31″ H (Conn. Historical Society). (Right) **464. c.1750–1780:** A later example in maple that uses fewer turnings, but has doubled the front box stretchers; 30⅝″ H (Author).

(Right) **465. CORNER CHAIR, c.1740–1760:** This illustrates the usual flat curved back with flaring handholds and a raised crest—above two concave arched slats; its sausage & ring legs are joined by ball-turned double stretchers; painted black (gold outlines are from the 1800s); 30$\frac{1}{2}$″ H (Private Coll.).

(Above) **466. CORNER CHAIR, c.1750:** A unique rural variation that includes a tapered splint seat and straight front; the continuous arm is mounted above curved slats, while its posts are of the vase-sausage-ring form; 33$\frac{1}{2}$″ H (Roger Bacon; Robert W. Skinner, Inc.).

(Below) **467. CORNER CHAIR, c.1730–1750:** A more formal chair that combines a Queen Anne cabriole leg (pad foot) and vase splats, plus block & turned rear legs (joined by an X-stretcher); maple; 30$\frac{1}{2}$″ H (Conn. Historical Society).

(Above left) **468. CORNER CHAIR, c.1760–1770:** A raised-back form having a peaked crest supported by baluster-turned spindles; concave slats; splint-woven seat; 41″ H (Deerfield Memorial Hall Museum, PVMA). (Above right) **469. CORNER (BARBER'S) CHAIR, c.1760–1770:** This chair adds a Windsor-like eared comb on spindles; also note its splayed Spanish feet, block & turned legs, and squared stretchers; 43$\frac{1}{2}$″ H (Private Coll.).

(Left) **470. CHAIR TABLE, c.1675–1700:** This form was an armchair with a hinged back that pivoted over onto the arms to create a table. It could be easily moved within a room and converted as required. This rectangular top is attached to a base of the Pilgrim period; it is an American-made (Mass.) English style in white oak plus a pine top; 19½″ H, top 53″ x 24″ (Metropolitan Museum of Art).

CHAIR TABLES: (Upper right) **471. c.1670:** A wainscot-type oak base (see **#397**)—with the usual shaped arms, turned posts, and plank seat—that is hinged to the top's two cleats; its feet are gone; 29″ H, top 42″ Dia (Smithsonian Institution). (Below) **472. c.1735–1770:** A similar form that includes a seat drawer; white oak, maple, and a pine top; 29″ H, top 50⅞″ Dia (Yale Univ. Art Gallery).

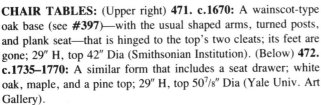

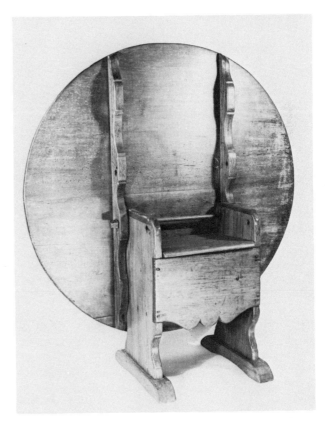

(Above) **473. CHAIR (HUTCH) TABLE, c.1710–1750:** Note the scrolled apron, legs, and cleats in this "hutch" table (i.e., its seat lifts for storage beneath); hard pine, with oak trestle feet; 26½″ H (Private Coll.).

(Below & right) **474. CHAIR TABLE** (two views), **c.1750–1770:** Block & vase posts are typical in this period; the two cleats on the oval (2-board) top are attached by wooden dowel hinges at the rear of the flat arms; notice the plank seat, straight apron, and rectangular ''boxed'' stretchers; pine top and seat, plus a maple base; painted red; 29″ H, top 45$\frac{1}{2}$″ x 41$\frac{1}{4}$″ (Author).

(Above, left, & right) **475. SETTLE-TABLE** (two views), **c.1770–1790:** This double-width seat creates a ''settle-table'' with a rec-tangular 3-board top; the plank ends are also scrolled like a settle (see **#534**); red painted pine; 28″ H, top 49″ x 36$\frac{1}{2}$″ (Author).

WINDSOR CHAIRS: These "stick chairs" were made of combined woods and normally painted (green, black, and red most popular); appearing c.1725, they were light, durable, and inexpensive—rapidly becoming favorites of all classes. **WINDSOR "SACK-BACK" ARMCHAIRS:** (Upper left) **476. ENGLISH, c.1750:** Note this heavy British design (they often added a center splat); 39″ H (Private Coll.). (Upper center) **477. c.1760–1790:** The long leg taper was common in New England; 34½″ H. (Upper right) **478. c.1765–1780:** A Philadelphia-type "knuckled" armchair with an elliptical seat; the legs were shortened 2″ in use; 35½″ H. (Lower left) **479. c.1790–1810:** A later date's lessened turnings; typical steam-bent arms; 38″ H. (Lower center) **480. c.1765–1780:** A variation associated with Independence Hall; it has reduced leg splay, flat arms, and a wide arched crest; 35″ H. (Lower right) **481. c.1795–1825:** The broad bulbous back form at century's end; 37½″ H.

(Left) 482. CONTINUOUS-ARM, BRACED WINDSOR CHAIR, c.1775–1800: The back rail and arms here are one piece of wood (steam bent) vs. the double-tiered sack-back style (see **#477**); also note the two V supports ("braces"; see **#487**); its single-board seat is carved ("saddled") to body shape; 36″ H (Private Coll.).

(Right) 483. SACK-BACK WINDSOR CHAIR, c.1795–1830: A late-period rural example that includes diminished turnings, shapeless arms, and a straight seat front; the legs penetrate its seat and are "wedged"; 38″ H.

484. BOW-BACKED WINDSOR CHAIR, c.1760–1780: A classic form with a continuous bow (nine spindles), saddle-shaped seat, boldly turned legs, and an H-stretcher; 36¼″ H (Private Coll.).

485. BOW-BACKED WINDSOR CHAIR, c.1780–1800: Note the incurving feet—a characteristic of Rhode Island chairs; seven spindles were the most common number for this style; painted black; 37″ H (Author).

486. BOW-BACKED WINDSOR CHAIR, c.1785–1790: A later narrow back that surprisingly uses nine spindles (they were usually draw-carved by a spokeshave); little form now remains in the seat; 36″ H.

(Left and above) **487. BRACED BOW-BACKED WINDSOR CHAIR** (two views), **c.1780–1800:** These long tapering legs are associated with New England, and the incurving feet with Rhode Island; two V braces reinforce the back (see closeup of their tailpiece); legs, stretchers, and spindles retain early bold turnings; 37 1/2″ H (Private Coll.).

(Upper left corner) **488. LOW-BACK WINDSOR CHAIR, c.1760–1780:** A form using flattened arms with spread ends and a low applied crest; the ball-ended legs are a Penn. characteristic; its woods include tulip, poplar, maple, and oak; 28″ H (Metropolitan Museum of Art).

(Left) **489. BOW-BACKED WINDSOR CHAIR** (two views), **c.1765–1780:** This style mortised its arms through the bow; it is branded by the maker (''B GILBERT'') under the seat (*above left*); 36″ H (Author).

(Right) **490. BOW-BACKED WINDSOR CHAIR, c.1790–1810:** A later version employing the newly fashionable ''bamboo'' turned legs; 38″ H.

COMB-BACK WINDSOR CHAIRS: (Upper left) **491. c.1775–1790:** These spindles continue through the arm to support an upper comb piece, while the vase & ring legs end in a tapering Rhode Island form; observe also the broad shieldlike seat and flaring knuckle arms; 43¼″ H (Deerfield Memorial Hall Museum, PVMA). (Upper center) **492. CHILD'S TABLE CHAIR, c.1770–1790:** Note the widely splayed legs, plus the rear rod that passed through arm holes to restrain the child; green paint; 44″ H (Private Coll.). (Upper right) **493. c.1770–1790:** A broad Conn. chair combines its wide leg splay with an oval seat; red paint; 36¼″ H (Private Coll.). (Lower left) **494. c.1765–1780:** This impressive Philadelphia chair mounts an arched crest rail (or comb) with scrolled ears; molded saddle seat; the baluster-ring legs end in blunt "arrow" feet; (*below*) its seat's underside shows old light green paint; "jack" plane marks, chamfered edges (to appear thinner); 45½″ H (Au.).

WINDSOR CHAIRS: (Upper left) **495. COMB-BACK, c.1775--1800:** A New England lobed comb style; 38″ H (Conn. Historical Society). (Upper center) **496. COMB-BACK, c.1780:** A rural Rhode Island form; note its thin comb, arms joined by the crest, and unique legs; 40$^{1}/_{2}$″ H. (Upper right) **497. FANBACK, c.1770–1800:** Uninterrupted spindles; mortised arms; 38″ H (Deerfield Memorial Hall Museum, PVMA). (Lower left) **498. ROD-BACK,** **c.1790–1830:** A common form by the 1800s reflecting the squared Sheraton profile, plus a ''bamboo'' base style; 34$^{1}/_{2}$″ H. (Lower center) **499. CONTINUOUS-ARM/COMB-BACK, c.1785–1810:** A combination chair; the legs were shortened in use; 44$^{3}/_{4}$″ H (Conn. Historical Society). (Lower right) **500. FANBACK, c.1765–1790:** Comb and turnings are typical of the Tracy and Allen families in eastern Conn.; 37$^{3}/_{4}$″ H (Author).

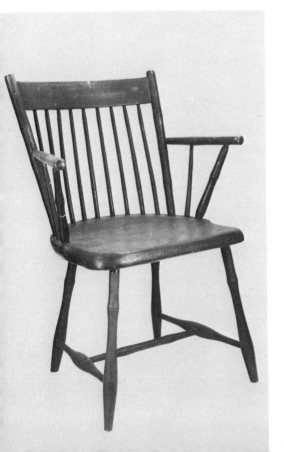

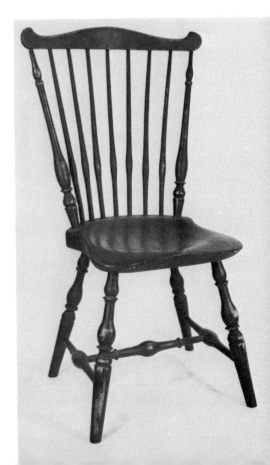

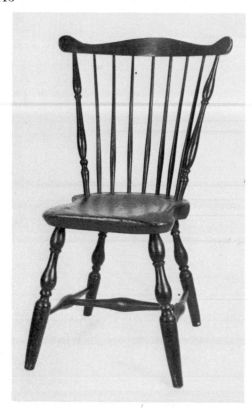

(Above) **501. FANBACK WINDSOR CHAIR, c.1770:** Note the seven spindles, vase-ring posts and legs, bulbous H stretcher, and long tapered leg endings common in New England and New York; 34¾″ H.

(Above) **502. FANBACK WINDSOR CHAIR, c.1780–1800:** This slightly later example shows less bulbous leg turnings, and the emerging bamboo shape in the center stretcher; eight spindles; 34¼″ H.

(Lower right) **504. ROD-BACK (BIRDCAGE) WINDSOR CHAIR; c.1790–1810:** A late-century style popular in the early 1800s; the upper back opening with one or more spindles is associated with its "birdcage" name; note the new squared-back Sheraton influence, its flatter squared seat, the bamboo legs and box stretchers that are now replacing the H shape—all typical of this transition period; black paint; 33½″ H.

(Above) **503. FANBACK WINDSOR CHAIRS, c.1770–1780:** A pair having carved scrolled ears, modified saddle seats, and the Rhode Island style of tapering feet; black paint; 36½″ H (Author).

WRITING-ARM WINDSOR CHAIRS: (Above) **505. COMB-BACK, c.1765–1803:** By Ebenezer Tracy, Lisbon, Conn.; accessory drawers are under its arm and seat; red paint; 45¼″ H (Deerfield Memorial Hall Museum, PVMA). (Right) **506. CONTINUOUS ARM, c.1775–1800:** Included are two drawers and a "candle slide" at the arm's end; 40¾″ H (Stanley-Whitman House, Farmington, Conn.).

WINDSOR SETTEES: Windsors also appeared as wide settees. (Lower left) **507. LOW-BACK, c.1760–1780:** A Penn. style using arrow-footed legs; 30½″ H, 53½″ W. (Lower right) **508. c.1770–1800:** Combined comb- and sack-back forms (both, Metropolitan Museum of Art).

120

WING (EASY) CHAIRS: These chairs had upholstered arms, back, wings, and seat. (Left) **509. QUEEN ANNE PERIOD, c.1725:** This arched back flows into wings and the vertical rolled arms of the period; its front cabriole legs have pad feet, while the rear legs are squared and canted; New England; original needlepoint; maple, walnut; 46³/₄″ H (Metropolitan Museum of Art). (Right) **510. CHIPPENDALE, c.1785–1800:** The wooden frame demonstrates the larger side wings of this dating (handy for draft protection or a nodding head); note, too, the squared Chippendale legs (box stretcher); 44¹/₂″ H (Private Coll.).

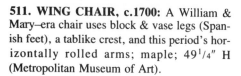

511. WING CHAIR, c.1700: A William & Mary–era chair uses block & vase legs (Spanish feet), a tablike crest, and this period's horizontally rolled arms; maple; 49¹/₄″ H (Metropolitan Museum of Art).

512. WING CHAIR, c.1725: The new Queen Anne influence employs cabriole legs with Spanish feet, ball & disc stretchers, plus horizontal arm rolls (an alternate to the vertical arm, see #509); walnut and maple (Metropolitan Museum of Art).

513. OPEN-ARM ("MARTHA WASHINGTON") CHAIR, c.1790–1800: A late century form includes open shaped wooden arms and square beaded Chippendale legs; 44¹/₂″ H (Metropolitan Museum of Art).

(Upper left) **514. FORM (BENCH), c.1660–1690:** Most 17th-century sitting was on "forms" (benches) and "joint" stools (see **#520**); this early English carved oak "form" includes melon-turned splayed legs and heavy stretchers; 18^1/$_2$″ H, 43^1/$_2$″ L (Private Coll.).

(Above) **515. LONG FORM, c.1670–1700:** A plain maple American bench (found with the table **#547**) that has a beaded top edge and mortised A-shaped legs; 19″ H, 104″ L (Private Coll.).

(Upper right corner) **516. SLAB BENCH:** A crude style used throughout our period; it combines the outer part of a tree trunk (some bark still remains) and socketed legs, which penetrate to the top.

(Right) **517. UTILITY (WEAVER'S) BENCH, c.1650–1850:** A common working style made from a slab seat (a recessed center included here) and chamfered legs (socketed); pine; 22^3/$_4$″ H.

(Left) **518. SCROLLED BENCH, c.1770–1790:** A Chippendale-period scrolled bench that used single-board legs (mortised through the seat), plus side aprons (see **#526**); pine; 17^1/$_2$″ H, 48″ L.

(Near left) **520. JOINT STOOL, c.1680–1700:** An American (N.Y.) version in applewood displaying simplified local turnings; 21″ H (Lillian Blankley Cogan).

(Above) **519. JOINT STOOL, c.1670–1690:** This English oak stool includes the usual thumb-molded seat, lunette-carved apron, baluster legs, and squared stretchers (the feet are gone); pegged mortise & tenon joints; 17½″ H (Author).

FOOT STOOLS: By the 1700s, stools served more for feet than sitting. (Far left) **521. c.1700–1720:** This William & Mary form (turned trumpetlike legs) has a restored rush seat; 13½″ H. (Near left) **522. c.1710:** A stool made like a chair base, using vase-turned legs, baluster stretchers, and a rush seat; 11½″ H (Lillian Blankley Cogan). (Lower left corner) **523. c.1730–1750:** A Queen Anne shape that includes scrolled aprons and cabriole legs (bottoms are worn, but were probably pad feet originally); the cyma-curved seat openings served as a handle; 8½″ H. (Lower right) **524. c.1760–1800:** A popular style that retains the earlier scrolled apron and single-board legs; its seat is chip-carved on the ends; 6¾″ H.

(Far left) **525. STOOL:** This primitive low work stool (for the hearth, milking, etc.) has a curved single-piece top and handle; 12½″ H. (Near left) **526. FOOTSTOOL, c.1770–1810:** Note the Chippendale scrolled-board legs and applied straight aprons; nailed joints; 6¾″ H. (Below) **527. STOOL, c.1650–1850:** A common 3-legged work stool; 10¼″ H.

STOOLS: (Left) **528.** A tree-formed seat with cuts underneath from its use as a handy chopping block. (Lower left) **529.** A work stool mounting octagonal legs; 19″ H. (Lower center) **530. c.1750–1800:** Like a weaver's stool, but possibly a table (i.e., little top wear); 23½″ H (Private Coll.). (Lower right) **531. CHILD'S NIGHT CHAIR, c.1740–1780:** A seat/potty form like a narrow settle; 24″ H (Merle E. Bouchard).

SETTLES: These were high-backed benches that protected the sitter from chilling drafts, and reflected the hearth heat. (Upper left) **532. c.1690–1750:** An early curved-back American form; 49″ H, 82″ W (Henry Whitfield House, Conn. Historical Commission). (Above) **533. c.1720–1730:** An alternate style with a pinned frame, raised panels, and open arms; American; 50″ H, 74″ W (Wadsworth Atheneum). (Left) **534. c.1770–1790:** A typical type using vertical backboards and ended by scrolled planks; 53$\frac{1}{4}$″ H (Conn. Historical Society). (Lower left) **535. c.1760–1800:** This smaller child's settle has a lift-up seat for storage; 26$\frac{1}{4}$″ H, 32$\frac{1}{2}$″ W. (Below) **536. c.1750–1770:** A double-facing design that shares its single back with opposite seats; 50″ H, 56″ W (Au.).

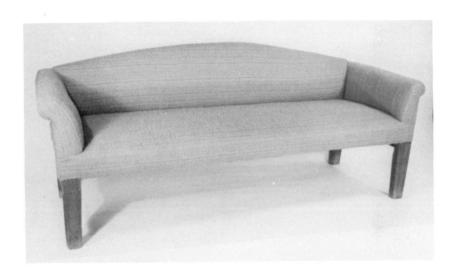

(Above) **537. CONVERTIBLE BED SET-TLE** (two views), **c.1790–1810:** A dual-use settle; the seat and front are hinged at the bottom to open forward and create a sleeping compartment (*upper right*); 33$^{1}/_{2}$″ H, 66$^{1}/_{2}$″ W. (Right) **538. SOFA, c.1760–1790:** The usual sofa had an upholstered seat, back, and arms; this rural Chippendale form includes an arched back, rolled arms, and chamfered legs (chestnut); 29$^{1}/_{2}$″ H, 72″ L. (Below) **539. SOFA, c.1770–1800:** A more formal Chippendale sofa that combines the serpentine (''camel'') back, roll-over arms, thin feather cushion, and reeded legs; 40″ H, 75″ L (Ballard Coll.).

(Below) **540. SOFA FRAME, c.1750–1825:** The surviving nailed frame from a rural sofa with its back edge broken off; it was possibly upholstered only on the arms originally; 20$^{1}/_{2}$″ H, 64$^{1}/_{4}$″ L (Private Coll.).

(Upper left) **541. WAGON SEAT, c.1760–1770:** This form served as a settee at home or an extra seat for the wagon; note its sturdy posts and thin slats; maple, ash; 31$\frac{1}{2}$" H. (Upper right) **542. WAGON SEAT, c.1780–1800:** A later seat with plainer styling; tops of the upper slats have broken off (common); the center leg is thicker to support sockets on three sides; 28$\frac{1}{2}$" H, 35" L.

(Right) **543. CHILD'S TRAINER, c.1750–1840:** A child's walking trainer; hickory; 15$\frac{1}{2}$" H (Thankful Arnold House). (Lower left) **544. BABY TENDER, c.1770–1820:** A nailed baby pen with an inside seat; pine (Deerfield Memorial Hall Museum, PVMA). (Lower right) **545. CHILD'S WALKER (STAND STOOL), c.1790–1820:** Pen for a standing and walking child; notice the period's wide wooden casters; 17$\frac{3}{4}$" H (Johnathan Dickerman House, Hamden [Conn.] Historical Society).

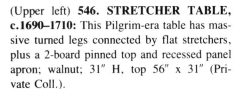

(Upper left) **546. STRETCHER TABLE, c.1690–1710:** This Pilgrim-era table has massive turned legs connected by flat stretchers, plus a 2-board pinned top and recessed panel apron; walnut; 31″ H, top 56″ x 31″ (Private Coll.).

(Second left) **547. STRETCHER TABLE, c.1670–1700:** This long table uses a center flat stretcher, turned legs, and removable single-board top (93″ x 31″); its two drawers have carved faces (never any pulls); walnut; found in the Hudson Valley; 31″ H (Private Coll.).

(Below left) **548. TRESTLE TABLE, c.1650:** "Trestles" were transverse feet holding a vertical column that supported the tabletop; the columns were pierced and joined by a large center stretcher (pinned and wedged); the top removed to dismantle the table for storage when not in use; New England; a pine top and oak frame; 36″ H, top 146½″ x 24″ (Metropolitan Museum of Art).

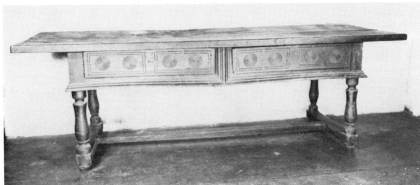

(Lower left) **549. TRESTLE TABLE, c.1700–1740;:** A hard pine table with scrolled trestles and columns; note wedges securing its stretcher; 2-board top; 31″ H, top 83″ x 31″ (Au.).

(Lower right) **550. TRESTLE TABLE, c.1690:** A small oval-top trestle form that incorporates block & turned legs and a stretcher; 25″ H, top 30½″ x 20½″ (Lillian Blankley Cogan).

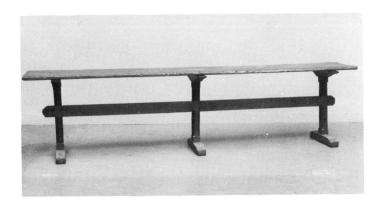

(Above) **551. TRESTLE TABLE, c.1700–1750:** A Penn. style employing an elaborately scrolled base, and adding a center drawer; walnut (Metropolitan Museum of Art).

GATELEG TABLES: This form used à center pivoting gatelike leg to support the table's hinged leaves; it was most popular c.1650–1720 (succeeded by the drop-leaf tables). (Upper right) **552. TRESTLE GATELEG, c.1690–1710:** Note the trestle feet and notched gateleg to fit into the stretcher when closed; maple and pine; 26¹/₂″ H (Stanley-Whitman House, Farmington, Conn.). (Right) **553. c.1690–1710:** A William & Mary period design in oak with an elementary Spanish-foot form and early long columnlike turnings; 27¹/₂″ H. (Lower left) **554. c.1680–1700:** Note these stepped trestle feet and spiraled ("twist") legs; 29″ H. (Lower right) **555. c.1690–1720:** Such heavy "ring & bobbin" turnings are of the William & Mary era; Conn. River Valley; hard pine top, maple base; 26″ H (Private Coll.).

(Upper left & right) **556. GATELEG TABLE** (two views), **c.1720–1750:** Note the popular vase & ring–style base on this maple table in its open and closed positions; an end drawer has been added; 27¼″ H (Author).

(Right) **557. TUCKAWAY (TUCK) TABLE, c.1690–1720:** An English oak version of the space-saving ''tuck'' table that folded the gate flat, and swung the hinged top down to create a compact form for storage; 26¼″ H (Private Coll.).

(Lower left) **558. SINGLE-GATE TABLE, c.1720–1750:** A variation with a wide top and single drop leaf—requiring only one gate; vase & ball turned legs; squared stretchers; pine; 27¼″ H.

(Lower right) **559. FLAT-GATE TABLE, c.1740–1760:** This style, favored by the English, mounts a flat-faced gate frame in a turned-leg base; 24½″ H.

(Left) 560. DOUBLE GATELEG TABLE, c.1680–1710: A long table made with one drop leaf supported by two gatelegs; notice its early block & column legs; cherry and pine; 30″ H, 88″ W (Conn. Historical Society).

(Below) 561. BUTTERFLY TABLE (two views), **c.1720–1735:** This American innovation used an in-place wing-shaped bracket (a "butterfly") that swung out to support a raised leaf; note the typical raked legs (vase & ring here), and flat stretchers; a slope-sided end drawer was added at some time; maple posts, cherry stretchers, and a birch top; 28³/₄″ H (Author).

(Right) 562. UNDERSIDE OF #563: The butterfly bracket is dowel-hinged into the stretcher and underside of the top; note its early butterfly hinges and normal bracket wear under the leaf.

(Below) 563. BUTTERFLY TABLE, c.1690–1710: This is earlier than **#561**, per its wider splay, and more bulbous William & Mary–style turnings; typical pinned mortise & tenon joints; 23¹/₂″ H (Lillian Blankley Cogan).

SAWBUCK TABLES: It was typically a rectangular top on X-shaped legs, connected by a stretcher. (Above) **564. c.1750:** A New England form (Mass.); the chamfered legs cross in a lap joint, while the stretcher is mortised through this joint, and secured by a wedge (i.e., easily dismantled); the 2-board top was later shortened at the far end; pine in red paint; 27″ H. (Right) **565. c.1700–1750:** A German-Penn. style using scrolled legs; walnut and oak (Metropolitan Museum of Art). (Lower left) **566. c.1750-1800:** A later hard pine table that includes nailed side stretchers in a trough design; 25$\frac{1}{2}$″ H (Private Coll.). (Lower right) **567. c.1750–1800:** This nailed sawbuck table is dovetailed to a pair of footrest-type stretchers. 27″ H (Private Coll.).

TAVERN (STRETCHER-BASE) TABLES: These low, sturdy utility tables normally had turned legs and low stretchers. Being light and movable, they were popular in home kitchens and inns (i.e., no booths, they moved the table to the customer). (Center left) **569. c.1740–1760:** Note the usual side drawer, and these later plain-turned legs; maple; 26¼″ H. (Center right) **570. c.1760–1780:** The top was often bleached from constant cleaning with lye soap; this base includes regional turnings and beaded stretchers; from western Mass.; 27½″ H. (Lower left) **571. c.1760–1790:** The drawer was omitted here; it has a pine top, walnut base, and typical pinned mortise & tenon joints; 27¼″ H. (Lower right) **572. c.1750–1760:** Note this turned middle H-stretcher table form; 28⅝″ H (Au.).

(Above) **568. TAVERN TABLE, c.1720–1750:** Note the Queen Anne period's scrolled apron; the common single-board top includes the transverse "breadboard" ends; vase & ring legs; pine; 27″ H, top 43½″ x 30″ (Author).

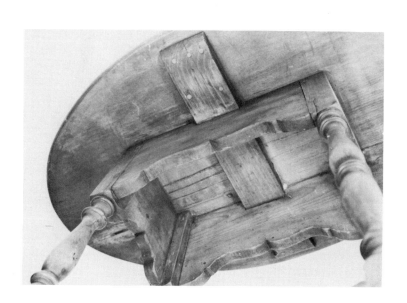

SIDE TABLES: (Left) **573. c.1740–1750:** A table with splayed legs and a scalloped apron in maple and pine; from N.J.; (*upper left*) note its supportive bottom cleat; 24″ H. (Upper right) **574. c.1750:** These legs have only a side splay; the American stretchers are typically flush with the leg blocks; 22$\frac{1}{4}$″ H. (Right) **575. c.1720:** An octagonal top above a squared frame; found in Mass.; 26$\frac{1}{2}$″ H (Wadsworth Atheneum). (Below) **576. c.1720–1760:** A single-board pine top (30$\frac{1}{2}$″ x 74$\frac{1}{2}$″; breadboard ends) on a maple base; 28″ H.

(Left) **577. WINDSOR TAVERN TABLE, c.1750–1770:** Windsor tables usually had open frames, turned legs, and spindle-like stretchers that suggest influence from the Windsor chairs; this one adds block forms in the legs; its rectangular pine top is pegged; 26³/₄″ H (Author).

(Upper right) **578. WINDSOR TABLE, c.1760–1790:** A round recessed top on three Windsorlike legs and stretchers; walnut; from Penn.; 26″ H (Israel Sack, Inc. N.Y.C.).

(Right) **579. WINDSOR TABLE, c.1780–1800:** These long tapering legs are in the New England Windsor form—joined by high double stretchers; pegged pine top; 25¹/₄″ H.

(Lower left) **580. SIDE TABLE, c.1740–1780:** The wide splayed tapering legs omit stretchers, but add a scrolled Queen Anne apron and breadboard-ended top; pegged mortise & tenon joints; New England.

(Lower right) **581. SIDE TABLE, c.1720–1740:** An oval 2-board top above a deep apron and splayed legs with pad feet; green paint; 24″ H.

SIDE TABLES: This later Queen Anne form that omitted stretchers found many uses—especially in catering to the new tea-drinking fashion. (Left) **582. c.1740–1760:** These tapering splayed legs end in button feet; note the cutout apron; maple; 25″ H (Private Coll.). (Center left) **583. c.1740–1760:** An oval top with block & turned legs plus disc feet; 28″ H (Private Coll.). (Center right) **584. c.1760:** A rural combination of uneven maple legs (pad feet) and a molded skirt; Conn.; 28″ H (Private Coll.).

TEA TABLES: More formal tables appeared in these longer rectangular forms or on tripods (see **#652**). (Lower left) **585. c.1740–1800:** This table mounts a scrolled apron, cabriole legs, and side molding on a birch top; maple base; 27″ H (Wadsworth Atheneum). (Lower right) **586. c.1740–1800:** The "porringer top" includes rounded corners reportedly for candles, porringers, etc.; 26¼″ H (Conn. Historical Society).

(Left) 587. UTILITY TABLE, c.1700–1725:
This long American utility table stands on an
early (Flemish) cabriole leg form with cushioned pad feet; it is all maple, with pinned
mortise & tenon joints; the 2-board top attaches
mortised breadboard ends (*close-up above*);
29″ H (Private Coll.).

(Right) 588. UTILITY TABLE, c.1740–1760: These heavy cabriole legs, large pad feet, removable top (3-boards; pinned to the
base;), and three drawers are typical of Hudson Valley, N.J., and
Penn.-"Dutch" areas; walnut; 28″ H (Author).

(Lower left) 589. UTILITY TABLE (two views), **c.1770–1800:**
A work-table form found across the Northeast that has a removable
top (pinned through its side cleats), unequal drawer widths, and
tapering legs ending in pad feet; notice the oval brasses and wood
inlays on the drawer fronts (Chippendale-Hepplewhite period);
(*lower right*) the removed top reveals the tongue & groove corner
joint now gaining popularity, a side pin for the top, plus a dovetailed drawer; 28″ H.

(Upper left) **590. UTILITY TABLE, c.1750–1790:** A work-table form found in Penn., N.J., and the Hudson Valley: it includes the characteristic removable top (side pins), uneven drawer widths, and disc-ended turned legs; cherry top, maple base; painted red; 26″ H (Author).

(Upper right) **591. UTILITY TABLE, c.1780–1800:** This apron retains earlier curved ends, yet its beaded legs show a Hepplewhite tapering profile; the top originally had a drop leaf; 26″ H. (Below) **592. UTILITY TABLE, c.1740–1800:** A variation made from an old "batten" door, plus plank legs joined by a center stretcher.

(Center left) **593. UTILITY (PLANK, BUTCHER'S) TABLE, c.1650–1850:** A heavy plank top mounted on faceted legs (socketed); the type is associated with butchering or heavy cutting, and at one time this one had six legs (four near one end; a Penn. style); 31″ H.

(Left) **594. UTILITY TABLE, c.1770–1810:** The center stretcher (dovetailed) and straight squared legs (beaded edges) are typical of the Chippendale period; its single-board pine top measures 60$\frac{1}{2}$″ x 29″; 29″ H.

(Above) **595. UTILITY TABLE, c.1760–1790:** This Chippendale period table has chamfered straight legs and a mortised center stretcher, while its rectangular top is made with two tongue & grooved boards; pine in red paint; 26″ H (Author).

(Above) **596. UTILITY TABLE, c.1770–1810:** The plain Chippendale lines continue here; its square-sectioned legs (beaded outside edge) join a straight apron with pinned mortise & tenon joints; maple; a single-board pinned top; 27$^1/4$″ H.

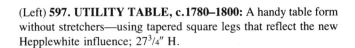

(Left) **597. UTILITY TABLE, c.1780–1800:** A handy table form without stretchers—using tapered square legs that reflect the new Hepplewhite influence; 27$^3/4$″ H.

(Right) **598. UTILITY TABLE, c.1790–1810:** A solid table having a better working height (higher); from the central Conn. River Valley; the top is typically scrubbed lighter, and its base is painted red; tapering round legs indicate the new Sheraton influence; heavy board stretchers are nailed to the legs; 32$^1/2$″ H.

DROP-LEAF TABLES: These tables were made with hinged leaves that folded down when not in use to save space. (Upper left) **599. c.1725:** This 3-legged variation has three leaves; the round top (when open) rotated to support them on the frame; mahogany (Metropolitan Museum of Art). (Left) **600. c.1720–1740:** Notice these baluster splayed legs and bottom stretchers; the leaves were supported by pull-out bars. (Lower left) **601. c.1750–1760:** A tea table with hinged leaves braced by pull-out supports; maple; 26¼″ H (David Bland).

SWING-LEG TABLES: This style swings out an end leg on each side (hinged near the apron's center) to support the raised leaves. (Upper right corner) **602. c.1750–1770:** Cabriole legs with pad feet; mahogany; from eastern Mass.; 27″ H. (Lower right) **603. c.1740–1760:** A popular Queen Anne cabriole-leg style mounting rounded leaves; 28¼″ H (Private Coll.).

(Upper left) **604. SWING-LEG TABLE, c.1760–1780:** This heavy walnut table has four fixed corner legs plus two additional swing legs; their squared Chippendale form includes chamfered inner corners; from central N.Y.; 28½″ H. (Above) **605. DROP-LEAF TABLE, c.1750–1780:** A tea-table base with button feet that had a later drop leaf added for heavier work; maple base with a pine top; 25″ H.

(Left) **606. SWING-LEG TABLE, c.1755–1770:** An elegant cherry table mounting reeded legs and hinged "rule-joint" leaves; because a swing leg pivoted out half of the apron, a second complete apron was usually installed behind it; 27½″ H. (Lower left) **607. SWING-LEG TABLE, c.1780–1820:** Note the early Hepplewhite tapered legs; birch; found in Maine; 30″ H. (Lower right) **608. DROP-LEAF TABLE, c.1785–1810:** These leaves are held up by arms pivoting from the apron; cherry; 28¼″ H.

CARD TABLES: (Upper left) **609. c.1770–1790:** This form includes a rear corner swing leg, plus a hinged leaf to rest against the wall or fold over the stationary top; its legs are fluted on the outside faces; 29″ H. (Upper right) **610. c.1720–1740:** An earlier version of the hinged-top form with a baluster-turned base (Au.).

(Above) **611. CARD TABLE, c.1790–1800:** An elegant mahogany-top table finished in maple veneer; 28″ H (Private Coll.). (Center right) **612. PEMBROKE TABLE, c.1795–1820:** Notice the narrow ''Pembroke'' leaves on this cherry table; 28″ H. (Right) **613. PEMBROKE TABLE, c.1785–1800:** These leaves have a serpentine outline; 27¹/₂″ H (Conn. Historical Society).

(Upper left) **614. PEMBROKE TABLE, c.1785–1800:** The "Pembroke" form—from the Chippendale and Hepplewhite periods—features narrow drop leaves (usually supported when open by hinged brackets); these tapering legs are typical, and are joined by arched crossed stretchers; 28½″ H (Private Coll.).

(Upper right) **615. PEMBROKE TABLE, c.1790–1810:** A small mahogany Pembroke form from Rhode Island that includes flat X-stretchers; the inside leg corners are chamfered.

SIDE TABLES: (Center left) **616. c.1680–1700:** Such side tables normally sat against a wall to hold serving vessels, or were used to extend a table's length; this early carved oak example has an arched center drawer, and turned columnar legs of the late l600s; 31½″ H.(Lower left) **617. c.1760–1770:** A simple triangular base (pine) supports a scrolled top; 29″ H. (Lower right) **618. c.1780–1800:** A slightly scrolled T-shaped apron is combined with tapering Hepplewhite legs; it has a 2-board pine top and a maple base; 26½″ H.

619. TABLE STAND, c.1710–1730: This unique broad top is supported by splayed baluster-turned legs; the top's bottom edge is chamfered to reduce its visible thickness; maple and pine; 25 1/2" H (Lillian Blankley Cogan).

620. TABLE STAND, c.1750–1770: These tapered round legs (pad feet) and straight aprons create a maple base for a small oval top; it also includes an end drawer, and pinned mortise & tenon joints; 27" H (Author).

621. SEWING STAND, c.1790–1810: This veneered and inlaid Hepplewhite sewing stand has a hinged lid, a lower front drawer, and slides for the newly fashionable cloth storage bag underneath; 29 1/2" H.

622. TABLE STAND, c.1780–1790: An attractive cherry stand with applied top molding, a lipped drawer, beaded outer corners on its legs, and pierced X-stretchers; 28" H (Conn. Historical Society).

623. TABLE STAND, c.1790–1820: A common utility pine stand with a drawer and tapering legs that remained popular well into the 1800s; 28 3/4" H.

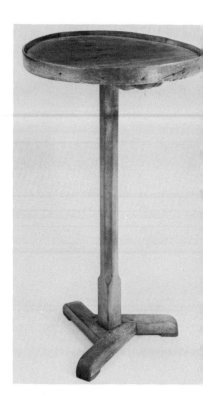

(Upper left) **624. X-BASE STAND, c.1710–1730:** The round top is a single piece of burl—supported by four diagonal braces mortised into the chamfered post; 24″ H. (Upper center) **625. TRI-BASE STAND, c.1700–1750:** This channeled and chip-carved post is socketed (and wedged) in a 3-footed base; 28¼″ H. (Upper right) **626. TRI-BASE STAND, c.1740–1780:** A top with an applied outer rim; the chamfers on its trunk terminate in "lamb's-tongue" ends; maple and ash; 26½″ H (Author).

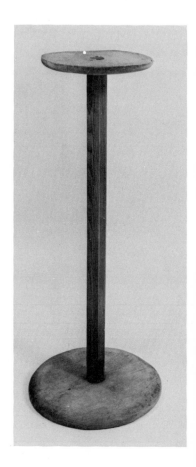

(Above left) **627. X-BASE STAND, c.1740–1810:** The octagonal post is socketed and wedged at each end; 24″ H. (Above center) **628. ROUND-BASE STAND, c.1750:** This turned stand includes a chestnut base, maple post, and pine top; 28½″ H (Private Coll.).

(Right) **629. ROUND-BASE STAND, c.1750–1810:** An elementary New England pine form with an octagonal post; 33¾″ H.

(Upper left) **630. PLATFORM STAND, c.1750–1770:** This turned trunk has a threaded end and a large wooden nut under the platform; walnut; found in N.J.; 25¹/₂″ H. (Upper center) **631. X-BASE STAND, c.1680–1700:** An attractive early baluster-turned post in a stepped cross-base; octagonal top; 24³/₄″ H (Lillian Blankley Cogan). (Upper right) **632. X-BASE STAND, c.1690–1730:** A unique base form—added to a gracefully turned trunk; maple; 25¹/₂″ H (Wadsworth Atheneum).

(Upper left) **633. PLATFORM STAND, c.1730–1750:** This footed stand unscrews into four parts; maple, cherry, pine; 29″ H (Private Coll.). (Upper center) **634. PLATFORM STAND, c.1780–1800:** A ball-footed Hudson Valley and New England form; its column edges are beaded; 27″ H. (Upper right) **635. X-BASE STAND, c.1720–1750:** A bulbous maple trunk socketed into a flat lap-joined base; square pine top; 27¹/₂″ H (Author).

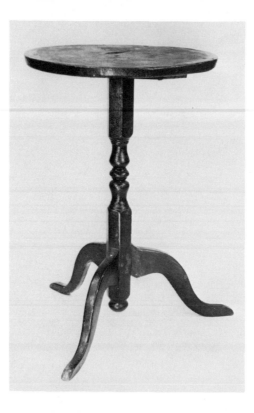

636. T-BASE STAND, c.1730: This turned maple post is mounted on a pinned T-shaped base with downcurving ends; from Mass. (David & Marjorie Schorsch, Inc.).

637. TRIPOD (CANDLE) STAND, c.1750: The faceted "vase & disc" trunk adds a turned "drop" below the leg joints; its round top is typical; 25″ H (David Bland).

638. TRIPOD STAND, c.1750–1770: The usual post extension that passes up into the cleat continues on through this top; pine, in mustard color paint; Conn.; 29½″ H.

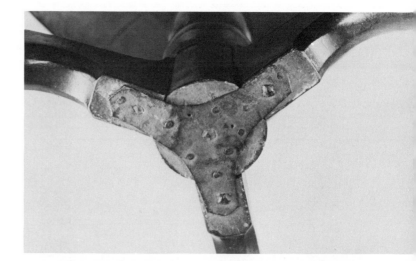

639. TRIPOD STAND, c.1760–1780: Note this inlaid top and the well-shaped snake feet; 25½″ H. (Above right) **639A.** The common iron brace that secured the legs in their dovetailed joints. (Right) **639B.** A cleat typically beveled to reduce its visibility.

(Left) **640. TRIPOD STAND** (two views), **c.1771–1780:** A cherry "candle" stand attributed to Eliphalet Chapin (East Windsor, Conn.); note the bulbous vase & ring post, graceful snake-headed feet, and (*upper right corner*) its decorative incised base rings and chip carving; the legs are typically dovetailed into the post from the bottom (and held by iron straps, per **#639A**); 26″ H (Author).

(Right) **641.** An alternate method of attaching the legs—by pinned mortised joints from the side; note this use of squared pins in round holes for staying power; and their tendency to project out with age.

(Left) **642. TRIPOD STAND, c.1765–1780:** Snake feet and a vase-turned trunk hold a scrolled top on this stand; (*lower right*) an underside close-up of the top's carved edges reveals early tool marks; cherry; 28″ H (Author).

(Lower left) **643. STAND DRAWER:** Double-ended drawers often passed through a stand's deep bracket ("cleat"); they were used for cards, candles, strikers, etc.

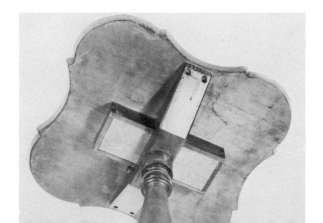

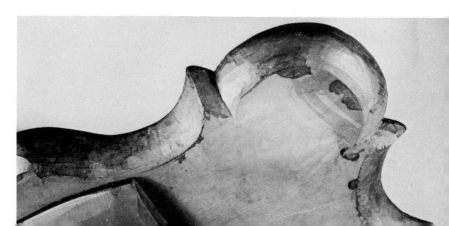

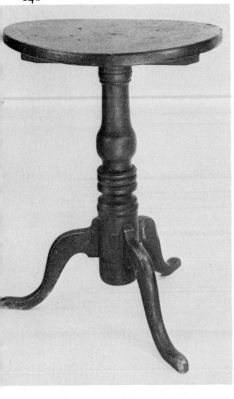

TRIPOD STANDS: (Upper left) **644. c.1780–1800:** A heavily turned regional form from Willington, Conn.; the warped round top is pegged; red paint; cherry; 24″ H. (Upper center) **645. c.1770–1780:** A rural cherry stand with vague ''cup'' or ''urn'' turnings, plus an applied edge on its square top; 27″ H. (Upper right) **646. c.1780–1790:** A crisply turned urn-shaped post of this neo-classical period; the square top is stationary; red paint; 27″ H.

TRIPOD STANDS: (Above left) **647. c.1780–1790:** A hinged top with mahogany, maple, and birch inlays; center probably a cylindrical ''peel'' (Au.). (Above center) **648. c.1780–1790:** Note the more modest urn & ring turnings in this maple stand; it also has a square top and well-formed snake feet; 26¹/₂″ H. (Above right) **649. c.1780–1790:** A transitional form that combines a heavily turned trunk and flat, shouldered legs; 25″ H (David Bland).

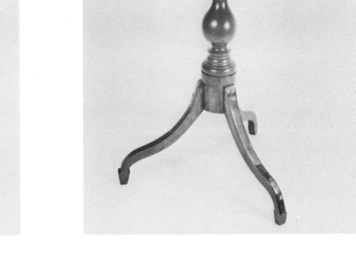

(Above) **650. TRIPOD STAND, c.1790–1830:** By the century's end, such convex (''spider'') legs were becoming popular; this stand is in maple, with a fixed oval top (24″ x 17″); its urn-style post retains a bold outline; 26³/₄″ H.

(Upper right) **651. TRIPOD STAND, c.1795–1830:** A transitional table having the multiringed turnings favored in the early 19th century, but the ''spade'' feet of the late 1700s; maple; fixed circular top; 27″ H.

(Lower left) **652. TIP-TOP (TILT) TEA TABLE, c.1750–1755:** Formal tripod tea tables had a larger and heavier Chippendale form than the candle stands—and most tops were hinged to tip; this unusual octagonal 3-board cherry top is painted with stippled designs (Metropolitan Museum of Art).

(Lower right) **653. TIP-TOP TEA TABLE, c.1760:** The broadly turned cherry center post is dovetailed with its three substantial legs that end in cushioned snake-head feet; 28″ H.

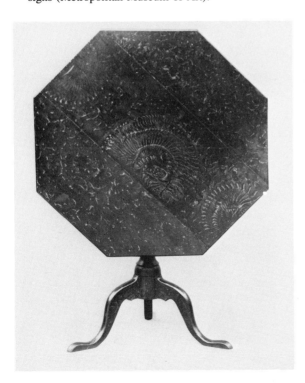

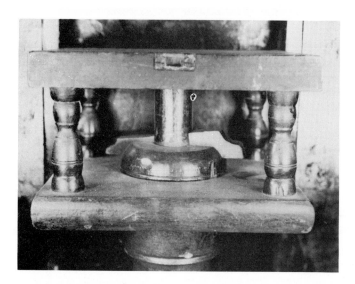

TIP-TOP TEA TABLES: (Upper left & right) **654. c.1760:** A modified "vase" or "cup" post with a 3-board top (see underside, *right*), i.e., the post terminates in a wooden block that is hinged (wooden dowel) to the top's cleats; its brass spring catch hooks onto the nail in the block; 26½″ H. (Left) **655. "BIRDCAGE",** **c.1760–1800:** A device that allows the tabletop to tip or rotate; four columns join its two platforms; the lower post is held by a key wedge, and its top is hinged to the upper platform. (Lower left) **656. "PIECRUST" TOP, c.1760–1780:** This more elegant table includes a "birdcage", and a raised-edge "piecrust" top; 29″ H (Private Coll.). (Lower right) **657. c.1780:** An unusual trunk turning that illustrates the wide range of regional variations; 30″ H.

TIP-TOP TEA TABLES: (Left) **658. c.1780:** Growing affluence in the 1780s is apparent in this mahogany example having snake feet and carved "gadrooning" in the trunk's lower cup; 27½″ H. (Right) **659. c.1780:** A similar single-board top mahogany table also adds gadrooning, and more heavily shouldered legs; it was found in Wethersfield, Conn.; 28″ H (Author).

Timekeeping

The time of day in modest homes of the colonies was normally gauged by the position of the sun, pacing of chores, or the local church bell being rung at a preset hour. Sundials found limited use (see **#660**), and sandglasses also helped to measure short periods (see **#662**). Yet, by the end of the 18th century, a surprising number of middle-class homes had acquired clocks. This trend had been greatly accelerated in the 1790s when America's clockmakers perfected inexpensive wooden works which launched one of our major industries for the 1800s.

The first domestic form in England was the 17th-century "lantern" clock (using weights on hand-set chains). It cannot be properly considered a "country" piece, but one is included here to help trace the clock's evolution during our period (**#666**).

About 1660 the pendulum was added. With this development, the "tall" or "case" clock came into being (since named the "grandfather's clock"). Its high case was needed to house the weights that drove the mechanism, as well as the long pendulum that regulated the speed-of-action (see **#669**). Most of the 18th-century works were brass and came from England (**#670**). The name found on a clockface may be the original maker of the mechanism, or the importing merchant who often had the wooden case made locally. By incorporating the prevailing succession of furniture style changes, this tall form continued to be popular as late as the 1850s.

Eighteenth-century clockfaces remained essentially square until about 1725, when an arched top was added to conceal the striking bell. This early dial was typically of brass with a silvered or pewter ring on which the numerals were engraved. By 1770, however, most faces were being enameled on an iron base—followed by less expensive practices from the growing American makers, such as painting directly on wood, or mounting an engraved paper dial. The usual tall clock of that century (English and American) had brass works, ran for eight days (wound by a key), and struck a bell on the hour or at regular intervals to relay its message through the house.

(Right) **660. SUNDIAL ("NOON MARK"), c.1730–1800:** Although accurate for little beyond indicating noon, such portable pewter sundials were commonly nailed to the window sill; this one was discovered in Albany, N.Y. and is marked, "I B"; 4⅝″ Dia.

(Left) **661. SUNDIAL-COM-PASS, c.1750–1780:** A compass and sundial were important for travel; the sundial is hinged to fold; its turned brass case uses a threaded cover; 2" Dia.

(Right) **662. SAND (TIME) GLASS, c.1750–1800:** This timer has two equal hand-blown conical bottles (joined by wax or cement) protected with a wooden frame; it still has the early green paint; 7½" (Lillian Blankley Cogan).

(Above left) **663. POCKET WATCH, c.1762-63:** A gentleman's silver pocket watch was not common among country people, but would have been owned by the higher end of our scale. Made in London by ''F PEACOCK'' with brass works, an enameled face, and silver cases—it typically used a key for winding, and a ''chain drive'' instead of a mainspring; (*above center*) the watch opens to reveal a protective outer case (with linen pad), and its central works (*above*) that include the glass face.

(Far left) **664. WATCH BOX (HUTCH), c.1780–1810:** Because pocket watches were expensive and not carried constantly, they were frequently hung in wooden boxes on the table or wall; small windows kept the watch face visible; note this pierced crest with an inverted heart design; 7¾" H.

(Near left) **665. WATCH BOX, c.1770–1800:** A rectangular form that includes dovetailed corners, a pegged back, and the rear hanging ring; 4" H (Author).

(Above) **666. LANTERN (BIRDCAGE) CLOCK, c.1660–1690:**
This first English domestic clock form saw little use in country
homes; powered by hand-set weights on ropes or chains, it is shown
here as part of the clock evolution; the brass case includes pierced
crests and a large domed bell (the side door is open); also note its
single pointer (the minute hand appeared c.1710); brass works;
13″ H (Henry Whitfield House, Conn. Historical Commission).

TALL (CASE) CLOCKS: The pendulum arrived c.1660, and by
1690 the tall (''grandfather's'') clock had developed to house it
and the windup weights. (Above left) **667. c.1720–1740:** By James
Hubert (London); note the early corniced flat top, square face, and
bull's-eye glass in the door; 83½″ H (Private Coll.). (Above right)
668. c.1760: This English mahogany case mounts a ''broken bonnet,'' and adds an arch to the face (now enameled on an iron plate);
81″ H. (Far left) **669.** The open case reveals two steadily descending weights (for the works and bell), plus its pendulum. (Near
left) **670.** Typical brass works behind the face; notice the bell at
top, the drums for winding up the cord for the weights (wound
by key), and its rear L form to attach the pendulum.

154

TALL CLOCKS: Cases were commonly made locally for the imported works. Sometimes the works were simply hung on the wall with their pendulum and weights in full view (called a "wag-on-the-wall"). (Above, left to right) (1) **671. c.1780:** An American case of butternut, chestnut, and pine—with a simulated broken-bonnet top that includes three wooden "spiked ball" finials (gilded); the floral-painted enamel face includes small hands indicating the seconds and calendar days (others often showed moon phases or a rocking ship); eight-day brass movement with an hourly "strike"; a Chippendale bracket base; 84″ H. (2) **672. c.1790:** Three carved flame finials appear here on urn bases (Chippendale); it is signed on the face, "S SIBLEY" (Great Barrington, Mass.); brass works,

cherry case; note the hood's typical side window; 89″ H. (3) **673. c.1790–1800:** Signed by "DANIEL PORTER" (Conn. and Mass.); the more elaborate top includes three urn finials; 83″ H (Private Coll.). (4) **674. c.1790–1800:** Inexpensive American tall clocks using wooden works began to expand the market in this decade; the typical example shown (by "GIDEON ROBERTS," Bristol, Conn.) reverts to the earlier flat-top form (see **#667**); pine, red stain; 81″ H (Conn. Historical Society).

(Right) 675. CLOCK KEY, c.1740–1820: A common form of clock-winding key; it combines a wrought-iron handle and a brass tube.

❧ VOLUME II ❧
COOKING & EATING

The kitchen hearth was the heart of a country home. Its fire was seldom allowed to expire—being raked apart to create slow cooking, accelerated for rapid heat, divided to prepare the oven or maintain small portions simmering on the side, and banked to survive the night. In the evening, its glow would reflect on the narrow tables, chairs, cupboards, hanging herbs, and white-washed walls as the family gathered for a brief time together in personal chores, camaraderie, or worship.

VARIETY OF IMPLEMENTS: Occasionally a prized object of silver or fine china might be displayed for a special event, but to live and survive in the developing colonies, tradition and ingenuity were called upon to provide a baffling array of functional items fashioned from wood, horn, pewter, brass, copper, iron, tin, leather, and clay.

During the 1600s, coarse pottery, wooden implements, iron pieces, and basic pewter forms dominated the kitchen scene. But as the homes expanded through the 1700s, so did their wares. Wrought and cast iron increased the variety of andirons, firebacks, kettles, pots, tools, lighting devices, and utensils. Pewter (mostly imported until after 1800) found uses beyond the early eatingware in clockfaces, sundials, measures, teapots, mugs—and continued to enjoy country popularity even after the more fashionable homes began to accept silver, Sheffield plate, porcelain, and glass substitutes near the end of the century.

Brass and copper were largely imported from Europe, but they too inspired brightness in rooms beyond the kitchen as the home expanded, by contributing slender candlesticks, teakettles, warming pans, tobacco boxes, and furniture brasses.

CERAMIC EVOLUTION: Ceramics further abetted this 150-year growth to a better life. The early colonists brought German stoneware, Dutch Delft, and English slipware. Successive years saw the infusion of local redware, English delft, white salt-glazed stoneware, and ivory-colored creamware (which displaced much of the earlier table pottery by 1780). Meanwhile, the Chinese porcelains and their European copies in "soft" and "hard" paste made steady inroads in the American market, so that by 1800 even many of the more humble homes treasured a few pieces of this delicate dinnerware.

The study of such household wares affords us an intimate insight into these extraordinary people. In our own age where colonial life is too often viewed in the serenity of nostalgia, it is essential to appreciate the enormity of their early accomplishments in conquering a wilderness, establishing communities, and making the most of simple pleasures.

Cooking

The woman spent a major part of her day at the hearth. While watching the flames in a colonial fireplace today, it isn't difficult to picture her at work in a broad linen apron, bent over in preparing the meal . . . stirring and tasting, adjusting iron pots or broilers to appropriate distances from the hot embers, testing smoke-blackened meat on a spit, or isolating coals toward a separate spot on the hearth to nurture a particular portion. There were also frequent turns to the portable work tables directly behind her on the kitchen floor. With practiced motions she would select from among the assembled ingredients, take a pinch of crushed herbs, or grind some additional seasoning in the mortar and pestle to complete the recipes handed down verbally from preceding generations.

(Below) **676. SKEWER REST, c.1680–1780:** A handwrought iron salamander figure for use on a skewer rest; 11″ L.

(Above) **677. LUG POLE:** The earliest fireplace ("hearth") in the kitchen ("hall") had a "lug pole" stretching from side to side inside and slightly above the opening; it was usually of hardwood (often 3"–4" Dia); as shown here, chains, trammels, and pot hooks hung from it to support kettles and pots over the embers.

(Above) **678. CRANE:** Aggravated by the lug pole's tendency to burn through and dump food into the flames, the settlers adopted an iron "crane" (early 18th century) that pivoted from side supports; it also allowed the cooking utensils hanging from it to be easily swung out to the proper distance from the fire.

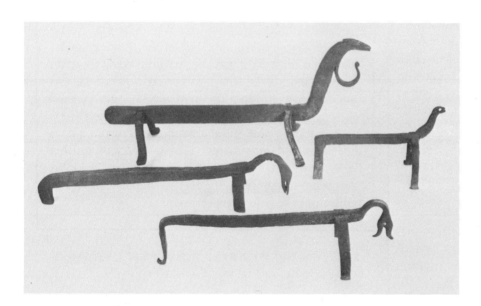

ANDIRONS (FIREDOGS, DOGS): Andirons were meant to hold logs for the fire and to provide air circulation under them. The earliest American versions were stones or bricks; yet cast- and wrought-iron forms had long been established in Europe, and were being imported or made here by the mid-1600s. (Left) **679. SPIT DOGS, c.1650–1725:** These were European-made wrought-iron forms with dog heads and legs that served as low andirons or rests for meat skewers (note a hook on the upper dog to cradle a spit); 9³/4"–22¹/2" L.

(Right) **680. SPIT (FIRE) DOG, c.1690–1725:** This addition of a vertical column to the dog illustrated their gradual conversion toward formal andirons; 21¹/4" L (Author).

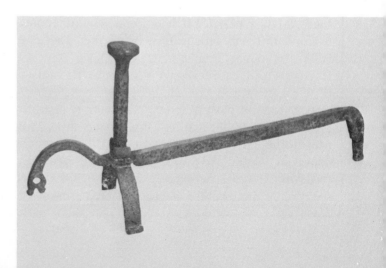

(Left) **681. ANDIRON, c.1640–1660:** An English cast-iron style excavated at Jamestown, Va.; it displays this type's typical spread legs, recessed panel post, expanded top knob, and raised cherub's head plus wings on the base (Colonial National Historical Park, Yorktown-Jamestown, Va.).

(Above) **682. ANDIRONS (SPIT DOGS), c.1670–1690:** A European 17th-century wrought-iron form that used scrolled legs; its adjustable hooks (positioned by the ratchet slots at the rear) support a horizontal ''spit bar'' (that held the meat); 27^1/$_4$'' H (Thankful Arnold House, Haddam, Conn.).

683. ANDIRONS, c.1670–1710: Tall Dutch-style andirons with arched legs, scrolled decorations, and permanent rear hooks to support a spit (or skewer) at the desired height; the upper iron extensions pass through the brass knobs and are then peened over; 24'' H (Author).

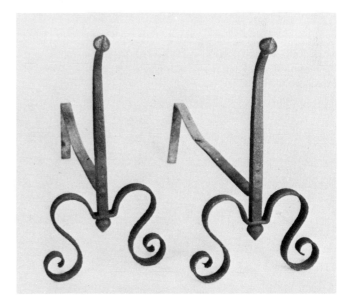

684. ANDIRONS, c.1660–1690: An English 3-piece andiron mounted on scrolled legs and extending a long rear log support; the squared column is already nodding forward with its conical top in anticipation of the later ''gooseneck'' form (see **#690**); 17'' H.

(Left) **685. FIREDOGS, c.1720–1750:** A variation made in America that contained the logs between raised posts as was done in medieval hall hearths—as well as providing hooks for skewers; 15″ H (Museum of Fine Arts, Boston).

(Right) **686. SKEWER (SPIT) REST, c.1690–1730:** A 3-legged stand with hooks to support skewers resting before the hearth; 12¼″ H.

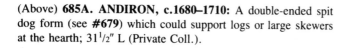

(Above) **685A. ANDIRON, c.1680–1710:** A double-ended spit dog form (see **#679**) which could support logs or large skewers at the hearth; 31½″ L (Private Coll.).

ANDIRONS: (Above) **687. c.1710–1730:** A 2-piece "scrolled-top" form mortised into an arched base; 9½″ H. (Lower left) **688. c.1720–1760:** Another flat-neck andiron with only a partial scroll; 12″ H. (Lower right) **689. c.1720–1760:** The evolving "goose-neck" form; note that its lobed end repeats the round "penny" feet; 14½″ H.

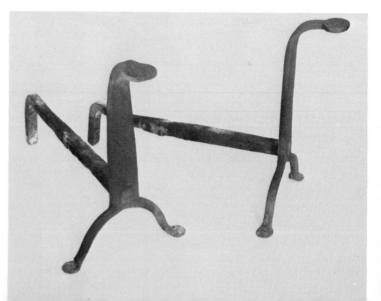

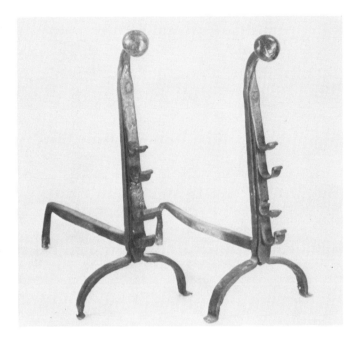

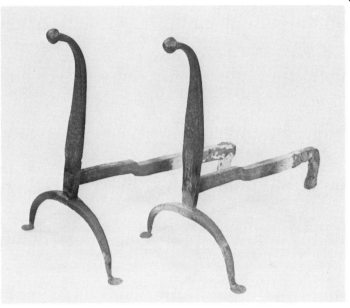

(Above) **690. ANDIRONS, c.1680–1720:** A tall design for the large hearth; note the gooseneck uprights that end in modified conical finials; the iron panels with spit hooks are riveted to the fronts; 24³/₄″ H (Author).

(Above) **691. ANDIRONS, c.1750–1790:** This 3-piece construction was becoming popular by midcentury, i.e., the column, arched legs (mortised to receive the upright), and log extension (notice its step-down to keep logs at the rear); 17″ H.

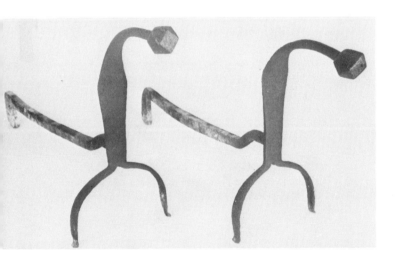

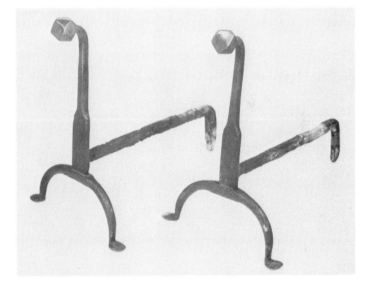

(Above) **692. ANDIRONS, c.1740–1780:** An extreme gooseneck with a faceted head—made in the early 2-piece form, i.e., its front was split at the bottom to forge integral legs and the rear extension added; note that feet are often burned short from long use in the coals; 14¹/₄″ H.

(Above) **693. ANDIRONS, c.1750–1790:** This straight retracted neck is a mature gooseneck example of the later 1700s; 15″ H.

(Left) **694.** Some andirons were cast, but most were of wrought iron (until c.1840), and still bear forging marks where the red-hot metal was pulled and hammered by the smith. Prolonged use in the hearth fire has exposed this wrought iron's longitudinal fiber and grain—which allowed it to stand twisting and strain not possible with the harder steel or brittle cast iron.

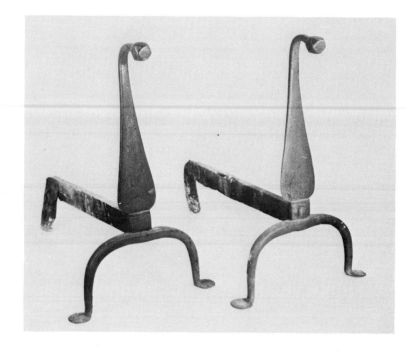

(Above) **695. ANDIRONS, c.1760–1790:** This 2-piece gooseneck design displays an inverted heart shape, twisted column, faceted head, and arched base; 15¼″ H (Conn. Historical Society).

(Upper right) **696. ANDIRONS, c.1760–1790:** A mature example of the 3-piece gooseneck style that anticipates the evolving "knife-blade" profile (see **#709**); note, too, its round ("penny") feet; 19¾″ H.

(Left) **697. ANDIRONS, c.1760–1800:** This "horse-head" form uses a "crook" neck that terminates in a finial forged to resemble the head of a horse or goose; 16¼″ H.

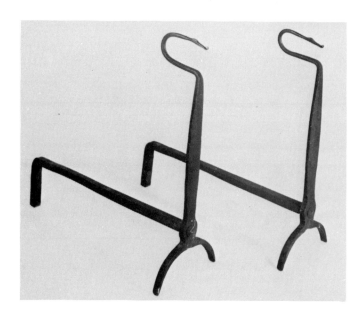

(Lower left) **698. ANDIRON, c.1740–1770:** Distinctive 2-piece "pig's tail" andirons from N.H.; the chamfered upright forms a flattened top that continues forward to create a curled pig's tail; 14¾″ H (Author).

(Lower right) **699. ANDIRON, c.1750–1790:** A modified pig's tail version that omits a decorative scrolled tip, but includes the popular penny feet; 17¼″ H.

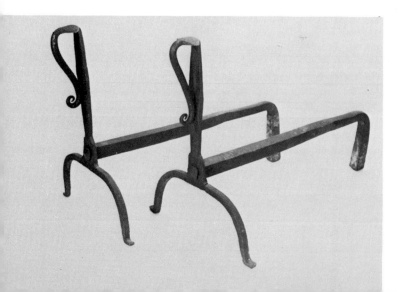

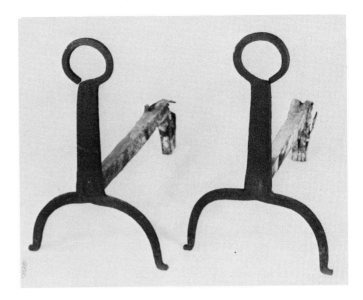

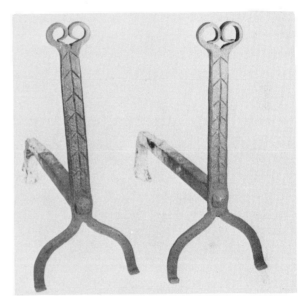

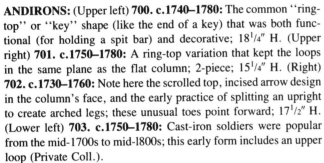

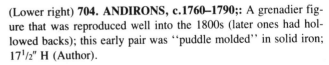

ANDIRONS: (Upper left) **700. c.1740–1780:** The common ''ring-top'' or ''key'' shape (like the end of a key) that was both functional (for holding a spit bar) and decorative; 18¼" H. (Upper right) **701. c.1750–1780:** A ring-top variation that kept the loops in the same plane as the flat column; 2-piece; 15¼" H. (Right) **702. c.1730–1760:** Note here the scrolled top, incised arrow design in the column's face, and the early practice of splitting an upright to create arched legs; these unusual toes point forward; 17½" H. (Lower left) **703. c.1750–1780:** Cast-iron soldiers were popular from the mid-1700s to mid-1800s; this early form includes an upper loop (Private Coll.).

(Lower right) **704. ANDIRONS, c.1760–1790;:** A grenadier figure that was reproduced well into the 1800s (later ones had hollowed backs); this early pair was ''puddle molded'' in solid iron; 17½" H (Author).

162

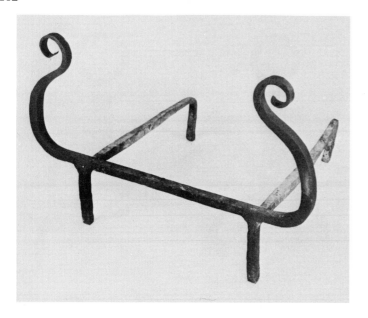

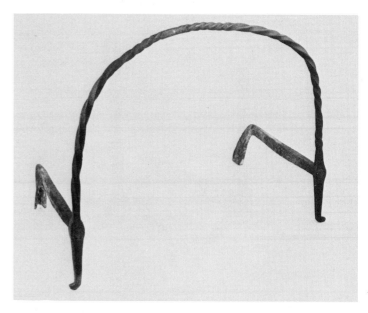

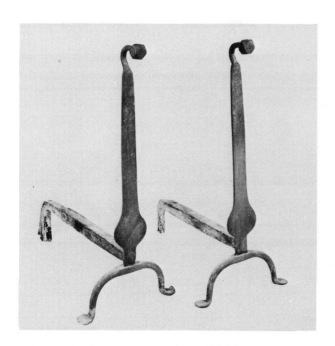

ANDIRONS: (Upper left & right) **705, 706. c.1750–1800:** Such single-piece andirons are usually found in N.H.; 14″, 16″ H. (Above) **707. c.1700–1800:** Primitive "serpent" andirons shaped from squared bars; 10¾″ H (Compton LaBauve, Jr.). (Left) **708. c.1750–1775:** Note these "crook" necks and the bulging "knife-blade" uprights; 24½″ H (Private Coll.). (Lower left) **709. c.1770–1790:** The thin "knife-blade" form with brass ball finials; 20″ H. (Lower right) **710. c.1775–1800:** Another knife blade—mounting a brass urn finial; 24½″ H.

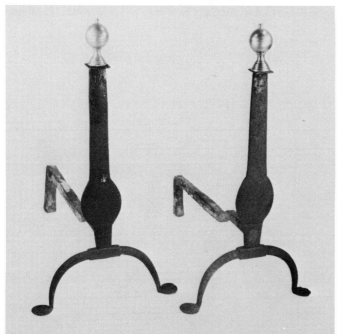

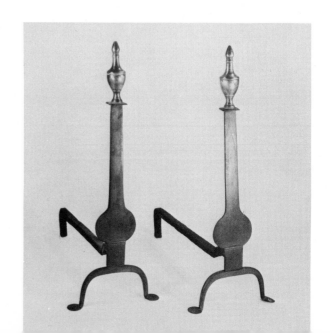

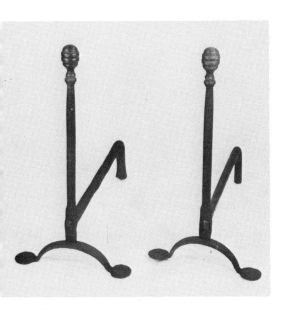

ANDIRONS: (Left) **711. c.1760–1800:** An elementary 3-piece pair having a low-arched base with penny feet; the thin uprights hold brass-ringed finials; 16¹/₂″ H. (Right) **712. c.1770–1790:** As neoclassical patterns gained favor, such brass "acorn" finials and columnar forms appeared—combined here with earlier arched iron bases; 18″ H.

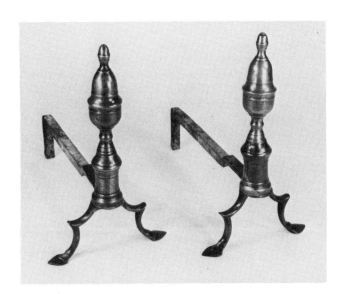

(Left) **713. URN/ACORN ANDIRONS, c.1785–1800:** As homes became better decorated after the Revolutionary War, brass andirons appeared in parlors and bed chambers; these have an urn/acorn shape and the new cast brass "spur" legs with hooflike feet; 13¹/₂″ H (Author).

(Lower left) **714. BALL ANDIRONS, c.1785–1810:** Such brass forms use a threaded iron bolt through the center to compile the cast sections; note the popular ball finials, spurred legs, and the new "slipper" feet; "log stops" also appeared at this time on the extensions; 17″ H.

(Lower right) **715. BALL ANDIRONS, c.1795–1815:** Closer to the century's end, this form anticipates the 1800s pagoda shapes and raised rings; scrolled log stops are present, and the spurred legs have acquired ball feet; 15″ H.

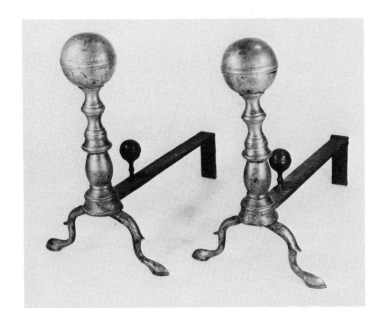

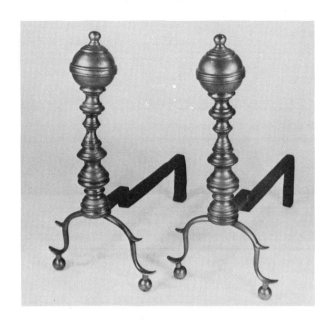

(Upper left) **716. BALL ANDIRONS, c.1795–1820:** The pagodalike rings increase here as the 1800s begin; their hollowed brass sections are now from halves soldered together; 17$\frac{1}{2}$″ H. (Above) **717. RINGED ANDIRONS, c.1800:** Note this last vestige of the 1700s ball form being consumed by the new styling; 15$\frac{3}{4}$″ H. (Left) **718. STEEPLE ANDIRONS, c.1790–1800:** Another innovation perched a steeple on the ball finial; brass; 17$\frac{1}{2}$″ H (Author).

(Left) **719. FIREBACK (FIRE PLATE, CHIMNEY BACK),** Marked **"1703"**: Firebacks were large flat cast pieces leaning against the fireplace back wall to protect its masonry, reflect heat, and serve as decoration (see above); this is an early American arched form; 27$\frac{1}{4}$″ H (Metropolitan Museum of Art).

720. FIREBACK, Marked "1746": These cast-iron plates bore a variety of armorial, religious, and floral designs in low relief; this one from Penn. records a country fiddler playing for a dancing couple, plus a sawbuck table and the date "1746"; its lower corner is broken; 26″ H (Mercer Museum, Bucks County Historical Society).

721. FIREBACK, Marked "1620": Above is the side from an old German 5-plate stove (i.e., an iron boxlike radiator with a fire inside or heat coming through a hole in the fireplace wall from an adjoining room) that was found in use as a fireback; note its biblical scene of the prodigal son, and the date "1620"; 37″ H.

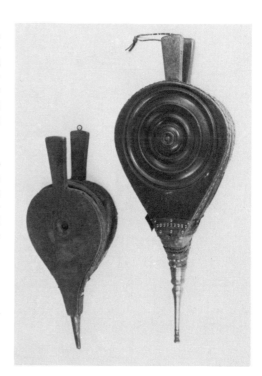

(Right) **722. BELLOWS, c.1700–1820:** Bellows were a necessity to fan a sickly blaze back to life; note these plain and elaborately turned examples; they consist of wooden faces, tacked leather sides, and a brass or iron snout; 17½″, 22½″ H.

(Left) **723. FENDER, c.1780–1800:** Fenders were fences before a hearth to keep coals from the floor; alternate forms used low sheet iron or brass, often curved and pierced (Lillian Blankley Cogan).

166

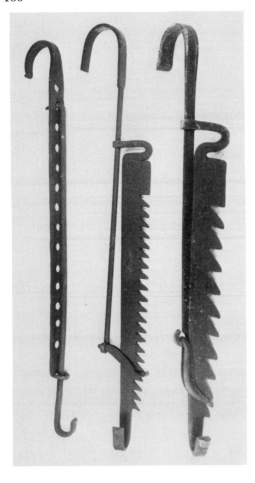

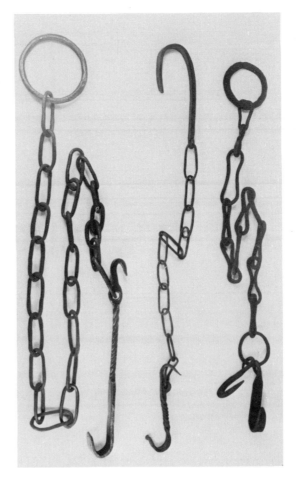

(Above) **724. TRAMMELS, c.1650–1740:** These adjustable suspensions hung from the fireplace lug pole (see **#677**), and held utensils above the embers; note their "hole & rod" and "saw-toothed" forms; 31"–35" H.

(Above) **725. CHAIN TRAMMELS, c.1640–1750:** Wrought-iron chains also served as trammels, looped over the lug pole and hooked into a link for the desired height of a vessel above the fire.

(Above) **726. TRAMMELS, c.1730–1800:** These are shorter versions for the later crane (see **#678**); (*left*) an elbow designed to project out from the crane; 10"–23" H.

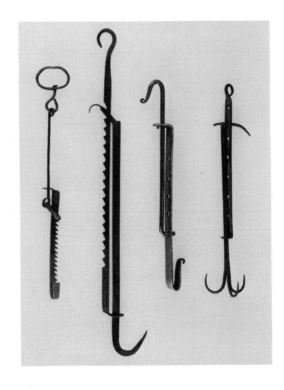

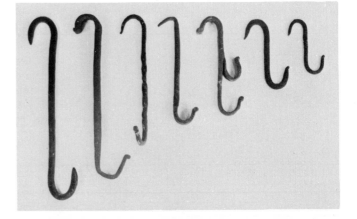

(Left) **727. TRAMMELS, c.1740–1800:** These small delicate trammels were used for lesser utensils, e.g., grease lamps, candle holders, small tea kettles, or (*right*) birds for roasting; 11½"–18" H. (Above) **728. POT (or S) HOOKS:** Handy extensions from a trammel or crane to hold utensils; 4"–12¼" H.

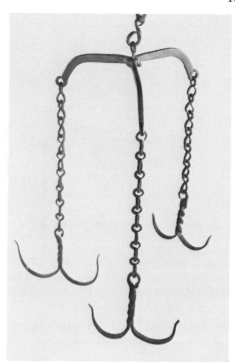

(Left) **729. DUTCH CROWN:** A crownlike iron form with hooks that was used in the larder (storage) to suspend meat or small game; 10″ Dia (Private Coll.).

(Right) **730. CROWN & HOOKS, c.1700–1800:** This variation of the Dutch crown used three arms to suspend chains with double hooks for the food.

(Above) **731. TINDER BOX, c.1660–1700:** Such small holders for flint, steel, and tinder were kept at hand to strike a fire; this early iron English box mounts a steel "striker" along its outer side; embossed sliding cover; 2¼″ H, 1¼″ W (Private Coll.).

(Left) **732. TOBACCO/TINDER BOX, c.1650–1680:** A domed oval iron tobacco or tinder box with a 17th-century design scratched into its surface—which was then filled with pewter and filed smooth; 1″ H, 3½″ L (Au.). (Above) **733. DRYING HANGER** (2 views), **c.1750–1850:** A pronged forged-iron form to dry herbs or corn; 19″ H.

(Above) **734. TINDERBOX, c.1750–1800:** Steel tinderbox with a hinged dome lid; 3″ W. (Below) **735. TINDER POUCH, c.1730–1780:** A leather pouch for flint and tinder; a steel striker is riveted along the bottom; brass applied corners; 3″ W.

(Above) **736. CANDLEHOLDER/TINDERBOX, c.1770–1820:** A popular tinned-iron drum form providing a tinderbox base (note the handled cover to douse sparks), and a candleholder cover; side-ring handle (see **#286**).

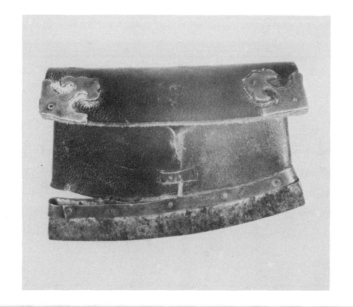

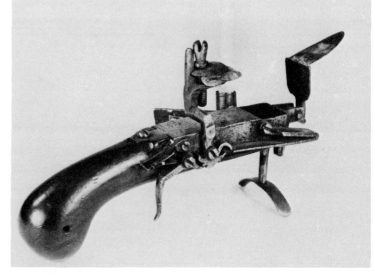

(Above) **737. TINDER LIGHTER, c.1750–1780:** The ''pistol'' lighter used ''flintlock'' ignition, i.e., an arm with flint in its jaws snaps forward to hit the L-shaped steel ''frizzen'' and spread sparks on the tinder beneath; the candle then picked up the flame (Private Coll.). (Left) **738. STRIKERS (STRIKE-A-LIGHTS, STEELS), c.1690–1800:** Creatively forged strikers; (*lower right*) a form copied from the ox-yoke key; 2¼″–5½″ W (Au.).

(Above) **739. FIRE PANS (FIRE SCOOPS, COAL CARRIERS):** The easiest way to kindle a flame was to carry coals from a nearby hearth or house; scoops like these served that need; (*left*) c.1750–1820, an open iron pan from N.H.; (*right*) c.1785–1830, a tinned-iron slanted style with a perforated hinged cover; 13³/₈″, 16″ L.

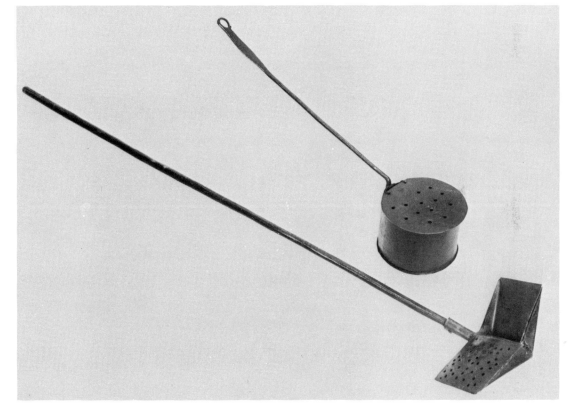

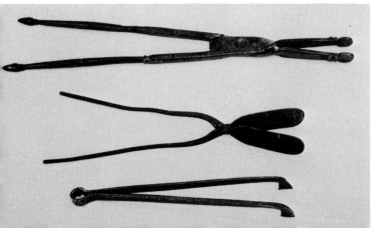

(Above) **740. FIRE PANS, c.1760–1820:** The tinned-iron drum-shaped body (*top*) has a hinged lid and forged iron handle; the V-shaped holder (*bottom*) has one side open to pick up the coals, and the other covered to hold them; 16″, 32³/₄″ L.

(Left) **741. EMBER TONGS, c.1750–1800:** Small tongs found many uses, including lifting coals to light pipes or start fires; both the scissors and tweezer types are shown; 9″, 12″, 17¹/₂″ L.

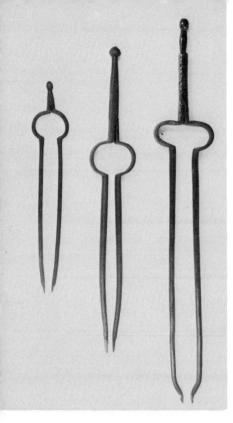

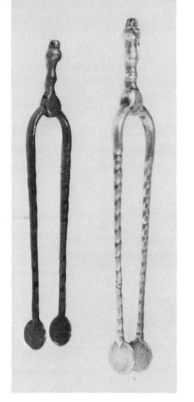

(Left) 742. FIRE TONGS: A basic form of iron hearth tongs used throughout our period; (*right*) c.1700–1750; (*two left*) c.1750–1820; 14³/₄″–28″ L.

(Right, left to right) (1 & 2) 743. EMBER (PIPE) TONGS, c.1750–1790: A small Dutch-English brass style; 8¹/₂″, 10¹/₂″ L. **(3) 744. IRON POKER, c.1750–1800:** Forged with an open heart handle; 18¹/₄″ L. **(4) 745. SCISSORS TONGS, c.1750–1800:** Unique, specialized prongs for lifting baked potatoes out of the ashes, etc.; 15¹/₂″ L.

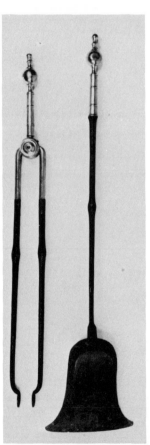

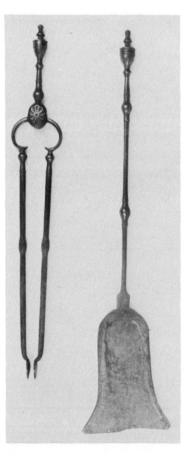

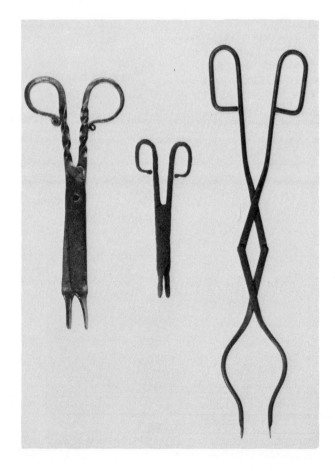

HEARTH TONGS & SHOVELS: The better country homes began acquiring matching fire tools in the late 1700s. (Left) **746. c.1780–1810:** A brass and iron pair of ball-headed tongs, and a typical wide-mouthed shovel; 30¹/₄″, 35″ L. (Right) **747. c.1780–1830:** Iron, with urn finials; some sets included pokers; 27¹/₂″, 31¹/₄″ L (Author).

(Above) 748. SCISSORS TONGS, c.1740–1790: (*Two left*) Wrought-iron utility tongs with twisted stems, scrolled finger loops, and small end nibs; 12¹/₂″, 7³/₄″ L. (*Right*) "Lazy Tongs," c.1780–1810—a latticelike form that contracted when open, and stretched to close (coals for pipes, etc.); 19³/₄″ L (max.).

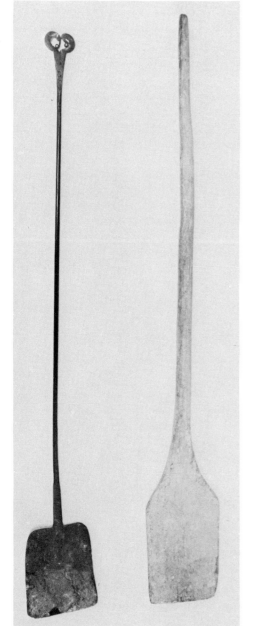

(Lower left) **749. PEEL (SLICE):** The bake oven was usually part of the fireplace. A fire was built inside to heat its walls; then the coals were raked out, food put inside, and the door covered (see **#766**); these two long shovel-like "peels" (iron, wood) placed baked goods in the oven and later removed them; both are 59″ L. (Above) **SERVING PEELS:** Short-handled wooden peels also fed the oven, and served hot foods; (Upper left) **750.** A thick wooden example; 16⅞″ L. (Upper right) **751.** A wide, thin peel of sycamore; also a cutting board per its knife scars; 15¾″ L.

(Lower center) **752. ASH PEELS:** These shorter iron "ash peels" were for baking or removing hearth ashes; 38″, 40″ L. (Lower right) **753. ASH (HEARTH) SHOVELS:** Short-handled shovels used to clean the bake oven or fireplace; 16¾″–22⅝″ L.

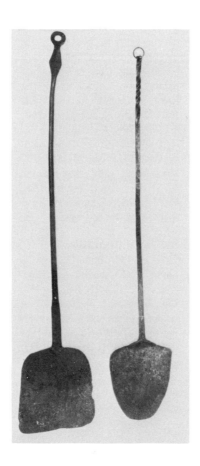

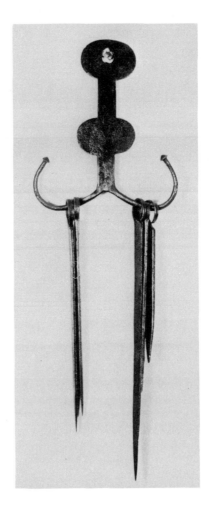

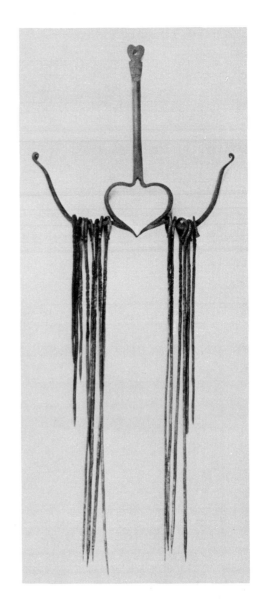

SKEWERS: These were iron rods or blades used to secure meat for roasting (a ''spit'' was the longer meat-holding bar); they were usually hung from these double-armed iron ''holders'' at the hearthside (see **#760**). **SKEWER HOLDERS:** (Upper left) **754. c.1740–1790:** A straight-arm design; 4¼″ H (Private Coll.). (Upper center) **755. c.1750–1800:** The lobed form with curved arms; 6½″ H. (Upper right) **756. c.1730–1780:** A long open heart shape; 9½″ H (Author).

SKEWER HOLDERS: (Left) **757. c.1750–1800:** The ''diamond''-and ''shank''-type holders; 4¼″, 5¾″ H. (Right) **758.** This handsome pierced skewer holder has incised designs plus the initials ''MH'' and the date ''1759''; 9¼″ H (Author).

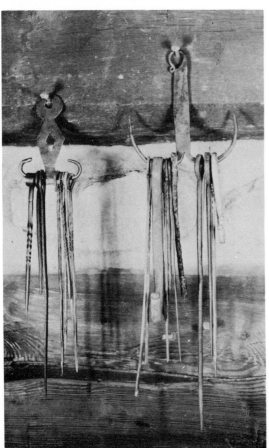

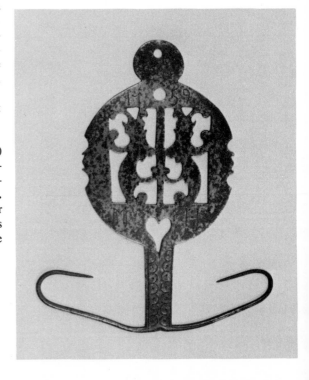

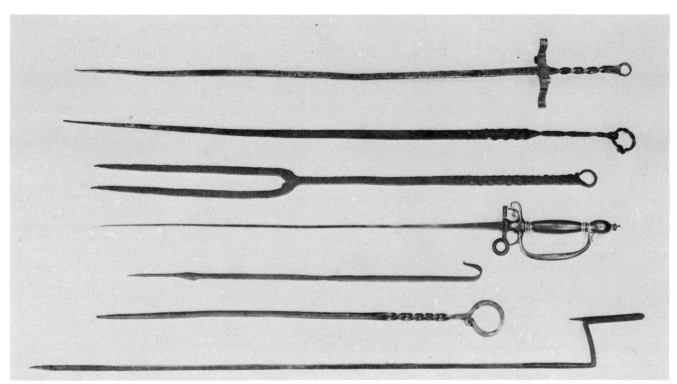

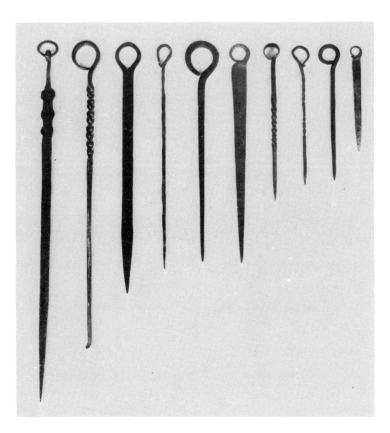

(Above) **759. SPITS, c.1700–1800:** Spits were usually the long rods for roasting large pieces of meat; note the variety shown here that ranges from a remounted sword hilt to a right-angled spit from a reflector oven (see **#822**) with its sharp handle projection for inserting into holes to hold at various roasting positions; 19″–32″ L.

(Left) **760. SKEWERS:** Typical variations of the smaller wrought-iron skewers that held meat portions for cooking; 8½″–26½″ L.

(Below) **761. DOUBLE-ENDED SKEWERS, c.1750–1800:** Two handwrought skewers having double-pointed ends and a spiraled center; 10″, 11″ L.

TEAKETTLES: Their primary purpose was to boil water. Cast-iron kettles were mostly used at the hearth, copper or brass in the parlor. (Above) **762.** (*left*) **c.1720–1780,** the early 3-legged squat profile in cast iron that includes the typical notched spout; body 6^1/$_2$″ H; (*right*) **c.1770–1820,** a later high-shouldered form in copper with its usual dovetailed bottom; body 6″ H. (Right) **763. KETTLE TILTER (IDLE-BACK, LAZY-BACK), c.1700–1800:** This device held a teakettle as shown; pulling the extended arm tipped the hot kettle to pour; 20″ H. (Lower left) **764. KETTLE-TILTERS, c.1750–1810:** Three variations showing an arched iron lever, an open spiraled handle, and a wooden grip; 19^1/$_2$″–25^1/$_2$″ H (Author).

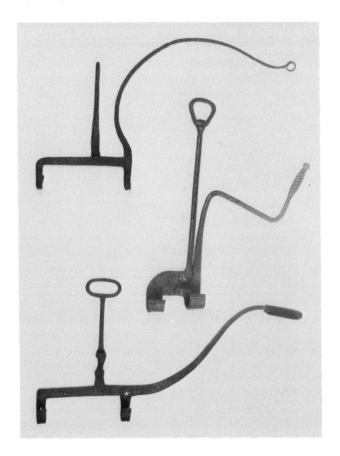

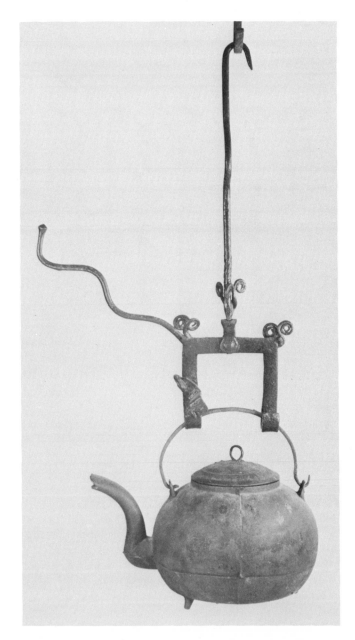

(Upper left) **765. BRANCH HANGER:** A common method of creating hooks for hanging was to suspend a section cut from a tree with its branches appropriately positioned; 13″ H.

(Upper right) **766. HEARTHSIDE, c.1650–1720:** A typical early hearth of brick (often whitewashed) with two oven openings at the ends of the rear wall (the oven door covers are in the center of the rear ledge); note the variety of implements, the accumulation of ashes, andirons for separate cooking locations, and the large wooden ''blanket crane'' at the top (that pivoted out for drying items or to separate the kitchen with hangings for sleeping—especially in midwinter after closing off the other rooms) (Private Home).

768. POT CASTING MARKS: Cast iron is smelted in a blast furnace and, while still in a molten state, poured into a hollowed mold. Most 18th-century pots were made in this manner; the process left a raised mark where the iron entered the mold. During the first half of the 1700s this was typically a round mark (''sprue'') on the bottom (*left*); by midcentury, a new elongated line (''gate'') had become normal, and continued into the 1800s (*right*).

767. POT (FLESH POT), c.1640–1690: A European bronze cooking pot of ancient form, cast in a 2-part sand mold (note the vertical filed lines); its ears show the early angled slope; the legs are faceted (and probably shortened by long use in the embers); notice the addition of oriental-style symbols to its side; 6½″ H.

176

(Left) **769. POTS:** Bulbous cooking pots were workhorses throughout our period, and ranged in capacity from a half gallon to ten gallons shapes; (*right*) c.1670–1740, the early round profile with a circular bottom sprue (see **#768**) and long legs to sit in the coals; the cover is not original; (*left*) c.1740–1780, by now the pot had acquired a flatter ovoid outline, shorter legs (i.e., often hung from a crane), and the bottom gate scar; note the wooden handle replacement; both 9″ H to rim.

(Right) **770. POTS, c.1730–1750:** Two small midcentury pots with their original domed covers (ring handles) retain the earlier round form; note the seams from a typical 3-piece mold (cast bottom up), i.e., the vertical seams separating two horizontal sections, and the base piece that terminated at the encircling ridge near the bottom; the arched handles (''bails'') are normally of wrought iron; their pointed ''ears'' holding the bails at each end became rounded during the 1800s; 7$^{1}/_{2}$″, 7$^{3}/_{4}$″ H.

(Below) **772. POT MARKING:** English and American 18th-century pots were seldom marked, but some do bear raised initials of the maker or brief designs as seen here.

(Above) **771. POTS vs. KETTLES:** By definition, a ''pot'' was bulbous, and narrowed near the top before flaring out (*left*), c.1780–1820; the ''kettle'' had straighter sides that widened at the rim (*right*), c.1770–1810.

(Upper left) **773. POT, c.1780-1820:** A large (13$\frac{1}{2}$″ W) cooking pot showing the low squat form that evolved about 1780; it retains the original cast-iron cover bearing raised foliate designs. (Upper Center) **774. KETTLE, c.1750–1820:** The usual straight-sided cast-iron kettle incorporating a heavy wrought-iron bail; 8″ H. (Upper right) **775. HANGING SPIT, c.1700–1800:** An iron ''game hanger'' with a long stem that could sit in a base.

(Left) **776. CALDRON, c.1720–1800:** The caldron was a very large kettle; this one measures 10″ H, 20$\frac{3}{8}$″ W. (Below) **777. POT COVERS:** A display of pot covers including both cast- and wrought-iron forms; 5″–13″ Dia (Author).

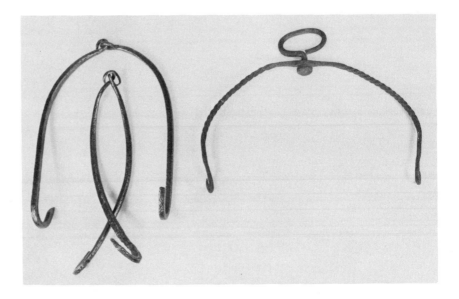

(Upper left) **778. KETTLE, c.1760–1820:** A kettle with a double-arched handle from which a second smaller vessel could be suspended—usually a perforated "steamer" (used like today's double boiler); 21″ Dia.

(Upper right) **779. DETACHABLE HANDLES, c.1650–1800:** For moving large vessels heated by the fire, it was convenient to use removable bails that hooked into the side ears; (*left*) two pairs of adjustable "pot tongs"; 15″ L; (*right*) a rigid handle with a swiveled hanging ring.

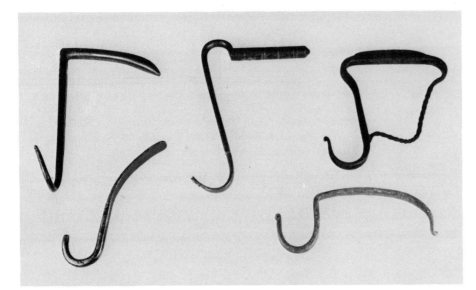

(Above & right) **780, 781. POT LIFTERS:** A simple hook with a handle was a practical and necessary utensil to lift hot kettles or pots at the hearth; this variety of forms testifies to the creativeness of the colonial blacksmith, whitesmith, and handyman. (*Below*) A close-up of a unique pot-lifter finial (Author).

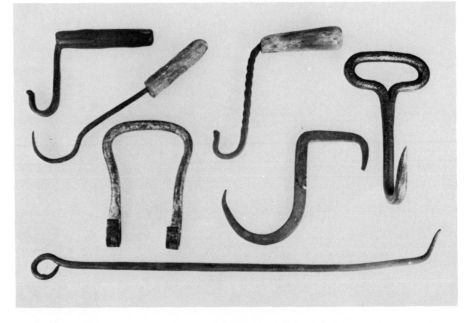

(Above) **782. BRASS KETTLES, c.1740–1840:** Examples of legless kettles (i.e., for hanging) formed from a brass body that had been hammered into a mold, and attached by rivets to a wrought-iron rim and handle; 5⅝″, 9″, 16½″ Dia.

(Below) **783. BRASS ROASTER, c.1740–1780:** A dry roaster (for chestnuts, etc.) that has an open curving brass handle riveted to the perforated drumlike body (hinged lid); 21″ L (Au.).

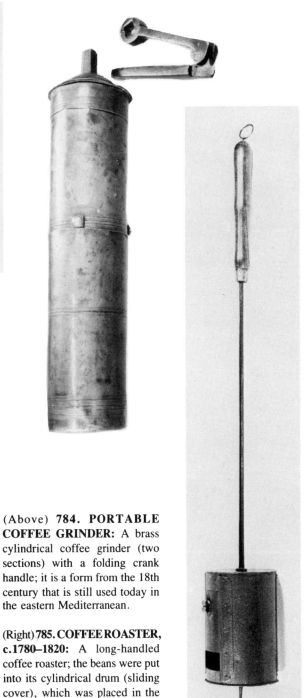

(Above) **784. PORTABLE COFFEE GRINDER:** A brass cylindrical coffee grinder (two sections) with a folding crank handle; it is a form from the 18th century that is still used today in the eastern Mediterranean.

(Right) **785. COFFEE ROASTER, c.1780–1820:** A long-handled coffee roaster; the beans were put into its cylindrical drum (sliding cover), which was placed in the hearth and rotated.

(Left) **786. COFFEE ROASTER, c.1780–1820:** A coffee-roasting drum (see #785), but mounted in a boxlike brazier (includes a bottom grate and space for charcoal); the handle is restored; 14½″ H.

(Left) **787. FRYING PANS, c.1775–1820:** The short-shouldered handle at the left is riveted to the pan, while the other handle is welded as an extension; both pans were hammered to shape in a mold; 13$^{1}/_{2}''$ Dia. (Right) **788.** This was a common marking on utensils—the top letter is the family name; those below represent the husband's and wife's first names.

FRYING PANS: (Two, lower left) **789. c.1700–1800:** Early long-handled pans with iron and wood-extended handles; 48″, 46″ L. (Two, lower right) **790. c.1775–1820:** One of these handles is welded to the pan (*left*), the other is riveted; 38″, 37″ L.

(Above) **791. SAUCEPAN, c.1740–1770:** Saucepans were used for sauces and meat accompaniments; this is made of copper with a long wooden Queen Anne turned handle; its cover extends over the pouring spout; 3¼″ top Dia (Private Coll.). (Right) **792. FRYING PAN, c.1750–1800:** An alternate design that has an arched reinforcement riveted to the pan and handle; 16¼″ L.

(Left) **793. SKILLET, PAN:** (*Left*) c.1750–1800, a broad-lipped Dutch-style brass skillet with a turned cherry handle; (*right*) c.1790–1820, a later vertical-sided copper pan; 8⅝″, 6⅝″ Dia.

SKILLETS (PIPKINS, POSNETS): These were small cooking pots with a handle. (Lower left) **794. c.1650–1700:** An English gravel-tempered earthenware example (excavated) with three stubby legs (Colonial National Historical Park, Yorktown-Jamestown, Va.).

(Lower right) **795. c.1720–1810:** Small cast-iron skillets having three short legs and integral handles (normally one-third distance down from the rim); 5″–8″ Dia.

(Above) **796. SKILLETS, c.1700–1800:** These popular shallow flat-bottomed skillets on legs were cast as single units; 8″–10″ Dia.

(Right) **797. PAN, KETTLE, c.1750–1800:** (*Left*) A heavy-footed iron pan and cover with a wrought-iron bail; (*right*) an iron kettle hammered to shape in a mold; the forged-iron handle is held by riveted ears; 10³/₈″ Dia.

(Right) **798. SKILLET (POSNET), c.1700–1800:** This deep-bodied variation of the skillet is cast in "bell metal" (80% copper, 20% tin; bronze—90% copper, 10% tin); note its typical three splayed legs (reeded outer faces) and the practice of casting raised initials or designs into the handle's upper face; the bottom has a round sprue mark (See #768); 9³/₈″ Dia.

(Left) **799. SKILLET (POSNET), c.1700–1800:** Another bell-metal skillet in this form which stretches back to the Middle Ages; the taller legs permit it to sit deeper in the hot embers; the piece is cast as a single unit; 8¹/₄″ Dia.

(Left) 800. DUTCH OVEN, c.1700–1800: Most small baking was done in cast-iron "Dutch ovens" such as this modified skillet; the sunken cover held embers heaped on it as the base sat on its legs deep in the coals of the hearth—to absorb heat from all sides; 8″ Dia.

(Right) 801. SPIDER, c.1750–1800: This form of frying pan or skillet on high legs was called a "spider"; the large example here has a series of star, crescent, and circle designs struck into the handle, and terminates in an open heart finial; the legs and handle are riveted to its sides; 14″ Dia (Author).

(Below left) 802. SPIDERS, c.1750–1800: Flat-bottomed spiders; the handle at the right has a socket for a wooden extension (would not carry heat); 7³/₄″, 11″ Dia.

SPIDERS: (Above right) **803. c.1775–1840:** This style using a rounded bottom was popular in Penn. well into the 19th century; 6¹/₂″–9³/₄″ Dia. (Left) **804. c.1750–1800:** European-made examples using copper or brass with rims turned over reinforcing wire; the iron legs and handles are attached by rivets; 5¹/₂″, 6¹/₂″ Dia.

(Upper left) **805. HANGING PANS, c.1750–1780:** Notice the ring swivels here for hanging; (*left*) a cast-iron body and integral legs, plus the wrought-iron handle; (*right*) a frying pan that omits the legs; 10⁵/₈″, 11″ Dia.

(Above) **806. POT STAND, c.1740–1800:** An open iron stand with three footed legs that was sized to hold the large pot; it allowed the pot to cool away from the hearth, or to sit above the embers; 17″ H, 12″ Dia (Thankful Arnold House, Haddam, Conn.).

TRIVETS: These were stands on three or more legs that supported kettles, skillets, and other cooking vessels at the hearth. (Above) **807. c.1650–1800:** Note the variations of even these elementary forms; 6¹/₂″–7⁵/₈″ Dia. (Right) **808. HANDLED TRIVETS, c. 1750–1800:** Three-legged trivets with attached handles; all are of wrought iron; 4³/₄″–8¹/₂″ Dia (Author).

(Left) 809. TRIANGULAR TRIVETS, c.1700–1800: These 3-legged trivets were typically forged by the smith in wrought iron; the legs are often found substantially shortened from sitting in hot embers for many years; their sides measure 8″–9″ L.

(Right) 810. TRIVET, c.1700–1760: A practical form of iron trivet, which extended one leg to support a forked arm that steadied the handle of a pan or skillet whose base rested on the circular stand; 15¾″ L.

(Left) 811. POT PUSHERS, c.1660–1800: This implement is basically a semicircular footed bumper with a rear handle; it was used primarily to push hot vessels on the hearth, or to maneuver coals back into the fire area; note the variety of small embellishments; 4″–6¼″ W.

(Right) 812. TRIVET, c.1790–1810: An elegant late-century English-made trivet using a decorated pierced brass plate on top of the iron base that ends in "arrow" feet; notice also the turned wooden handle, and the front hooks for attaching to a low fender or other frame; it was intended for a parlor or bedchamber instead of the kitchen; 14½″ L.

(Left) **813. POT STAND (WARMING TRIVET), c.1740–1800:** A squared framelike stand that probably stood in the corner of the fireplace to keep large vessels warm, or near the dining table with hot containers for serving; its feet are pointed in four directions; 14″ H.

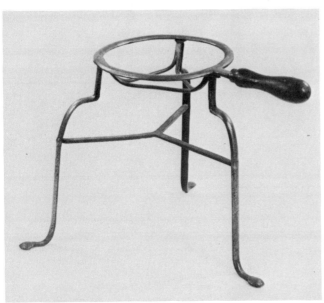

(Above) **814. TRIVET, c.1730–1780:** An English "warming" trivet (i.e., too fine to stand in the embers); note the iron cabriole legs with pad feet (Queen Anne), and its inner frame that holds a brass disc to support a narrow vessel; 10¼″ H. (Left) **815. Trivet, c.1780–1800:** This formal English design includes shouldered iron legs, as well as a wooden handle; 11¾″ H. (Lower left) **816. BIRD BROILER/TRIVET, c.1780–1810:** Another British form that mounts adjustable double forks for roasting small game; the sunken center could hold a pot, or even a pan of coals as a brazier; 12¼″ H to the ring. (Below) **817. TRIVET (FOOTMAN), c.1790–1820:** An elegant English trivet with side handles—dressed in a brass top over the iron frame; it is a style designed for the bedroom or parlor; 11⅜″ H.

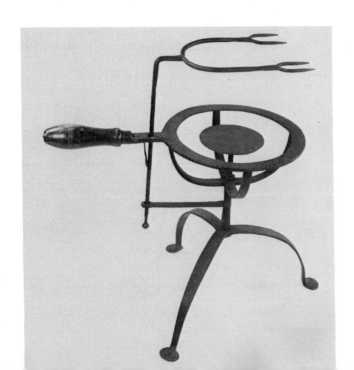

187

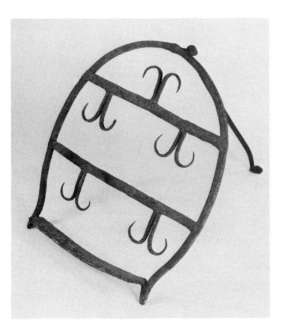

(Two left) **818. BROILERS, c.1750:** These wrought-iron easel forms are often called "Scottish broilers"; meat, fish, or bread was placed on the sloping front and set facing the fire; note their innovative scrollwork; 16″, 14½″ H (Author).

(Right) **819. WARMING SHELVES (POT WARMERS), c.1720–1800:** Such forged-iron shelves hung against the fireplace sides to keep food warm; their rear extensions provided clearance from the wall; both are 10″ H.

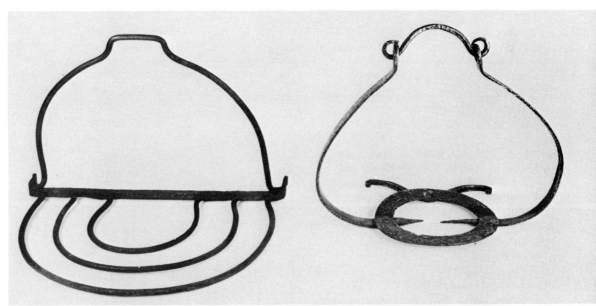

(Below) **820. WARMING SHELF, c.1720–1800:** A hinged innovation that rotates the platform to a vertical plane when not in use; 11½″ H.

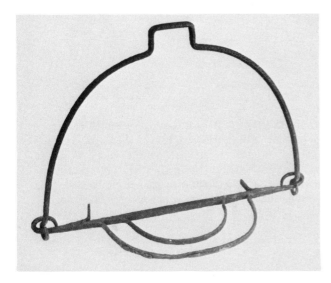

(Right) **821. APPLE ROASTER, c.1740–1810:** It was popular to roast apples at the hearth, and this iron frame was constructed to support two rows of them; note its center hanging ring, as well as the short legs; 13″ L.

(Above, top row) **822. REFLECTOR OVEN (ROASTING JACK, ROTISSERIE)** (two views), **c.1780–1820:** This portable open oven held meat on a rotating spit bar; it reflected heat onto the roasting meat, and protected from spattering grease; note the two handles plus a hinged cover for observing and basting; tinned iron; 16″ H.

(Above, second row) **823. WARMING OVEN** (two views), **c.1780–1820:** A reflecting oven for warming food or baking; the top includes a hinged door; 15½″ H.

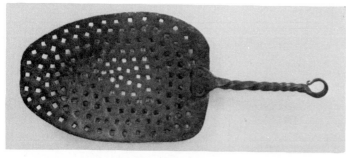

(Above) **824. BIRD ROASTER** (two views), **c.1750–1830:** A reflector oven for birds or fish; meat was held on the hooks, and heat was reflected on it from the back—while juices were caught in the fenced bottom; flat handle; 9⅝″ H. (Left) **825. FISH BROILER, c.1730–1780:** A simple iron broiler made from the twisted handle riveted to a concave perforated body; no feet were added; 12¾″ L.

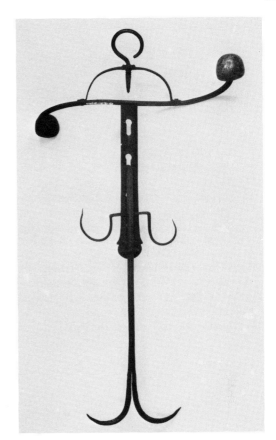

(Left) **826. BIRD SPIT, c.1760–1820:** A hanging frame that includes an adjustable cross bar (with a thumbscrew) supporting hooks for small game; the bottom projections probably held a pan to catch the meat drippings; 15³/₄″ H (Author).

(Right) **827. BIRD SPIT (DANGLE SPIT), c.1780–1820:** A double-level adjustable spit that can rotate for equal exposure (note the curving handles); 24″ H (Conn. Historical Society).

(Above) **828. GRIDDLE, c.1660–1730:** Colonial cooking embraced boiling, baking, roasting, broiling, and frying; the griddle served as a general hot plate; this early cast-iron form has faceted legs and a fluted handle; 22¹/₈″ L.

(Lower left) **829. GRIDDLE, c.1750–1820:** This consists of a cluster of cast-iron cooking surfaces that create a shallow version of the deeper "pattypan"; 16″ L. (Lower right) **830. CAT, c.1750–1790:** A portable plate holder or warming stand; its arms and balls are numbered for disassembling; 15″ H (Private Coll.).

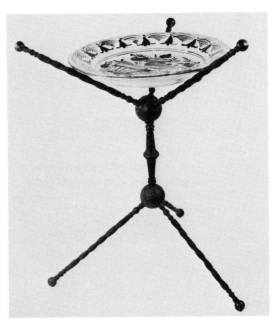

(Upper left) **831. HANGING GRIDDLE (BROILER), c.1680–1750:** An early hanging broiler; the flat iron griddle was puddle molded, while its arched handle and swivel ring were forged; there are no footings; 18″ Dia.

(Upper right) **832. HANGING GRIDDLES:** (Left) c.1750–1800, note this round cast-iron griddle's raised edge, three short feet, and ears for the wrought-iron handle; 14″ Dia; (*right*) c.1760–1810, an oval shape with a ridged footing; 13½″ H.

(Left) **833. SINGLE-ARM GRIDDLE, c.1750–1800:** A forged-iron variation using an abbreviated handle to hold its swiveling ring; 4¾″ H.

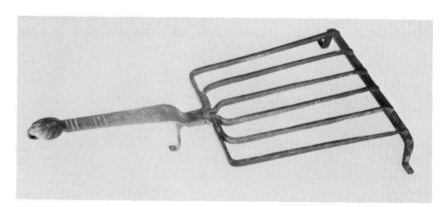

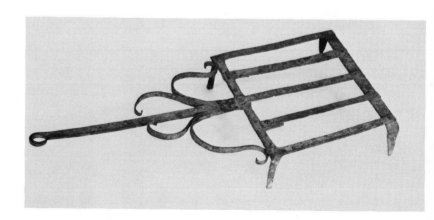

(Above right) **834. GRIDIRON, c.1640–1700:** The gridiron was a portable grate to lay meat or fish on for broiling, or to use as a semitrivet; it is an early 3-legged continental European form with a shell and hanging hook on the handle; wrought iron; 21″ L (Author).

(Lower right) **835. GRIDIRON, c.1730–1760:** The Queen Anne influence is seen in these scrolled additions to the squared grid and handle; 19″ L.

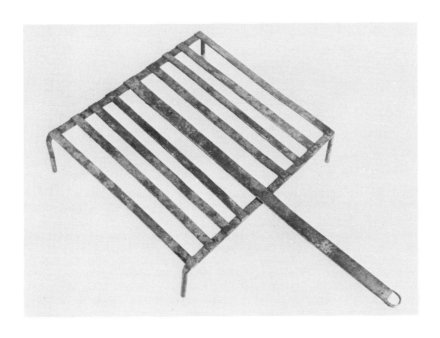

(Left) **836. GRIDIRON, c.1750–1800:** Flat iron bars have been riveted at each end to simple leg frames; the handle is an extended bar with a hanging-loop terminal; 21¼″ L.

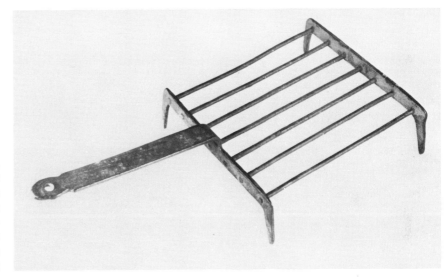

(Below) **837. GRIDIRON, c.1750–1800:** Iron rods penetrate the two end frames and are peened on the outer side; its flat handle is welded in position; 15¾″ L.

(Lower left) **838. GRIDIRON/GRISSET, c.1750–1800:** When broiling meat or fish, the hot juices and fat released were needed in the home (for soap, candles, grease lamps, etc.); these rods are V-shaped to catch such drippings, and let them flow down to the trough (or "grisset") at the rear (the front legs are higher); also note the pouring spout at its end; 25″ L.

(Lower right) **839. GRISSET ATTACHMENT:** Some of these attached grissets were removable by thumbscrews as shown.

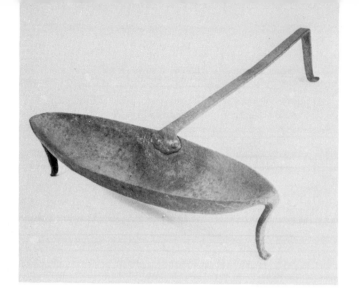

(Upper left) **840. GRISSET, c.1650–1720:** This forged grisset with end legs and a long riveted handle extension caught meat drippings at the hearth; it was also used when coating rushes in melted tallow for rushlights (see **#213**); 17″ W (Author).

(Upper right) **841. GRISSET, c.1720–1740:** A unique iron design probably intended to catch meat juices as a grisset; yet the high legs could place it in the embers as a griddle, or the four corner spouts might serve as grease lamps (see **#202**); from eastern Mass.; 22″ L.

(Left) **842. ROTARY GRIDIRONS, c.1740–1800:** To complement the squared stationary gridirons (see **#836–#838**), these rotary types mounted a round rotating grill on the center rivet of a 3-legged frame and handle; 28″, 20″ L.

ROTARY GRIDIRONS: (Above) **843. c.1750–1800:** A rotating variation on four short legs, plus a looped handle for hanging; 14″ Dia. (Left) **844. c.1750–1800:** Ironwork embellishments have been added here to the handle; 25¾″ L.

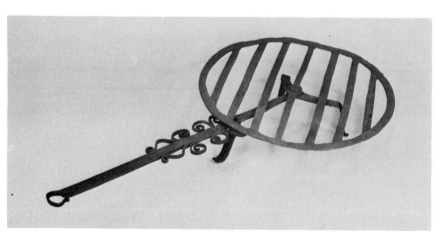

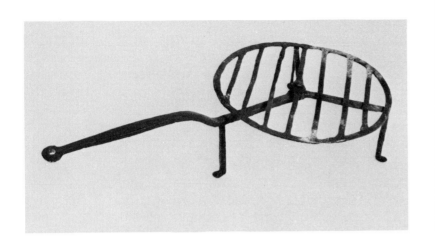

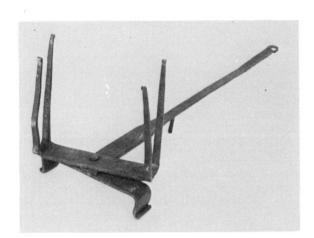

ROTARY GRIDIRONS: (Upper left) **845. c.1750–1800:** Note the "shouldered" handle here; because of the gridiron's low height, fat drippings could spatter from the coals to sear the meat— suggesting more gridiron use for light cooking and warming than broiling; 22″ L. (Above) **846. c.1750–1800:** This handle extends to add a 2-pronged toasting fork (see **#894**); 15³/₈″ L. (Left) **847. c.1750–1800:** A solid rotating griddle or warming tray; 24″ L.

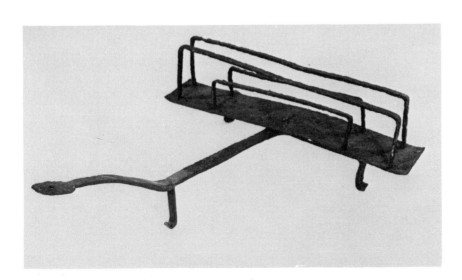

SWIVEL TOASTERS: Because bread was not baked daily, toasting was common; these 3-legged frames (wrought iron) held bread slices (or other foods) on a rotating bar before the fire and swiveled it to heat both sides. (Upper left) **848. c.1680–1740:** An early crude example that held one slice; 18″ L. (Upper right) **849. c.1740–1800:** A scrolled double-arched fence and shouldered handle; 17³/₄″ L. (Left) **850. c.1760–1790:** Note the twisted iron fences; 14¹/₈″ (Author).

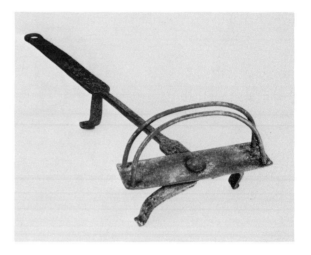

SWIVEL TOASTERS: (Upper left) **851. c.1750–1800:** An impressive toaster that is fenced in elaborate ironwork including ram's-horn finials; 19″ L. (Above) **852. c.1770–1820:** This is a simple arched toaster for a single slice of bread; 12³/₄″ L. (Left) **853. c.1750–1800:** The vertical-post fence form; 12¹/₄″ L. (Lower left) **854. c.1760–1800:** This rotating crossbar bends up its ends to receive the horizontal side bars; the handle is shouldered; 17″ L.

(Below) **855. STATIONARY TOASTER, c.1760–1800:** A rigid frame of wrought iron that could hold a single portion of bread, biscuit, meat, or cheese for heating; 11³/₄″ L.

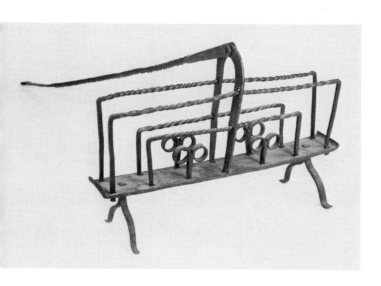

DROP-HANDLE TOASTERS: This alternate "drop" form retained the bar, but substituted a long handle hinged to a top support; the footed bar did not swing, but changed sides to the fire by reversing and turning the handle. (Upper left) **856. c.1750–1800:**

Note the long rotating handle, and ram's-horn scrolls—all in wrought iron; 26¾″ L. (Upper right) **857. c.1780–1820:** A later toaster with plain rod sides; 26″ L. (Below left) **858. c.1785–1820:** Another late example includes thinner rods in a 3-tier fence.

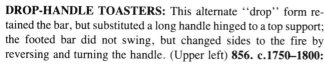

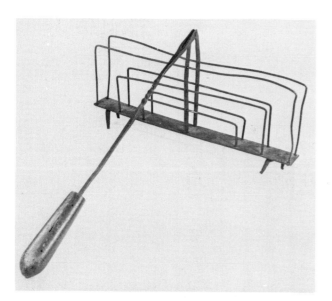

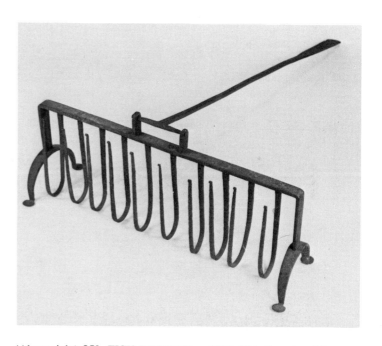

(Above right) **859. FISH BROILER, c.1750:** This forged multi-pronged rack with a drop handle was designed to hold fish, meat, or other foods before the fire, either inside the hooks or on them; 25″ L (Author).

(Left) **860. WAFER IRON, c.1680–1710:** Using two heated iron griddles (with long scissors handles) to make wafers or waffles predated America's settlement, and became very popular here; note these early wafer designs in the griddle; although originally intended for church communion, the thin flat wafers soon became common fare; 35″ L (Private Coll.).

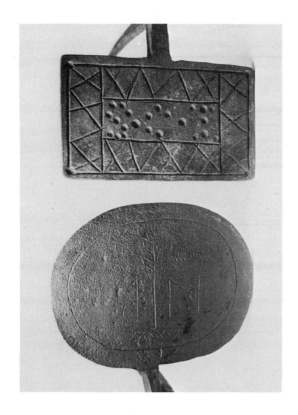

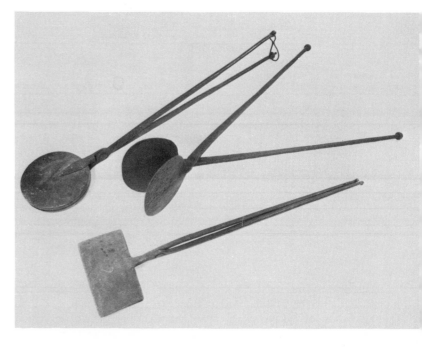

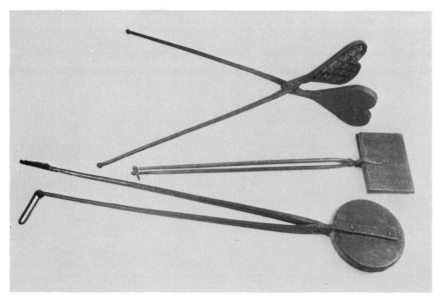

(Left) **861. WAFER DESIGNS:** Popular as wedding gifts, wafer "irons" were often incised with designs, e.g., the initials on both of these, as well as the "tree of life" on the oval griddle.

(Upper right) **862. WAFER IRONS, c.1750–1800:** Full-length wafer irons with the typical long scissors handles and round, oval, or rectangular plates; unlike the waffle irons (*below*), these wafer griddles were usually of wrought iron; the flat wafer was often dipped in honey, or rolled into cones or cylinders to hold preserves or other sweets; 28″–32″ L.

(Above left) **863. WAFFLE IRONS, c.1750–1820:** The Dutch introduced the waffle to America—and acceptance quickly spread; they usually split and buttered them, but the English soon added maple syrup, honey, or homemade "brown sugar" syrup; 27″–33″ L.

(Right) **864. WAFFLE PLATE DESIGNS:** As today, the thicker waffle required deeper designs in cast-iron plates, which were heated in the fire and buttered for use.

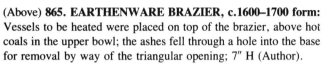

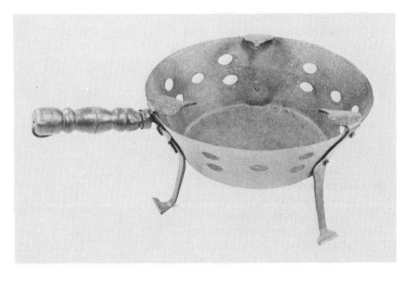

(Above) **865. EARTHENWARE BRAZIER, c.1600–1700 form:** Vessels to be heated were placed on top of the brazier, above hot coals in the upper bowl; the ashes fell through a hole into the base for removal by way of the triangular opening; 7″ H (Author).

(Upper right) **866. BRASS BRAZIER (CHAFING DISH), c.1680–1750:** The brazier was a portable stove for cooking, keeping food warm, making tea, adding to room heat, etc. (usually with charcoal). This Dutch form was for heating food at a table; the brass pan held coals, and its three raised arms supported the cooking vessel; an iron tang penetrates the wooden handle; 13^{1}/$_{2}$″ L.

(Left) **867. WROUGHT-IRON BRAZIER, c.1740–1780:** The flat-bottomed pan for coals has splayed legs riveted to its side; note the pointed holders at the rim; 12^{1}/$_{2}$″ L.

(Lower left) **868. COPPER-PAN BRAZIER, c.1740–1800:** This dished copper pan mounts iron legs and pointed supports, plus a wooden handle (Neumann Coll.; Valley Forge National Historical Park). (Lower right) **869. IRON-PAN BRAZIER, c.1750–1800:** Note the unusual added fence, three hinged holders, and twisted-iron leg reinforcements; wrought iron; 15″ L (Conn. Historical Society).

198

(Upper left) 870. WROUGHT-IRON BRAZIER, c.1750–1800: The most common form found in America consists of a square perforated iron box (to hold the coals) that sat on a footed platform and had a hinged grid top with a handle; note these supportive corner lobes for large vessels, and scrolled lift bars on the grid; its tang originally pierced a turned wooden handle (Private Coll.).

(Upper right) 871. WROUGHT-IRON BRAZIER, c.1750–1800: Here is a more common version of this style; its round corner supports, hinged grid, and bulbous wooden handle are typical, while the short ribbon legs extend as curled feet; 7″ H (Author).

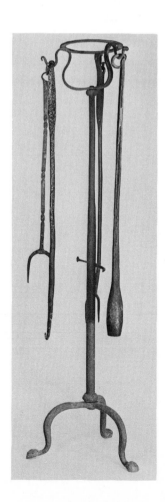

(Left) 872. CAST-IRON BRAZIER, c.1770–1820: This cast-iron body includes three integral legs, a platformed hearth opening, and a removable internal grate; the iron handle is forged. It was a form also popular on shipboard, as well as in 19th-century wagon trains—although the later versions had straighter sides; 8½″ H.

(Right) 873. HANGING STAND, c.1680–1720: A tall iron stand with hooks that hold flesh forks, a poker, and a heavy mulling iron; note the upper frame for a bowl or cup; 40″ H (Thankful Arnold House, Haddam, Conn.).

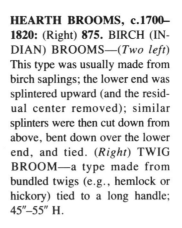

HEARTH BROOMS, c.1700–1820: (Right) **875.** BIRCH (INDIAN) BROOMS—(*Two left*) This type was usually made from birch saplings; the lower end was splintered upward (and the residual center removed); similar splinters were then cut down from above, bent down over the lower end, and tied. (*Right*) TWIG BROOM—a type made from bundled twigs (e.g., hemlock or hickory) tied to a long handle; 45″–55″ H.

874. HEARTH BRUSHES, c.1750–1800: (*Left*) This is made from tied fibrous plant sections; (*right*) a shaved stick form tied with a splint; 17″, 21½″ H.

(Above) **876. HOOK RACK, c.1780–1820:** Utensils hanging from a wrought-iron rack at the hearth; 14″ W.

(Right) **877. HOOK RACKS, c.1760–1800:** Note their typical spiked ends for driving into a lintel or post, and the scrolled-iron decorations; 10¼″–14″ W.

200

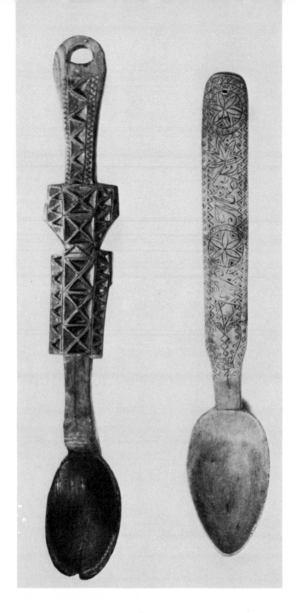

(Upper left) **878. CARVED MARRIAGE SPOONS:** One of the common bridal gifts was a carved wooden cooking spoon; (*left*) c.1640–1700, an early form with expanded decorative side panels (one corner gone); 16″ L; (*right*) c.1700–1820, a long enduring style showing incised carving that includes the bride's initials; 14″ L (Author).

(Upper right) **879. WOODEN COOKING/ SERVING SPOONS,** (Two left) **c.1690–1740,** early plain and decorated spoon forms; 16″, 12³/₄″ L; (right) **c.1700–1750,** another example of typical incised handle carving; 20¹/₂″ L. (Left) **880. WOODEN COOKING/TASTING SPOONS, c.1700–1800:** These hand-carved spoons testify to the local variances that existed even in such a simple utensil; 7⁵/₈″–12³/₄″ L.

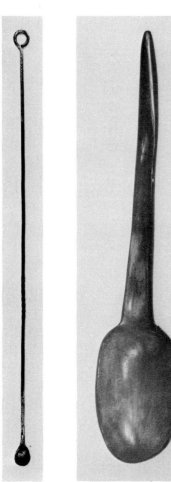

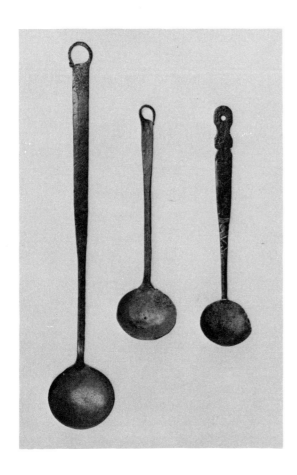

(Upper left corner) **881. IRON TASTING SPOON, c.1700–1800:**
A long-handled forged-iron tasting spoon; 32″ L. (Upper center)
882. HORN SERVING SPOONS, Marked **"1791," "1798":**
(*Left*) A spoon with a concave handle that is carved in the back
"1798 W L"; (*right*) a punched-dot design visible in this bowl
includes "1791"; 15⁵/₈″, 13³/₄″ L (Joan W. Friedland).

(Upper right) **883. IRON COOKING SPOONS, c.1750–1850:**
Most long spoons at the hearth were used for stirring, tasting, and
serving: (*Left to right*) (*1*) An iron handle riveted to a sheet brass
bowl; 18″ L; (*2 & 3*) flat handles that include terminal hanging
hooks; each is one piece of iron; 13″, 16¹/₄″ L; (*4*) a better finished
spoon by a "whitesmith"; 17³/₄″ L; (*5*) a twisted handle is riveted
to the bowl; all wrought iron; 22¹/₄″ L (Author).

(Left) **884. IRON TASTING SPOONS, c.1750–1850:** These
are shorter-handled tasting spoons with shallow round bowls;
8″–13″ L.

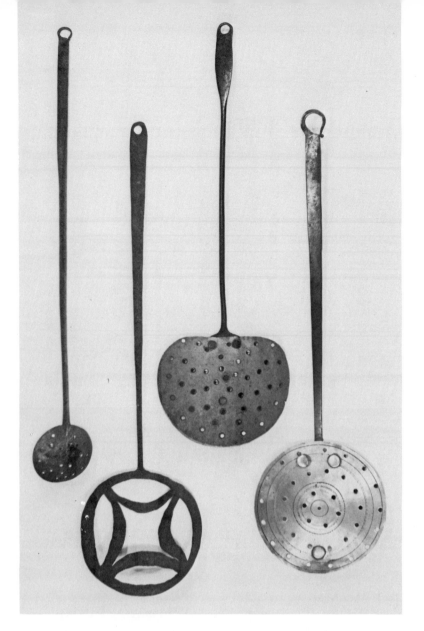

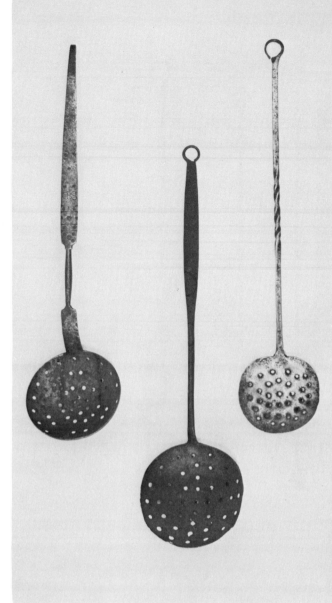

SKIMMER: This consisted of a long handle attached to a shallow perforated bowl or pan; it was used to skim grease or scum from a simmering pot, lift solid pieces from a liquid, and remove the cream layer from milk. (Above) **885.** (*Two left*) **c.1730–1770:** both are forged iron; 24^1/$_2$″, 25″ L; (*two right*) c.1750–1840, by 1750 the iron handle was being riveted to broad bodies in brass or tinned iron; these two are from Penn.; 22^1/$_2$″, 23^3/$_4$″ L. (Upper right) **886. c.1750–1840:** Three single-piece iron skimmers typical of the later 18th and 19th centuries; 19^1/$_4$″–19^3/$_4$″ L.

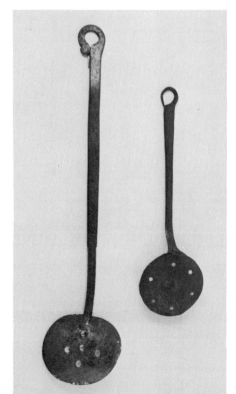

(Near right) **887. IRON STIRRERS, c.1750–1800:** A near-skimmer form forged in iron for stirring; both "bowls" are flat, and include holes to minimize turbulence; 12^3/$_4$″, 8^1/$_4$″ L. (Far right) **888. WOODEN SKIMMER, c.1700–1800:** A rare surviving early wooden skimmer (they usually split through the holes); from Mass.; 14^1/$_2$″ L.

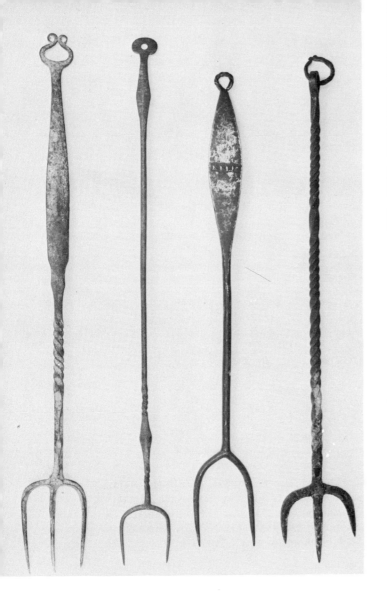

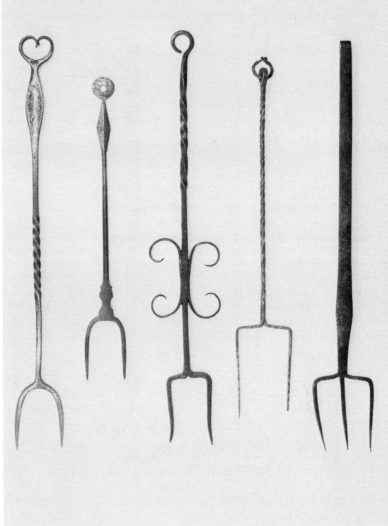

COOKING FORKS: Long wrought-iron forks were mostly used to lift meat or to toast food (see **#893–#895**); many were made by a "whitesmith," who tinned or filed and finished ironware—vs. basic blacksmithing; forks remained a typical part of Penn. dowries until the mid-1800s. (Upper left) **889.** (*Fork at left*) c.1660–1700; (the others) c.1700–1820; 21″–23¹/₂″ L. (Upper right) **890. c.1740–1800:** A variety of smaller cooking forks; 15¹/₂″–18¹/₂″ L.

(Right) **891. SPOON MARKINGS:** (Left) A close-up of some stamped and filed designs, plus the initials "CHS" (probably a bride or owner); (right) the maker's marking, "ELLIS," inside a rectangular cartouche. (Below) **892. WOODEN SPOON/ LADLE, c.1700–1800:** A maple spoon for household and cooking chores in deep vessels; 35″ L.

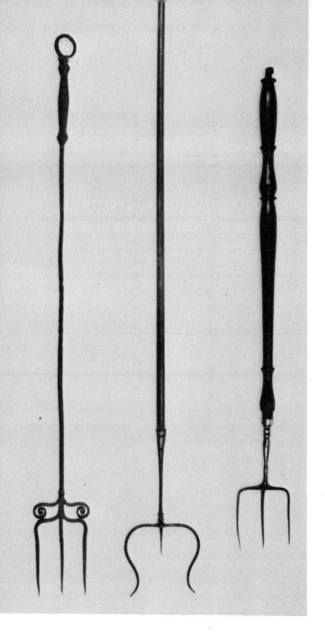

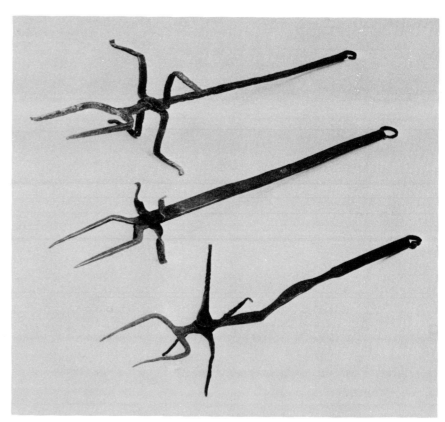

TOASTING FORKS: (Upper right) **894. DOUBLE-FOOTED, c.1730–1800:** Some forks had legs to help position portions of meat, fish, biscuits, bread, etc. at an angle to the hearth fire; 15"–19$\frac{1}{2}$" L. (Lower right) **895. SINGLE-FOOTED,** The bottom fork is c.1680–1710; the other two are c.1700–1800; 17$\frac{1}{2}$"–22$\frac{1}{2}$" L.

TOASTING FORKS: (Upper left) **893.** These 2- or 3-tined iron forks with long handles were used to toast a piece of bread or other food at the hearth. (*Left to right*) (*1*) c.1680–1700, wrought iron; 25$\frac{3}{4}$" L; (*2*) c.1650–1700, an iron head on a wooden rod; (*3*) c.1730–1760, a turned wooden handle (Queen Anne form), plus a brass collar and iron tines; 22$\frac{1}{2}$" L (Au.).

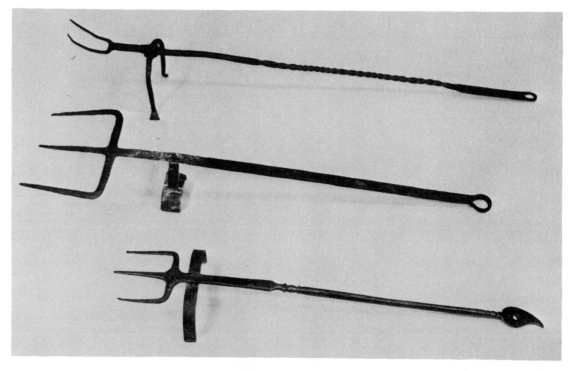

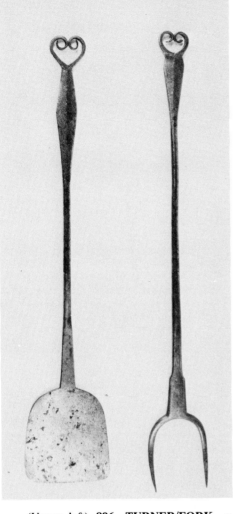

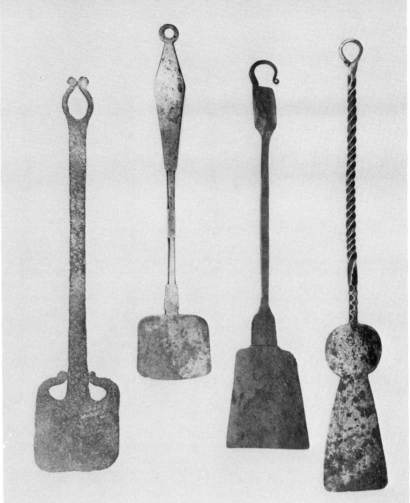

(Upper left) **896. TURNER/FORK, c.1750–1800:** A paired "turner" (spatula) and cooking fork with heart-scrolled finials; found in New England; 16″ L. (Upper right) **897. TURNERS (SPATULAS, SCRAPERS):** (*Turner at left*) c.1680–1720; (the others) c.1750–1800; these shovel-faced spatulas were used to turn food over on a griddle or in an oven and to serve as scrapers; 13″–16³/₄″ L.

(Lower left) **898. TURNERS, c.1700–1800:** Forged short-handled variations; 7″–10¹/₂″ L.

(Lower right) **899. TURNER/FORKS, c.1750–1800:** Double-ended examples with pierced hearts (from Penn.); both measure 10¹/₄″ L (Author).

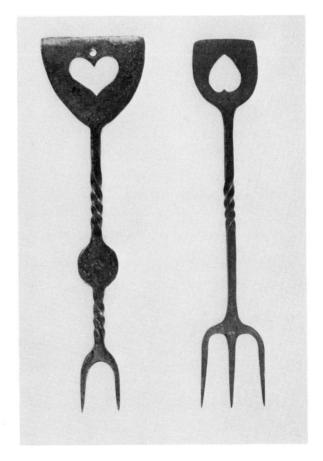

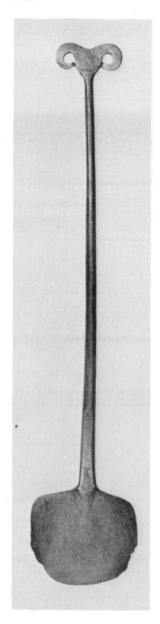

SALAMANDER: A long-handled browning iron having a near-round blade to help brown or toast surfaces of roasts or pastry (probably also used as a turner and peel). (Upper left) **900. c.1750:** This long iron salamander includes a "ram's-horn" finial; 23³/₄″ L. (Upper center) **901.** (*Salamander at left*) c.1680–1710; (the others) c.1730–1800; all are wrought iron; 8⁷/₈″–18″ L.

(Upper right) **902. BUTTER PATTERS, c.1740–1800:** These iron spoonlike forms are completely flat, and were used to "pat" butter into containers to prevent spoiling; 6¹/₄″, 13⁵/₈″ L.

(Left) **903. GOURD DIPPERS:** Gourds were dried out and transformed into implements such as spoons, funnels, bowls, canteens, dishes, cups, and dippers; (*far left*) an uncut gourd probably used for a baby's rattle (seeds inside), or a darning ball; 9″–16″ L.

(Above) **904. BURL LADLES (DIPPERS):** These are "treen" (i.e., wood) dippers made from burl (see **#980**); because burls were usually small in size, some ladles combine their burl "bowl" with a contiguous handle of normal wood grain; 7″–19″ L (Devere Card).

(Above) **905. LADLES:** Various ladle forms, each cut from a single piece of wood; the handle's hooked end caught the rim to keep it from sliding into a pot or bucket; 9³/₄″–17″ L.

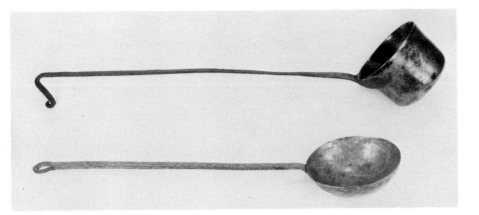

LADLES: (Above) **906. c.1760–1810:** (Top) A cast brass ladle cup with a forged-iron handle that splits for riveting to the side; 20″ L; (bottom) a copper bowl beaten into a mold for shaping; it is riveted to an iron handle; 16¹/₄″ L. (Right) **907. c.1770–1830:** As metals became plentiful in the late 1770s, they replaced many wooden implements; these brass bowls turn rims over a wire, and have riveted iron handles; 27″–34¹/₄″ L.

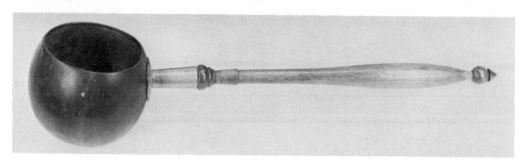

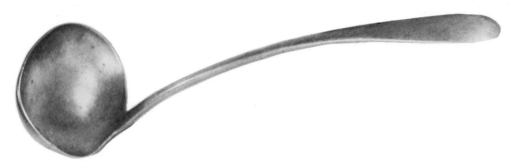

(Left) **LADLES:** (Top to bottom) (*1*) **908.** A single-piece wooden ladle with a gentle spout in the rim; 20½″ L. (*2*) **909. c.1760–1830:** This coconut-shell bowl is attached by a metal ferrule to a turned wooden handle; 15″ L. (*3*) **910. c.1760:** An English pewter ladle with an oval bowl; 13″ L (Private Coll.). (*4*) **911. c.1740–1760:** A pewter form that includes an extended pouring spout and a turned handle mounted in the socket; 15″ L.

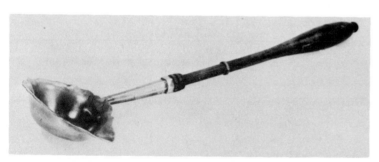

HERBS: Almost every established home had its herb garden; the herbs were dried, ground up, and employed in many uses from seasoning and preserving food to medical applications. (Lower left) **912. HERB DRIERS, c.1650–1850:** A common X form from which herbs and other items were hung to dry (Private Coll.).

(Below) **913. COUNTRY HERB GARDEN:** A typical profusion of herbs required to meet the needs of a colonial family.

(Upper left) **914. MEDICINAL HERBS:** For common ailments, country people usually trusted native plants and home remedies in preference to a physician; note the typical glass storage bottles, mortar & pestle, and balance scales. (Upper right) **915. SPICE CHEST (CUPBOARD), c.1730–1760:** Chests of small drawers kept spices separated yet at hand in the busy kitchen; note the drawer string pulls; oak and pine; rabbeted and nailed joints (Private Coll.).

(Right) **916. SPICE CHEST, c.1750–1780:** A more refined walnut chest that includes six tiers of double-graduated drawers, and bracket feet of the Chippendale period; $13^3/4''$ H (Israel Sack, Inc., N.Y.C.). (Below) **917. FOOD CHOPPERS, c.1760–1850:** These troughlike grinders were used for cutting up herbs, vegetables, and seasonings by rolling the sharpened circular iron blade back and forth; their base is of cast iron—the blade is forged (with a wooden handle); each has an end pouring spout; both 18″ L.

(Above) **918. COMMON HERBS:** (*Left to right*) (*1*) Sage—used for seasonings and medicinal teas, also to soothe and reduce itching; (*2*) Hyssop—mostly medicinal (e.g., coughs, sore throats); (*3*) Lemon Balm—helpful in cooking and medicinal needs; (*4*) Southernwood—usually used as a medicine, air freshener, or moth repellent.

(Below) **919. COMMON HERBS:** (*Left to right*) (*1*) Spearmint—primarily for stomach disorders; (*2*) Savory—a cooking herb; (*3*) Marjoram—mostly for cooking; (*4*) Thyme—both cooking and medicinal needs (e.g., coughs, shortness of breath).

MORTARS & PESTLES: In this day of automatic mixers, it is hard to believe that the colonial housewife spent several hours every week just pulverizing and powdering common items such as sugar, salt, herbs, spices, vegetables, and medicines. It was done by mashing the ingredients in cuplike mortars with a hand-held pestle; most country homes had wooden versions in maple, cherry, pine, burl, or lignum vitae (a dense, dark imported wood from the West Indies and Central America). (Upper left) **920. c.1700–1800:** (*Left*) A low-faceted cup form; lignum vitae; $3^1/_8''$ H; (*center*) the reinforced chalice shape with incised carving and initials; 6″ H; (*right*) a splayed-base mortar; $6^1/_2''$ H.

(Left) **921. WOODEN MORTARS & PESTLES:** (*Left*) c.1700–1800, a raised-ring design in cherry; 5″ H; (*center*) c.1750–1820, a burl form turned with a heavy rim; $6^1/_2''$ H; (*right*) c.1790–1810, a late tall functional shape; $9^1/_8''$ H.

(Lower right) **922. MORTAR & PESTLE, c.1750–1810:** A smaller turned wooden mortar & pestle for limited portions; 3″ H.

(Near right) **923. TREE MORTAR & PESTLE, c.1750–1825:** Hollowed tree trunks were commonly used to pound and grind grain or corn when mills were unavailable; note the malletlike pestle for this large mortar; $14^1/_2''$ H (Harrison House, Branford [Conn.] Historical Society).

924. BRASS MORTARS & PESTLES: (*Left*) c.1670–1700: Mortars were made from iron, brass, bronze, wood, stone, and ceramics; this early flared-rim brass example includes the period's typical raised-surface decorations (pressed into the molds by dies and stamps); its bottom is convex from repeated pounding by the stout brass pestle; 3″ H; (*right*) c.1750–1800, a later version that is higher, and has added body rings; 3¹/₂″ H (Author).

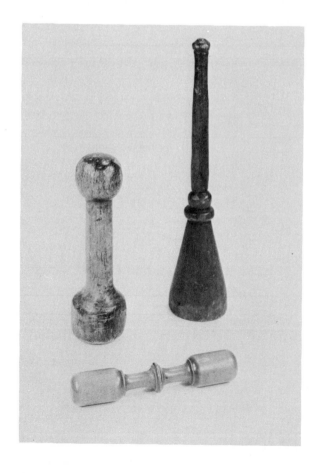

(Left) **925. PESTLES & MASHERS, c.1700–1800:** Note the variety of designs in these simple wooden pestles/mashers; the lower one resembles a later knife rest, but the wear is on its ends; 7¹/₄″–13″ H. (Above) **926. c.1650–1800:** (*Left*) A large pestle with a natural branch handle; 12¹/₄″ L; (*right*) a smaller "masher" from a single piece of burl; 6³/₄″ L.

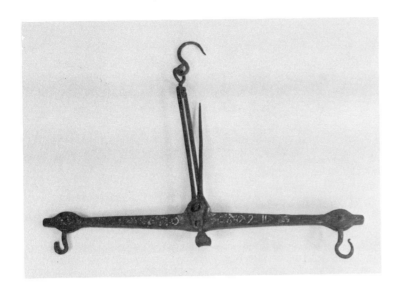

(Upper left) **927. BALANCE SCALE, 1699:** Material to be weighed was balanced against weights at the opposite end of the scale; this arm is marked "Anno 1699"; 20½" L. (Upper right) **928. BALANCE SCALE, c.1750–1820:** A later scale that retains its brass pans; 13¼" L.

(Below) **929. BALANCE SCALES, c.1750–1800:** Portable scales and weights in a hollowed wooden case having cotter-pin hinges and stamped decorations; 6½" L (Conn. Historical Society).

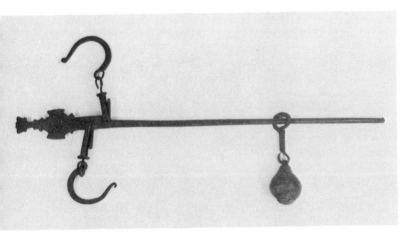

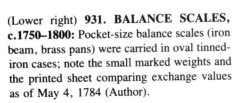

(Above) **930. SLIDING BALANCE SCALE, c.1730–1800:** Another early scale form; the upper hook suspends the scale, while the lower one holds the item being weighed; its sliding weight (*right*) is moved along the measured arm to achieve balance; 23¼" L.

(Lower right) **931. BALANCE SCALES, c.1750–1800:** Pocket-size balance scales (iron beam, brass pans) were carried in oval tinned-iron cases; note the small marked weights and the printed sheet comparing exchange values as of May 4, 1784 (Author).

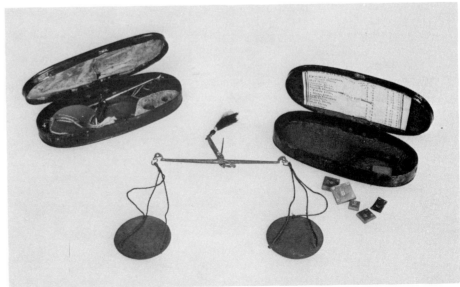

214

(Right) **932. FOOD GRATER, c.1760–1820:** This was made by perforating a sheet of tinned iron and curving it to fit a base of wood (nailed at the side); 11¼″ L (Merle E. Bouchard).

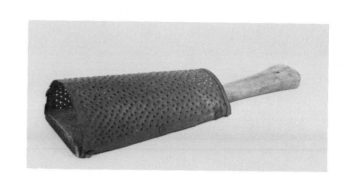

(Below) **933. NUTMEG GRATER, c.1770–1800:** A tall turned grater for nutmeg, cinnamon, etc.; its three separate sections (below right) include a top with perforated disc, a center container, and a bottom receptacle for the final seasoning; 7¼″ H.

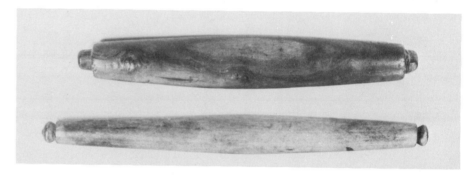

(Right) **934. ROLLING PINS (PASTE ROLLERS):** Early rolling pins had a bulge in the middle (more control), and no formal handles; (*top*) c.1750, cherry; (*bottom*) c.1780–1810, notice the later one's less bulbous profile; 13⅜″, 16¾″ L.

(Lower right) **935. PIE CRIMPERS:** The crimper was simply a handle holding a wavy cutting wheel (for the piecrust edge). (*Left to right*) *(1)* c.1680–1720, all iron; *(2)* c.1720–1770, brass; *(3)* c.1750–1810, wooden handle, bone wheel; *(4)* c.1750–1800, cherry handle, bone wheel; *(5)* c.1780–1830, pie crimper and "pastry jigger" (a curved cutter on the opposite end to cut out flat dough or cookies); iron with a tinned wheel; 4⅛″–6¼″ L (Au.).

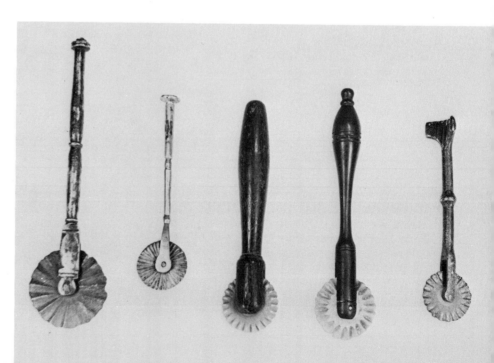

(Left) **936. BUTTER PRINTS, c.1750–1800:** These three hand-carved wooden prints were used to press designs into butter (''cookie'' prints were similar, but usually cut deeper); the typical oval, round, and rectangular forms are shown; 2¼″–7″ L.

(Center, left) **937. LEMON BORER, c.1750–1800:** This wooden implement pushed juice from a lemon as its deep corrugations pierced the center and ground the pulp; 4″ L.

(Right) **938. c.1750–1800:** (*Right*) Butter/Cookie Print Wheel—The wooden pegged wheel includes designs and serrated edges; 5¾″ L; (*top*) Cheese Cutter—The whittled handle mounts a thin arched blade; 4¼″ L; (*bottom*) Corn Husker (Shucker)—a pointed hickory tool with a leather strap to encircle the fingers; 4″ L.

(Lower left) **939. CUTTING BOARDS, c.1750–1850:** Here are two formal cutting boards—although blade marks on the backs of stools, candle boxes, tables, and trays indicate that almost any flat surface served this purpose in the home; 10½″, 10″ Dia.

(Lower right) **940. IRON DOUGH SCRAPER, c.1750–1850:** A common wrought-iron form for mixing dough.

216

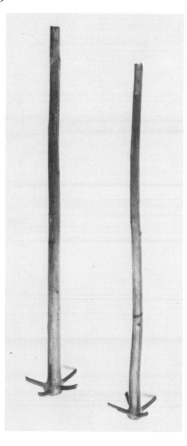

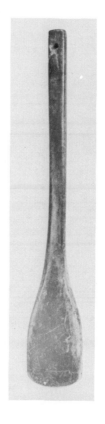

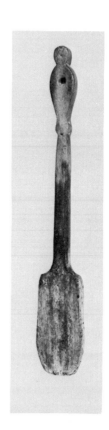

(Left) **941. WOODEN BEATERS/STIR-RERS, c.1750:** Light "beaters" (e.g., cream, eggs) were often cut branches with twigs positioned as arms; 15¼", 14¾" L (Author).

(Right) **942. WOODEN STIRRERS, c.1700–1850:** Kitchen stirrers were commonly fashioned from wood because of its availability, and to minimize abrasion to ceramic or cast-iron vessels; 23½", 14½" L.

(Below) **943. BUTCHER KNIVES, c.1740–1810:** Working knives usually consisted of a blade with a long tang that pierced a cylindrical handle, plus a bandlike ferrule at the juncture to prevent splitting; these handles are of wood; the bottom one is leather covered (see **#1323**); 12¼"–17½" L.

FUNNELS: (Lower left) **944. c.1680–1700:** An early wooden hand-carved chestnut example; 9¾" H (Private Coll.). (Lower center) **945. c.1740–1780:** A stepped profile cut from burl (Devere Card). (Lower right) **946. c.1750–1820:** A later lipped funnel of copper with an interior strainer; 5¼" H.

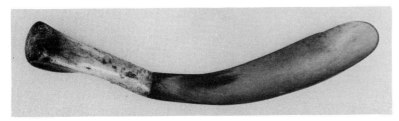

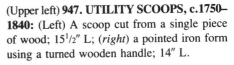

(Upper left) **947. UTILITY SCOOPS, c.1750–1840:** (Left) A scoop cut from a single piece of wood; $15^{1}/_{2}''$ L; (*right*) a pointed iron form using a turned wooden handle; $14''$ L.

(Left) **948. SCOOP, c.1750–1800:** This narrow scoop combines a bone handle and curved horn blade; $8^{7}/_{8}''$ L.

(Upper right corner) **949. SCOOP, c.1750–1800:** A shallow single-piece wooden scoop for light work, e.g., soft soap, suger, or skimming cream for butter (the remaining milk was usually fed to the animals).

(Above) **950. BRUSH/BEATER, c.1700–1800:** A cleaning brush or light beater; pieces of broom corn are tied around the handle; $14''$ L (Private Coll.).

(Right) **951. BUTTER PADDLES, c.1750–1800:** Such shallow spoonlike forms were employed to press down on butter after removal from the churn to force out water or whey (see **#902**); $8^{1}/_{8}''$, $10^{1}/_{4}''$ L.

(Left) **952. FOOD CHOPPERS, c.1700–1820:** Typical food choppers made with a curved cutting blade and one or two tangs for a wooden handle; blades $5^{1}/_{2}''$–$8^{1}/_{2}''$ W.

(Above) **954. DOUGH BOX, c.1780–1800:** A dough box painted in the Penn. fashion; it has dovetailed corners, as well as handles on the ends and lid; poplar wood (Metropolitan Museum of Art).

953. DOUGH BOX (TROUGH), c.1750–1840: A form in which to mix and knead dough—and then allow it to rise; mounted on this splayed Penn.-style base, it also served as an interim work table; pine, painted red; 27″ H (Private Coll.).

CHURNS: Such vessels were used to coagulate and separate butter from milk by the action of a long-handled agitator. (Lower left) **955. c.1650–1750:** An early European form using a hollowed tree trunk; its cover admits the plunger through a hole; the base is 12³/₄″ H. (Lower right) **956. c.1750–1850:** A common barrel-like churn of banded staves; note the applied handle for carrying or holding it steady when in use; the base is 23″ H (Webb-Deane-Stevens Museum, Wethersfield, Conn.).

(Above) **957. HORIZONTAL CHURN, c.1770–1820:** An iron-banded barrel-shaped churn using a horizontal agitator with an iron crank; it sits in a sawbuck frame having chamfered edges and lap joints; painted red (Author).

(Above) **958. CHEESE PRESS, c.1770–1810:** This press squeezed liquid out of the working curds (usually left overnight); note its windlass type handle (removable) with tension ropes—as well as the maple frame and ash trestle feet; 34″ H.

(Above) **962. WOVEN BASKET, c.1700–1800:** A typical splint utility basket using early wide random-width ash splints and a draw-shaved handle; 4⁷⁄₈″ H (Private Coll.).

BASKETS: Woven of rushes, grass, twigs, or splints, baskets filled innumerable needs in chores, storage, and transportation. (Lower left) **959. STORAGE, c.1750–1850:** A covered bulbous shape popular for storing feathers, wool, flax, etc.; 20″ H. (Lower center) **960. SPLINT CHEESE, c.1650–1850:** A traditional open form for cheese; 19¹⁄₂″ L. (Lower right) **961. STORAGE, c.1750–1850:** This is woven in splint, with sloping shoulders and a narrow neck; 20″ H (Conn. Historical Society).

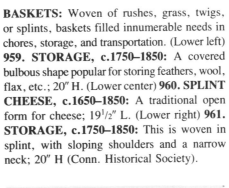

GRASS (RYE) BASKETS: A method used since ancient times; ropes of grass were tied together in layers (as in beehives). (Upper left) **963.** A heavily rimmed grass basket tied with splint; 4″ H, 8³/₈″ Dia. (Upper right) **964.** A lower oblong form, also splint tied; 2³/₄″ H, 5″ W (Author).

(Left) **965. DRYING BASKET, c.1700–1820:** An open, concave splint form for drying herbs, apples, etc.; note the end insets for handles; 39⁵/₈″ L (Conn. Historical Society).

(Right) **966. WALL (QUILL) BASKETS, c.1775–1830:** A high-backed style that hung on the wall; the smaller size often held "quills" for weavers (a reed or paper center wound in yarn or thread); also note its painted design; 11¹/₂″, 6¹/₂″ W (Conn. Historical Society).

(Lower left) **967. SPLINT BOX, c.1750–1790:** A small delicate storage box and cover made from tied splint; 2″ H, 8³/₈″ L.

(Lower right) **968. SIEVE (SIFTER), c.1700–1800:** This round sieve is made from the basketlike weaving of splint (some used woven horsehair); principally for grain; 18¹/₂″ Dia.

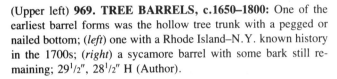

(Upper left) **969. TREE BARRELS, c.1650–1800:** One of the earliest barrel forms was the hollow tree trunk with a pegged or nailed bottom; (*left*) one with a Rhode Island–N.Y. known history in the 1700s; (*right*) a sycamore barrel with some bark still remaining; 29$^{1}/_{2}$″, 28$^{1}/_{2}$″ H (Author).

(Upper right) **970. STAVED BARREL/KEG, c.1700–1850:** The common staved-barrel form was made by a cooper; this is bound by saplings (iron bands were also used); 10$^{1}/_{2}$″ L.

(Center right) **971. HOLLOWED KEG, c.1750–1850:** Another method for a container was to hollow a log and insert the two ends; its outside surface was usually turned, as shown; 10″ L.

(Center left) **972. STAVED BUCKETS, c.1650–1850:** The sides were usually held by interlocking wooden hoops (mostly ash or hickory), and the liquid contents would swell the staves to render them tight; 11″, 9$^{1}/_{4}$″ H.

(Lower left) **973. HOLLOWED BUCKETS, c.1650–1800:** Hollowed logs also had bottoms inserted to create buckets (see **#969**); note the unusual pouring spout from a tree's natural form, and the ears for handles carved from the sides; 5$^{7}/_{8}$″, 8$^{1}/_{2}$″ H.

(Upper left) **974. PIGGIN, c.1700–1800:** This was a staved bucket having one stave extending higher as a handle; it was often used as a dipping vessel or a grain measure; 9$\frac{1}{2}$″ H. (Upper center) **975. COVERED BUCKET, c.1700–1800:** A sapling-bound style that used extended staves to receive a sliding wooden latch on the lid; note the corn cobs plugging the side knot holes; 11$\frac{7}{8}$″ H. (Upper right) **976. COVERED BUCKET (FIRKIN, SUGAR BUCKET), c.1760–1860:** A popular covered form with a swiveled handle and interlocking hoops; the body is 10″ H.

(Left) **977. FIRE BUCKETS:** Fire buckets were in use here as early as the 1600s; by the 18th century, many urban areas required them in each house by law for self-protection and community needs; all types were used, but the heavy hand-sewn leather forms predominated. (*Left to right*) (*1*) This is marked "Stephen Randall, No. 4, 1786, Providence" (R. I.); restored braided handle; 10$\frac{3}{8}$″ H; (*2*) c.1750–1830, the painted tapering-body type; its flat bail is replaced; 13$\frac{3}{4}$″ H; (*3*) c.1780–1840, a typical later form with a stitched-leather bail; the rim bends over an iron ring; 12$\frac{1}{4}$″ H (Author).

Woodenware

The ancient word *treen* ("from trees") is used today to describe small antique household untensils made of wood. In colonial days, the more familiar terms were "woodenware," "cooper's ware," or "turner's ware." Many families made their own treen, but the commercial woodenware was traditionally fashioned by artisans known as coopers and turners.

The cooper created staved articles such as barrels, kegs, tubs, churns, and buckets. In more populated areas, his work was even subdivided among the "tight cooper" (articles to hold liquids), "slack cooper" (dry products), or "white cooper" (small items and boxes). The turner made bowls, trenchers (plates), chargers (platters), and similar pieces turned on a lathe. Although the English apparently preferred beech and sycamore for these items, the Americans favored such woods as maple, poplar, butternut, and hickory.

(Above) **978. TINNED BUCKET:** A re-created tinned bucket from remains (*foreground*) excavated at Fort Ligonier, Penn.; (1758–1766); plating sheet iron with tin to resist rust was well established in the 1700s; body $9^{1}/4''$ H (Fort Ligonier, Penn.).

(Lower left) **979. SHOULDER YOKE:** A yoke carved to fit across the shoulders was a practical method for carrying two heavy buckets; pine; $31^{1}/4''$ W.

(Right) **980. TREE WITH BURLS:** Burl is an abnormal tree growth (a mild tumor) that protrudes from the trunk or limbs; being more dense and harder than the host tree, it was favored for bowls, mortars, dippers, scoops, salts, etc. Americans preferred white ash or maple, while Europeans favored oak. "Burl" is a modern term—the colonial references were to "knot" or "root" ware (see **#981**).

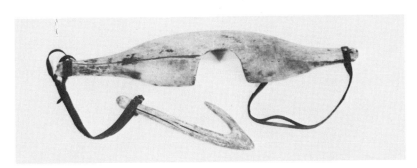

(Above) 981. BURL MIXING BOWLS: Typical colonial mixing bowl forms, i.e., wide openings, gently sloping sides, and low round footings; (*two left*) these are early "hewn" examples (probably chopped or burned out in the center, and then shaped with an adz and wood chisel); unlike normal wood, burl was seldom turned until about 1750. (*Left to right*) (*1*) c.1650–1720, $16^1/2''$ Dia; (*2*) c.1700–1800, $7^1/8''$ Dia; (*3*) c.1750–1810, 10" Dia (Author).

(Above) 983. WOODEN MIXING BOWL, c.1700–1800: This straight-sided (slightly concave) bowl form was used throughout the 1700s; pine; $11^3/4''$ Dia (Private Coll.).

(Below) 982. WOODEN MIXING/CHOPPING/SERVING BOWLS, c.1680–1800: Some of these are turned, others are carved; the deeper ones tend to be earlier; (*right*) the bowl with a handle has added a later flat base—having worn through its original bottom; $13^1/2''$ Dia.

(Upper left) **984. WOODEN MIXING BOWL, c.1750–1800:** A deep birch bowl with its horizontal turned lines still visible; the other side is cracked, and has early iron staples as a repair; 13$^{1}/_{2}$" Dia (Private Coll.). (Upper right) **985. HANDLED BURL BOWL, c.1750–1760:** A handsome form incorporating ram's-horn scrolled handles; 15$^{1}/_{2}$" Dia (Devere Card).

WOODEN MIXING BOWLS: (Second left) **986. c.1750–1800:** This hewn bowl includes end handles; cut scars in the bottom indicate its additional use for chopping food; 21$^{1}/_{4}$" L. (Third left) **987. c.1750–1800:** Similar to the bowl (**#986**), but with indented finger grips at the ends; 21" L. (Lower left) **988. c.1750–1800:** A crude form that retains pine bark on its underside; note the recessed pouring outlet in the left handle (probably to drain buttermilk from butter); 23$^{1}/_{2}$" L.

(Lower right) **989. WOODEN UTILITY BOWLS, c.1750–1800:** Two small versions of the **#988** form; 15$^{3}/_{8}$" L.

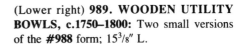

(Above) **990. TRENCHERS, c.1660–1720:** Tableware was initially functional wooden bowls, platters (''chargers''), and crude earthenware; round trenchers (wooden plates) gained acceptance in the mid-1600s as a size large enough to hold double portions—being set between two diners, who ate with fingers and knife; these early trenchers were usually thick and gently concave—without a brim or recessed center; (*lower row*) these reversed sides show the typical flat turned bottoms; two are maple, the other cherry; $10^{1}/2''$–$11''$ Dia (Author).

(Above left) **991. SQUARE TRENCHER:** A reproduction of the alternate ''squared'' trencher—an earlier c.1600–1680 form with a depressed center and corner ''salt'' cavity. (Above right) **992.**

ROUND TRENCHERS, c.1680–1720: Individual-size trenchers of the early thick style that omit a flat brim (see **#990**); $8''$ Dia.

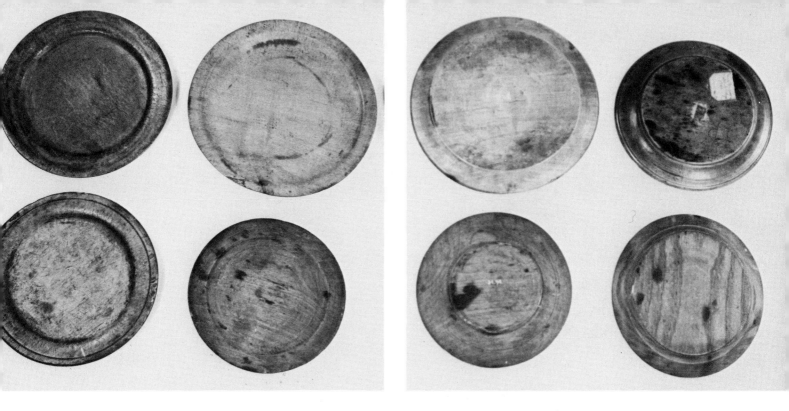

(Upper left) **993. ROUND TRENCHERS, c.1700–1800:** Examples of the more familiar flat-brimmed type that imitated the pewter plates then gaining acceptance (see **#1210**); note the normal wood shrinkage (perpendicular to the grain) into an oval form; maple, ash, chestnut, and cherry were the most popular woods; trenchers were disappearing by 1800 in favor of pewter and ceramics (easier to clean; did not split); (*upper right*) the reverse sides of similar trenchers reveal their usual flat turned base; knife marks on some of the backs support the tradition of turning over a trencher to eat the dessert; $7^1/2''–9^1/4''$ Dia.

(Near left) **994. UTILITY BOWL, c.1650–1800:** A hand-carved wooden bowl with an integral projecting handle; it could be used as a bowl, cup, porringer, or scoop; $3^1/4''$ H.

EATING BOWLS: (Above) **995. c.1650–1780:** This turned eating bowl includes incised decoration, a tinned-iron repair, and the usual raised flat footing; $5^1/4''$ Dia. (Right) **996. c.1680–1800:** Typical of the colonial era; (*two left*) these were turned with a low raised footing; (*two right*) both were adzed and carved (flat bottoms); $7''–9^1/2''$ Dia.

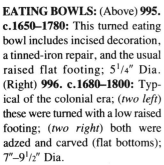

(Left) **997. EATING/UTILIT** **BOWLS, c.1700–1800:** This versed view reveals the decotive raised and incised rings add by the turner on these slight convex outer sides; their bottor are typically flat; 5″–7″ Dia.

(Right) **998. FOOTED SERVING PLAT-TER** (two views), **c.1700–1800:** A broad turned cherry serving tray on a raised concave base; 2¹/₂″ H, 10¹/₂″ Dia. (Author).

(Below) **999. SERVING BOWLS, c.1680–1800:** The principal meal in country homes was at the middle of the day; food was put on the table at one time in an array of bowls and platters; these serving bowls (i.e., low and wide) are turned, and have flat footings; 3–3¹/₄″ H, 8¹/₂″–15″ Dia.

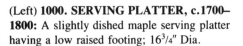

(Left) **1000. SERVING PLATTER, c.1700–1800:** A slightly dished maple serving platter having a low raised footing; 16³/₄″ Dia.

(Center left) **1001. TEA TRAY, c.1740–1760:** A Queen Anne–period walnut serving tray that adopts the pewter-style raised brim and flat center; tea had become universally popular by 1740; 13″ Dia.

(Right) **TANKARDS:** Most early wooden tankards had bound staves, a hinged lid, and an inserted bottom; the handle was usually carved as part of a stave. (Right) **1002. c.1750–1780:** A pine example with interlocked sapling bands; New England; 8³/₈″ H. (Lower right) **1003. c.1740–1790:** A larger tankard from Penn.; 10¹/₄″ H (Author).

(Above) **1004. DRINKING CUPS, c.1680–1740:** (*Left*) A footed cup with thick walls and rim; (*right*) this pedestal-base style adds incised designs on the side; 3¹/₄″, 4¹/₂″ H.

(Upper left) **1005. PITCHER, c.1680–1800:** A large pitcher cut from a single piece of wood; 11¹/₂″ H.

(Upper right) **1006. PITCHERS (NOGGINS), c.1720–1790:** Two different size "noggins" (small pitchers or mugs) found together in N.J.; note their characteristic faceted sides and hesitant spouts; each is cut from one piece of maple; 9¹/₂″, 5¹/₂″ H (Author).

(Near right) **1007. HANDLED CONTAINER, c.1750–1800:** This is constructed like the early tankards (see **#1002**), using wooden staves (one includes the handle) and iron bands; there is no pouring spout nor lid; 13″ H.

(Above right) **1008. PITCHER, c.1790–1820:** A later walnut example with a pedestal base that exhibits the more severe silhouette of early 19th-century ware; 7¹/₄″ H.

(Left) **1009. BURL CUP, c.1750–1790:** A long-handled cup cut from a single piece of burl; its large size suggests use in drinking, mixing, scooping, serving—or as a porringer for eating; 3⁵/₈″ H.

CANTEENS (WATER BOTTLES): Canteens were used within the house, in the fields, during travel, and on military duty. (Upper left) **1010. c.1740–1790:** The common barrel type with staves (usually pine, white oak, or cedar) bound by hoops (mostly hickory, ash, willow, or iron); red paint; 6³/₄″ Dia. (Upper center) **1011. c.1760–1840:** A single-band form popular in New England (pegged or nailed); note the tab marks for a shoulder strap; 6¹/₄″ Dia. (Upper right) **1012. c.1750–1840:** A staved canteen in a tapered profile; pine, held by hickory saplings; 8″ Dia. (Right) **1013. c.1750–1870:** This iron-banded example has carved legs extending from its bottom staves in order to stand upright; 8¹/₂″ Dia.

CANTEENS: (Left) **1014. c.1760–1850:** Typical cylindrical canteens which were usually carried to the fields; 5¹/₂″, 8″ L. (Lower left) **1015. c.1720–1820:** A traditional Germanic form from Penn.; the center disc was removed to carve its interior; painted; 6¹/₂″–10¹/₂″ Dia. (Lower right) **1016. c.1760–1870:** A large storage canteen; 10¹/₂″ Dia.

(Left) **1017. CANTEENS, c.1750–1840:** As with kegs (see **#971**), another method was to hollow a tree trunk and insert two end discs; as shown, they were cut in a variety of depths; the outer surface was usually turned, and often added raised or incised rings; $3^5/8''$–$7^3/8''$ L.

(Above) **1018. RUNDLETS (SWIGLERS, RUM KEGS), c.1750–1840:** These small hollowed and sealed wooden cylinders were commonly reserved for spirits; note their greater use of decorative rings and lines; $4''$–$8^3/4''$ L (Author).

(Right) **1019. STORAGE CONTAINERS, c.1700–1800:** Such small barrel-type containers were commonly used for salt or sugar; they illustrate both iron-band and interlocked sapling hoops; $6^7/8''$, $6^1/4''$ H.

COVERED BOWLS: (Far left) **1020. c.1700–1790:** A turned wooden body with an oval cover that locks when rotated in its oval opening; 3″ H. (Near left) **1021. c.1750–1790:** This later form has now acquired abrupt shoulders and a domed cover; 3¼″ H.

(Above) **1022. ROUND STORAGE BOXES, c.1760–1820:** Early examples of these popular round containers; later versions usually have narrower cover overhangs; also note their straight pegged and nailed seams; green paint; 4¼″, 5⅝″ H.

(Above) **1023. COVERED BOWL, c.1760–1790:** A large storage bowl and cover—turned from single pieces of wood; 13½″ W. (Lower right) **1024. SUGARLOAF (CONE):** Sweeteners included maple sugar (as syrup, hard cakes, or granules), molasses, honey, and sugar; white refined sugar (from the South) arrived paper-wrapped in this cone shape, and was broken with plierslike "cutters" (as shown and see **#1026–#1029**) before being ground to granules in a mortar & pestle.

(Above) **1025. ROUND STORAGE BOXES, c.1770–1790:** These smaller boxes (vs. **#1022**) illustrate straight nailed seams and pointed laps; their bases and tops are pegged; 2″, 3⅞″ H.

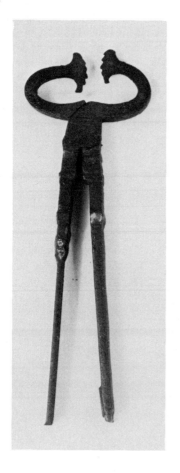

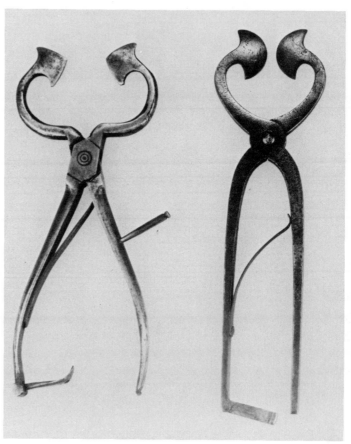

(Far left) **1026. SUGAR CUTTERS (NIPPERS), c.1670–1700:** A spread-end pliers form which was used to break up the hard sugar cone (see #1024); this early forged-iron example includes a repaired handle (Private Coll.).

(Center left) **1027. SUGAR CUTTERS, c.1760–1820:** These more common sugar cutters include arrowlike points, an inside spring, a rod extension to help break up chunks, and a bottom locking clasp; $8^3/8''$ L.

(Near left) **1028. SUGAR CUTTERS, c.1760–1820:** Modified simple country nippers; 9″ L.

(Right) **1029. MOUNTED SUGAR CUTTERS, c.1750–1810:** Sugar cutters were often mounted on a board with a turned wooden handle, as shown; the base is 12″ L.

(Below) **1030. TURNED CONTAINERS** (two views): (*Left*) Sugar Bowl, c.1790–1810—a late period form (i.e., squat, heavy profile) in rosewood; $6^1/4''$ H; (*right*) Pharmaceutical Container, c.1780–1820—made of sections from lignum vitae (a hard, dark imported wood); $10^1/4''$ H; (*lower right*) both containers are shown separated.

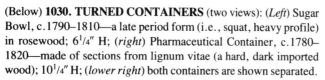

SUGAR BOWLS: Such small footed bowls held herbs, seasonings, tea, sugar, salt, etc. but are known as "sugar bowls" today. (Above) **1031.** (*Two left*) Pedestal-based bowls that date c.1740–1780; (*right*) the more severe form is later—c.1780–1810; 4½"–5½" H. (Upper right) **1032.** A burl sugar bowl (white paint over red) with a family label, "Made in Vermont in 1780"; 5⅛" H (Private Coll.).

SALTS (SALTERS): Salt was critically needed as a seasoning and preservative. Being broken off a block and pulverized in a mortar, its crystals varied from powder to rock salt. Storage boxes normally kept this supply in the kitchen (see **#125, #1019**), but during meals small open "salts" held it on the table (taken between two fingers and applied to the food); these containers were also used for condiments. (Above right) **1033. c.1700–1800:** Three basic styles of wooden salts are shown (the center one is whittled, not turned); 1¼"–3½" H. (Right) **1034. c.1700:** (*Left*) A low early form; the other two are c.1780; 1⅜"–3¼" H (Author).

(Above) **1035. SALTS:** (*Left*) **c.1760–1810,** an English pewter salt; (*right*) **c.1780–1810,** a similar shape in wood; 1⅝", 1¾" H. (Left) **DOUBLE SALT, c.1700–1750:** These twin cups were cut from one piece of wood; 5½" W.

(Left) **1036. CARVED SALT, c.1680–1720:** A small tapering wooden cup with early carving; it probably held salt or condiments; 1³/₄″ H. (Right) **1037. HORN CUP, c.1700–1740:** A cup from a cow's horn with an inserted horn base; note its early incised rings and punched-dot design; 2⁵/₈″ H. (Below left) **1038. HORN CUPS:** Their use was widespread and spanned our period; 1⁷/₈″–6⁷/₈″ H. (Below right) **1039. PERSONAL SALT HORN, c.1750–1800:** A form used when traveling and visiting; 2⁵/₈″ L.

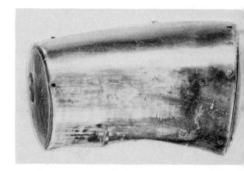

HORN: Cattle provided an abundant supply of horns, which were light, strong, and waterproof; after the inner material was boiled out, they were scraped and even separated into layers for use. (Center right) **1040. STORAGE HORN, c.1740–1820:** It is cut and plugged at both ends. (Below) **1041. HORN BOWL, c.1750–1850:** A bowl made from a single piece of horn; 8¹/₄″ L (Deerfield Memorial Hall Museum, PVMA). (Near right) **1042. BELT DRINKING CUP, c.1750–1820:** It resembles a farmer's honing-stone holder, but the lack of wear suggests a drinking cup; 7³/₄″ L. (Far right) **1043. SHAPED CONTAINER, c.1750–1830:** Horn could be heated and shaped as in this oval carrying form with shoulder cord loops; 7¹/₂″ H (Author).

(Left) 1044. COCONUT-SHELL CANTEEN, c.1750–1790:
Coconuts are found in surprising numbers among colonial ware; most arrived from the West Indies and southern trade; this one has a dovetailed pewter spout added; 5$^1/8$″ H.

(Above right) 1045. LEATHER "BLACK JACKS" (Flagons), c.1640–1720: England had a tradition of leather vessels reaching back to medieval days; these tankardlike flagons were of heavy leather with raised bases and applied (sewn) handles; (*left*) an English form, shaped by steam in a mold, then waxed, varnished, or tarred for waterproofing; (*right*) a simple "jack," not wet-pressed but sewn together in a simple oval construction (possibly American); 8$^1/2$″ H (Author).

(Right) 1046. LEATHER CANTEEN (BOTTLE), c.1650–1725:
This early molded form is made of thick cowhide held together by heavily stitched seams; notice center raised spout (it held a plug) and two flanking holes for shoulder cord; 7″ H, 7$^1/4$″ L (Au.).

Ceramic Tableware

A rapid succession of variations in ceramic tableware flooded into America from Europe and the Orient beginning in the 1600s. Because it arrived in an overlapping sequence, which can be extremely confusing to student collectors, an outline of the primary types is included here.

Most pieces are classified according to: (1) the *body* of clay which forms the basic vessel; (2) the *glaze*, a shiny glasslike coating applied to the body and then fired in a kiln to make the vessel impervious to moisture, enhance the color, and strengthen the clay (it can be transparent, colorless, or tinted); and (3) the *decoration*, usually done with slip, transfers, or painting by metallic compounds beneath or on top of the glaze ("underglaze", "overglaze").

TWO BROAD CATEGORIES: These ceramics are best defined by designating them as either *Pottery* or *Porcelain*. The most evident difference is that pottery is opaque, while porcelain appears translucent when held up to the light. ⟶

238

A. POTTERY: Early pottery vessels were made from common clay which was shaped by hand or turned on a potter's wheel before being glazed, decorated, and fired in a kiln. Great amounts were imported from Europe or produced here in similar forms. Although their coarse character deprived them of mention in most surviving home inventories, pottery shards found on 17th- and 18th-century American domestic sites are among the most frequently encountered artifacts. There are two basic subdivisions of pottery, *Earthenware* and *Stoneware:*

1. **EARTHENWARE:** This has a soft base which is usually porous until glazed. It includes a broad variety of the most common wares used in the colonial home:

    a. **Coarse Earthenware:** A low-fired, crude pottery made from ordinary red or brown clay for use in everyday chores. Its most typical variations were:

      • **Basic Redware:** A thick mundane earthenware that bore a minimum of decoration. It was usually covered inside (and sometimes all over) by a colorless lead glaze which gave a sheen to the surface and enhanced the red or brownish hue of the clay after firing (thus the name, "redware"). (See **#1055.**)

      • **Slipware:** A decorated redware covered with line or dot designs of contrasting-color slip (a creamlike clay applied as when icing a cake). A coating of lead glaze was then added over the slip, and the piece fired (see **#1049**).

      • **Sgraffito:** A slip-covered redware with extra designs created by scratching through the slip to expose the red clay beneath (see **#1050**).

    b. **Delftware:** A soft porous body that was dipped into a "tin glaze" (or "tin enamel"; created by the addition of tin oxide to the lead glaze). Firing produced a hard white opaque surface that could have designs painted on it in bright enamel colors (and then fired again). This type of colorful earthenware was known by various names, e.g., *Delft* in Holland; delft in England; *faience* in France; and *maiolica* (majolica) from Spain, Portugal, and Italy (see **#1115–1140**).

    c. **Creamware and Pearlware:** Created and supplied by England during the 18th century, this finer-quality earthenware led to the establishment of more delicate dinnerware as we know it today—better suited for the table than

the kitchen. It used a light-colored clay which provided a white or buff body that acquired a sparkling finish when covered with a lead glaze. Although not common in the more humble homes, these lighter ceramics were adopted by many of the middle class in America during the later half of the 1700s. The two basic variations were:

  • **Creamware (also queensware):** Perfected in the 1760s by Josiah Wedgwood, this creamy lightweight earthenware was moderately priced, available in matched sets for table use, and became the most popular of English imports here circa 1760–1800. Creamware was employed in a variety of decorative finishes: *plain*, with a clear sparkling ivory-colored surface (see **#1160**); *polychrome*, decorated with enamel colors (**#1167**); *Whieldon ware*, mostly 1750–1775, named for a former partner of Wedgwood who marketed this distinctive splashed or mottled finish usually in greens and browns (**#1176**); *transfer printed*, effected by engraving a pattern on copper from which a black impression was taken on a thin tissue paper, which was then transferred to the already glazed creamware body (popular in the U.S. circa 1785–1815 (**#1170**).

  • **Pearlware:** Actually an evolution from creamware in England that was being accepted in America by the 1790s. It presented a cleaner, shiny white surface better adopted to the popular blue decorations, overglaze colors, and transfer printing. Pearlware is the most common ceramic found here on most sites of the early 1800s (see **#1173**).

2. **STONEWARE:** This was a hard, heavy, nonporous ceramic (vs. redware's soft porous base) that acquired some degree of vitrification (i.e., a glasslike character) from high firing. It was usually given a salt glaze created by throwing salt into the kiln during firing. The salt burned to a vapor which was deposited as a shiny coating (with a slightly grainy surface texture). There were three primary types of salt-glazed stoneware in the American colonies:

    a. **Rhenish Stoneware:** A gray product developed in Flanders and the Rhine area of Germany. It was in common use here throughout the 17th century and up to the Revolutionary War, mostly as mugs, jugs, crocks, and chamber pots. The decoration usually consisted of incised, molded, stamped, or applied designs—often with cobalt blue added under the glaze (see **#1156**).

b. English Stoneware: Late in the 1600s, Britain developed this capability and produced salt-glazed "brown" stoneware, which was most evident here from 1690 to 1775. It ranged in color from dark buff to gray. Similar wares were also produced by a number of potters in the colonies (see **#1150**).

c. White Salt-glazed Stoneware: In contrast to the two utilitarian stonewares above, this variation presented a fine whitish color with a clear shiny salt glaze (although retaining the slightly rough surface). It was produced in England and achieved popularity as tableware in America circa 1730–1770 (at which time creamware gained favor). Adaptations of it varied among *plain white* finishes, *molded plate edges and forms* (**#1157**), *scratch blue* (incised decorations whose lines were colored with cobalt blue before firing (**#1159**); and *polychrome* (enamel color designs over the glaze).

B. PORCELAIN: The second broad category of ceramics is this exquisite ware which is white, thin, light in weight, delicate in decoration, hard, and nonporous. A high firing fused the glaze with the body to render the piece vitrified (near glass) and translucent. It was first made in China about A.D. 600 and exported in great amounts during the 18th century, so that by 1800 a total of as many as sixty million pieces of Chinese porcelain are estimated to have been sent to the West. This reasonably priced quality ware was supplied to America mostly through Europe until direct shipments became common after the Revolution. Although used as dinnerware by the more affluent families, individual pieces were prized in many of the lesser households as a prideful touch of elegance. Today, we normally consider porcelain of the colonial period in three categories:

1. **CHINESE EXPORT PORCELAIN:** This is the original "hard paste" variety described above. It was decorated by hand, beginning as simple underglaze blue designs, which evolved to polychromes and huge custom-decorated dinnerware sets by the end of the 1700s (accompanied, unfortunately, by a general decline in quality) (see **#1180–#1187**).

2. **"SOFT-PASTE" (or "ARTIFICIAL") PORCELAIN:** The Europeans made valiant efforts to reproduce the Chinese product up through the first half of the 18th century. In the process, they developed this "soft-paste" substitute by mixing ground glass with the clay for hardness, and coating the body with a shiny lead glaze. The result was an inexpensive ware that was white surfaced, light in weight, and easily decorated—although not quite as hard or translucent as the Chinese hard paste. The difference between the two is not always apparent (see **#1199**).

3. **EUROPEAN "HARD-PASTE" (or "TRUE") PORCELAIN:** The secret of Chinese porcelain was chiefly the ingredients of the paste and glaze. By the mid-1700s, this hard-paste product was finally being duplicated in Germany and rapidly copied across Europe—usually with Chinese-type decorations (known as "chinoiserie"). Most shards of English porcelain found on 18th-century American sites are hand painted in underglaze blue from the 1755–1775 period (see **#1201**).

Despite this succession of ceramic variations from abroad, it should be kept in mind that throughout the 1700s, the basic kitchen and tableware in America's lesser homes remained the durable woodenware, coarse earthenware, and pewter.

(Above) **1047. NARROW-NECKED JUGS (BOTTLES), c.1600–1700:** Mediterranean-style forms of the 17th century; (*left to right*) (*1 & 2*) unglazed stoneware; air holes are included in their hollow handles; note the decorative incised lines; (*3*) unglazed red earthenware with double handles; (*4*) a brown earthenware jug that is glazed inside and outside to the shoulders; 8″–14$\frac{1}{2}$″ H.

(Below) **1048. NARROW-NECKED REDWARE JUGS:** (*Left to right*) (*1*) c.1750–1780, slip-decorated redware; its lead glaze covers the outside down to the shoulder; (*2*) c.1760–1790, an interlocking slip design on redware; lead glaze; note the more bulbous outline of this later jug; (*3*) c.1740–1760, clear lead-glazed redware; the decorative lines were tooled into the sides as it revolved on a potter's wheel; (*4*) c.1760–1790, slip decoration covers this exterior; 9$\frac{1}{2}$″–14″ H (Author).

(Left) **1049. NARROW-NECKED SLIPWARE JUGS, c.1700–1800:** Note these squat-neck profiles of the 1700s; this red earthenware had slip "trailed" onto its sides by the potter from a spout, quill, or slip cup (often daubed on the shoulder and allowed to run down); 6$\frac{1}{2}$″–9$\frac{3}{4}$″ H.

(Upper left) **1050. SGRAFFITO WINE JUG, c.1690–1750:** A continental European form with sgraffito decoration, scratched through a yellow slip coating; 9″ H. (Upper center) **1051. WIDEMOUTHED JUG, c.1670–1690:** An English sgraffito-decorated jug; white slipware covers the red body—bearing the period's line/dot scratched designs. (Colonial National Historical Park, Yorktown-Jamestown, Va.). (Upper right) **1052. WIDEMOUTHED JUG, c.1680–1710 Form:** A two-handled jug that includes the early straight ringed neck (*see at left*); green-tinted glaze; 9¹/₂″ H.

(Above) **1053. WIDEMOUTHED JUGS:** (*Left to right*) (*1 & 2*) c.1600–1680, note the 17th-century tapered body and ribbed outer surface; glazed only inside the rim; (*3*) c.1690–1730 Form, a later, less severe profile; lead glaze inside and on the lip; (*4*) c.1720–1760, this redware is covered in a clear lead glaze, plus some green glaze around the neck; 6¹/₄″–10″ H.

(Left) **1054. DECORATING, c.1750–1800:** Uncontrolled color changes occurred from the clay and glaze impurities, as well as irregular kiln burning; the potter also added his own color, e.g., (*left to right*) (*1*) crossing lines of green and yellow slip; tan splotches; (*2*) clear glaze is spread above the shoulder (note drip line) over a white slip decoration; (*3*) this lead glaze is covered with a mottled green glaze and spattered black spots (Author).

NARROW-MOUTHED JUGS: (Above) **1055. c.1750–1800:** These bulbous squat-necked redware jugs were common during the second half of the 18th century; $7^1/4''$–$8^1/2''$ H. (Right) **1056. c.1775–1800:** Note the straighter sides and squarer lip profile in these later redware jugs; $8^1/2''$, $11''$ H.

(Above) **1057. WIDEMOUTHED JUGS, c.1700–1800:** The popular raised neck of the early 1700s slowly shortened during the century. (*Left to right*) (*1*) white slip was added here around the rim and as body "flower" decorations; (*2*) glazed inside and out, plus a vertical slip design; (*3*) a clear glaze was applied to the interior and rim, allowing the excess to flow unevenly down the outside; (*4*) a late-century shape with its shortened neck; glazed inside only; $9^1/2''$–$12^1/2''$ H (Author).

(Left) **1058. REDWARE VESSELS, c.1790–1830:** These forms near the end of our period now bear the squared-profile collarlike rims carried into the 1800s; their lead glaze is also thicker by this time; note the black splashed designs (manganese added to the glaze)—daubed with a brush or fingers by the busy potter; $6^1/4''$, $5^3/4''$ H (Private Coll.).

(Above) **1059. DOUBLE-HANDLED JUGS:** The double-han-dled earthenware jug generally disappeared in America by 1800. (*Left to right*) (*1*) c.1650–1700, a clear glaze inside and down to the shoulders; (*2*) c.1750, white slip is trailed on the sides and neck; (*3*) c.1680–1710, incised wavy-line decorations; the interior and rim are glazed; (*4*) c.1790–1800, mottled green and brown glazes cover the entire jug; notice the neck shortening and base broadening through the 1700s; 7″–11¹⁄₂″ H.

(Near left) **1060. DOUBLE-HANDLED POT, c.1650–1800:** This bulging earthenware pot (unglazed) includes a spout in its raised rim; it was a utility form applicable throughout our period (the body shape resembles iron pots, see **#769**); 8¹⁄₂″ H.

(Above) **1061. DOUBLE-HAN-DLED JUG, c.1650–1800:** A small example glazed down to the shoulders and bearing an early lunette-neck design in white slip (that usually yellowed in the kiln's fire); 4³⁄₄″ H.

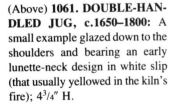

(Above right) **1062. JUG HANDLE VARIATIONS:** (*Left to right*) (*1*) c.1600–1700 form, this Mediterranean style has four applied crescent handles, a disc rim, and raised decorations; (*2*) c.1760–1790, note these double handles on the same side, plus a bulbous outline of the later 1700s; (*3*) c.1770–1790, a loop-handle form in a tan slip coating under vertical green streaks; (*4*) c.1780–1820, dark redware; the applied crescent handles and raised collar re-mained popular into the 1800s; 5³⁄₄″–10¹⁄₄″ H.

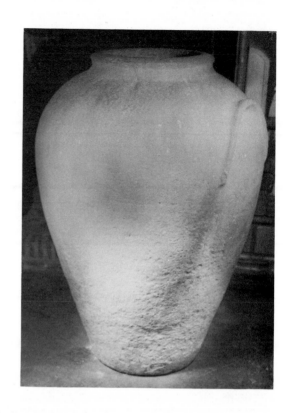

(Above) **1063. EARTHENWARE CANTEENS, c.1650–1800:** (Left) A narrow convex canteen having sgraffito designs scratched through its yellow and green slip; the holes next to the spout are for a shoulder cord; stubby toes appear at the bottom; 6^1/$_2$″ H, 2^1/$_2$″ D; (*right*) a rounded unglazed jug with raised ears that hold a rope handle; 6^1/$_4$″ H (Author).

(Upper right) **1064. UNGLAZED STORAGE JAR:** A common Mediterranean form since ancient times; after being shipped here containing merchandise (olive oil, etc.) they were reused throughout our period; 32″ H (Mercer Museum, Bucks County Historical Society).

(Left) **1065. WIDEMOUTHED JUGS, c.1690–1730:** A popular dark red earthenware shape bearing bands of incised decoration on the upper half; 6^7/$_8$″, 9″ H.

(Below) **1066. STORAGE JUGS:** (*Left to right*) (*1*) c.1650–1720, unglazed, thick walled, and crudely potted; (*2*) c.1740–1800, unglazed (i.e., absorbs heat in cooking), it resembles the Chinese "ginger jar" form; (*3*) c.1770–1800, a dark brown clay color is enhanced by its glaze; (*4*) c.1780–1810, redware that is glazed only on the inside; 6^3/$_4$″–10^1/$_2$″ H.

(Above) 1067. COOKING JARS (BEAN POTS), c.1750–1850: Such earthenware was used in the hearth coals or bake oven (beans, puddings); the interior is glazed to create a seal between food and clay; the outside remains unglazed to better absorb heat; 5″–10″ H.

(Upper right) 1068. DECORATED JUG, c.1700–1750: An attractive green-glazed earthenware jug displaying three bands of applied decoration; 13″ H. **(Left) 1069. FRENCH PROVINCIAL EARTHENWARE:** French Canada's earthenware have been excavated in New England; these utility vessels of the mid-1700s include integral handles; $4^{1}/_{4}$″–$6^{1}/_{2}$″ H (Private Coll.).

(Below) 1070. REDWARE STORAGE JARS, c.1760–1810: Common earthenware storage "jars" (i.e., cylindrical, no spout or handle) that gained favor in the later 1700s; note their incised decoration, and knob-top lids.

(Lower right) 1071. REDWARE STORAGE JAR, c.1780–1820: This example has the heavier glaze of the late 1700s and a splashed black glaze decoration; its broad rim allowed paper, cloth, or leather to be tied on as a cover; $8^{3}/_{4}$″ H.

246

(Left) **1072. COOKING POT, c.1766:** A cooking pot with three feet and a hollow handle—attributed to the ''Bean Hill Pottery'' in Norwich, Conn,; 7$\frac{1}{2}$'' H (Conn. Historical Society). (Below) **1073. PITCHERS:** (*Left to right*) (*1*) c.1680–1720, only the rim and handle are glazed; a brief pouring lip; (*2*) c.1710–1730, red slip designs appear on an orange slip; (*3*) c.1760–1780, the raised-neck form; a black glaze is daubed over the red base; (*4*) c.1770–1800, a clear-glazed pitcher with the incised initials ''LC'' on the neck; 6$\frac{1}{4}$''–11$\frac{1}{2}$'' H.

(Lower left) **1074. PITCHER, c.1680–1720:** A pinched-spout shape; it is covered by yellow slip and flower shapes in brown slip under clear lead glaze; 8'' H (Au.).

(Lower center) **1075. PITCHER, c.1740–1780:** The clay is coated with yellow slip on which leaf and dot designs have been applied in a red slip; 6$\frac{3}{8}$'' H (Au.).

(Lower right) **1076. PITCHER, c.1750–1800:** A wide-based form also used at this time; it is covered by a brownish-green glaze that extends almost to the bottom; 8$\frac{1}{4}$'' H.

(Right) **1077. WIDEMOUTH-ED REDWARE JUG, c.1770–1830:** A jug form popular in Europe and America during these years; its clear lead glaze (which enhances the clay's red tone) covers the inside and outer surface to within 1″ of the bottom; note the active slip decoration of lines, dots, and leaf shapes, plus the usual applied handle; 7⁵/₈″ H.

(Upper left) **1078. BLACK-GLAZED PITCHER, c.1700–1800:** The soft black glaze was common on country earthenware, but few examples survive; this was found near Albany, N.Y., yet it was also known in New England and Long Island; 7¹/₂″ H (Private Coll.).

(Near right) **1079. SGRAFFITO CUP, c.1670–1690:** An excavated English (North Devon) sgraffito cup has its design scratched through a white slip coating (yellowed in the kiln) (Colonial National Historical Park, Yorktown-Jamestown, Va.). (Far right) **1080. SLIP-WARE CUP, c.1720–1780:** This slip-decorated redware cup displays a dot & vine design; note its evolution from the 17th-century cup at the left; 3³/₄″ H.

(Left) **1081. REDWARE "CIDER" MUG, c.1750–1800:** An American redware mug (lip is chipped) from a Lancaster, Penn., tavern; the bulbous profile is similar to jugs of this period; 6″ H. (Right) **1082. REDWARE CUP, c.1750–1810 Form:** Note the expanded rim and concave outline of this variation; 3⁷/₈″ H.

(Far left) **1083. REDWARE MUG, c.1770–1780:** An American mug with an applied handle; note the incised line decorations scribed by the potter as it turned on his wheel; 5″ H (Private Coll.).

(Near left) **1084. REDWARE MUG, c.1780–1800:** Later characteristics appear here in this expanded rim and base, plus the heavier lead glaze; 6″ H (Private Coll.).

(Right) **1085. PERSONAL DRINKING FLASKS, c.1790–1830:** A redware (spirits) flask form especially popular in Penn.; note that the lead glaze covers the red clay (and enhances the color) down to just above the base; both are 6³/₈″ H.

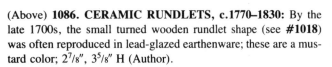

(Above) **1086. CERAMIC RUNDLETS, c.1770–1830:** By the late 1700s, the small turned wooden rundlet shape (see **#1018**) was often reproduced in lead-glazed earthenware; these are a mustard color; 2⁷/₈″, 3⁵/₈″ H (Author).

(Right) **1087. REDWARE TEA CADDY (CANNISTER),** Marked **"1767":** An interesting redware form with sgraffito and slip decoration; the front inscription includes, "Esther Smith . . . Her Tea Cannister . . . 1767''; from Penn.; 3³/₈″ H (Yale Univ. Art Gallery).

(Left) **1088. PUDDING MOLDS:** These center-post earthenware molds were used into the 19th century. (*Left to right*) (*1*) c.1725–1800, a sloping design (for molded gels) with a green-glazed interior and a side hanging ring; 9³/₈″ Dia; (*2*) c.1790–1840, a later rimless type having the straight fluting suited for cakes or puddings (i.e., easily removed); black and red glazes; 6³/₈″ Dia; (*3*) c.1750–1800, a higher baking mold that includes inside glazing; 8³/₄″ Dia (Au.).

(Above) **1089. SLIPWARE MIXING BOWL, c.1680 Form:** A later copy of a large c.1680 English slipware bowl covered by a clear lead glaze over red clay, decorated in white slip; it is not glazed on the outside; 4″ H, 13⁷/₈″ Dia.

(Above) **1090. PUDDING MOLD, c.1750–1800:** An earthenware example without fluting; it was not originally molded, but turned on a potter's wheel (finger marks are still visible); glazing appears only inside the bowl; found in Mass.; 3⁷/₈″ H, 10″ Dia.

MIXING BOWLS, c.1700–1800: (Far right) **1091.** An interior slip design; a clear lead glaze covers the inside and rim; 3³/₄″ H, 8¹/₄″ Dia. (Near right) **1092.** Note the red-slip interior decoration; the common iron staples to contain a crack do not penetrate to the inside; 5¹/₄″ H, 10⁵/₈″ Dia.

(Above)**1093. SLIPWARE MIXING BOWL, c.1740–1800:** A slip-decorated redware bowl attributed to the Moravian community in Penn.; it is glazed only on the inside; 2¹/₂″ H, 9¹/₂″ Dia.

(Above) **1095. REDWARE MIXING BOWL, c.1700–1800:** A sharply tapering form (slightly concave); the deeper bowls tend to date earlier; 6¹/₂″ H, 11″ Dia.

(Below) **1094. SLIPWARE MIXING BOWL, c.1750–1800:** A wavy and spiraled slip decoration on a dark red base; 3″ H, 12″ Dia (Private Coll.).

(Below) **1096. REDWARE MIXING BOWL, c.1770–1790:** A later 18th-century example (i.e., the sides are more bulbous); it is glazed inside and out, with an exterior decoration applied by a sponge; 4″ H, 11″ Dia (Private Coll.).

(Below) **1097. EATING/MIXING BOWLS, c.1700–1800:** Typical eating bowl forms; (*left to right*) (*1*) a high tapering outline; an orange glaze covers the inside and lip; 4″ H, 7¹/₂″ Dia; (*2*) a wavy interior design in green slip; note the excess yellow lead glaze that ran down the outside from its rim; 2³/₄″ H, 6³/₄″ Dia;

(*3*) this interior is covered by yellow slip, a red dot design, and a final layer of clear lead glaze; 2⁵/₈″ H, 7″ Dia; (*4*) a sharply tapered bowl; the exterior is blackened from cooking in the hearth; 2³/₄″ H, 9″ Dia.

(Above) **1098. UNGLAZED BOWL (or PAN), c.1625–1750**
Form: A coarse unglazed red earthenware bowl or "pan" (a broad shallow vessel) with a gentle spout, commonly used to pour off cream from the milk in cheesemaking; 4¹/₂″ H, 15¹/₂″ Dia. (Below) **1099. GLAZED BOWL, c.1700–1800:** A brown bowl with ear-like applied handles; 4″ H, 10³/₄″ Dia.

(Above) **1100. REDWARE PAN, c.1700–1800:** This double-handled pan has a pouring spout and is a type associated with dairying (*left*); 3¹/₂″ H, 13″ Dia. (Below) **1101. REDWARE PAN, c.1750–1820:** A shallow form that was favored for baking (pies, puddings), or serving (too small as a milk pan); 2″ H, 12″ Dia (Private Coll.).

(Left) **1102. UNGLAZED BAKING PAN, c.1750–1800:** A baking pan blackened from being buried in the coals; it was left unglazed to better absorb heat; the two raised nibs on its rim probably steadied a cover; 2³/₄″ H, 8¹/₂″ Dia. (Below) **1103. RED-WARE PLATES, c.1780–1820:** (*Rear*) These popular concave plates were pressed in a mold, with typical notched rims; (*right*) note the wavy slip decoration (normal wear in center); (*front*) a small (4″ Dia) pan decorated in black splotches.

(Upper left & right) **1104. SGRAFFITO PLATES, c.1670–1690:** Excavated sgraffito-decorated plates, i.e., the design was scratched through white slip to reveal the contrasting red clay; this was a common early style supplied by England (North Devon; see **#1105**); notice the popular tulip form and period line/dot designs (Colonial National Historical Park, Yorktown-Jamestown, Va.).

(Right) **1105. POTTERY FORMS, c.1650–1700:** Early heavily proportioned "gravel-tempered" (for hardness and durability) earthenware, also from North Devon (see **#1104**); (*left*) a rectangular baking pan; (*center*) a small 3-legged cooking pot ("pipkin"; see **#794**); (*right*) a 2-handled pot with cover (Colonial National Historical Park, Yorktown-Jamestown, Va.).

(Below) **1106. SLIPWARE PLATE, c.1700:** An English earthenware plate with period slip decorations; its press-molded form includes a notched rim; 12³/₄″ Dia (Smithsonian Institution).

(Right) **1107. SGRAFFITO PLATE,** Marked **"1793"**: A sgraffito-decorated plate (press-molded) from Penn.; the initials "HR" are probably for Henry Roudebuth (Montgomery County); note the opportunity in earthen vessels for personalized country artistry (Metropolitan Museum of Art).

ORNAMENTAL SLIPWARE: These slip-decorated pieces were a step between the coarse earthenware and refined tableware. (Far left) **1108. "MARBLEIZED" PLATE, c.1700–1750** Form: A reproduced pressed plate that was covered with a dark slip and then a swirled white slip to create this marbleized pattern; (Near left) **1109. c.1750–1760** Form: A reproduced plate coated in a dark brown slip, plus decorative lines of white slip.

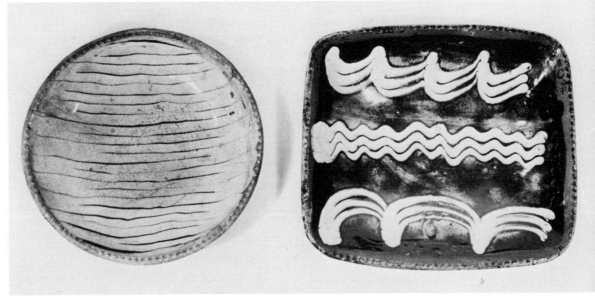

(Far right) **1110. SLIPWARE PLATTER, c.1720–1780:** This redware's heavy white slip decoration was probably applied by the potter's fingers; 11½″ x 13″ (Private Coll.). (Near right) **1111. COMBED SLIPWARE PLATE, c.1690–1740:** A combed design made by coating the body with colored slip, and (while still soft) drawing a toothed, "combed" instrument through it—before applying the lead glaze; 11¼″ Dia (Private Coll.).

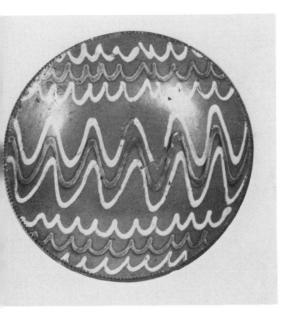

(Left) **1112. REDWARE PLATE, c.1750–1800:** A wavelike white and green slip decoration; 11½″ Dia (Private Coll.). (Lower right) **1113. "YELLOWWARE," c.1700–1770:** An English pattern using yellow slip coating plus brown spots; note the marbleized combing on the center piece (Roger Bacon; Robert W. Skinner, Inc.).

254

(Left) **1114. POSSET CUP,** Marked **"1702":** This early English technique by such potters as Thomas Toft and Ralph Simpson added a raised-dot slip decoration; the 2-handled cup form was used to drink "posset" (like porridge, mixed with wine and beer, see **#1138**), or "caudle" (a sweetened and seasoned wine or ale beverage) (Museum of Fine Arts, Boston).

DELFTWARE: Colorful delft pieces were established here in the 1600s, but lost much favor by the late 1700s (their surface frequently flaked and cracked). Although early production came from Holland, English delft was being imported by the mid-1600s. (Right) **1115. ENGLISH DELFT PLATE,** Marked **"1661":** An early octagonal delft form; similar freehand inscriptions were common; 8 1/8" W (Museum of Fine Arts, Boston).

(Lower left) **1116. ENGLISH DELFT CHARGER, c.1690–1710:** A wall and tower are painted in blue (popular cobalt-blue pigment) on the white delft surface; 13 1/2" Dia (Private Coll.).

(Lower right) **1117. ENGLISH DELFT CHARGER, c.1730:** A Bristol charger using an active design in orange plus dark and light blues (Private Coll.).

(Above) **1118. LIVERPOOL POLYCHROME DELFT, c.1700–1750:** The front and back of a pair of polychrome (i.e., multi-colored) plates; the face's floral motif is in purple, black, green, blue, and yellow; the reverse bears oriental-style markings; 10¼″ Dia (Author).

(Left) **1119. ENGLISH DELFT SOUP BOWL, c.1760–1780:** A freehand design in dark and light underglaze blue; 1½″ H, 8¾″ Dia.

(Lower left) **1120. ENGLISH DELFT PLATE, c.1760–1780:** A blue-decorated plate with flowers and double borders, plus the usual tin glaze; 9½″ Dia.

(Lower right) **1121. BRISTOL DELFT BOWL, c.1760–1780:** Another English cobalt blue–decorated piece; note its active floral design and lunettelike border; 2⅛″ H, 9″ Dia (Author).

(Far left) **1122. BRISTOL DELFT PLATE, c.1755–1770:** The Chinese porcelain's oriental influence on English patterns is apparent here; blue on white; 9″ Dia. (Near left) **1123. ENGLISH DELFT PLATE, c.1750–1770:** One of a pair of plates bearing this tree-inspired decoration in cobalt blue—plus a brown rim line; 8½″ Dia.

(Upper left) **1124. LAMBETH DELFT PUNCH BOWL, c.1700–1710:** An English polychrome bowl in blue, green, red, yellow, purple, and black; 4″ H, 8½″ Dia (Private Coll.). (Upper right) **1125. ENGLISH DELFT PUNCH BOWL, c.1760:** This more refined design illustrates progress in Britain's delftware (vs. #1124); the surface, too, is whiter and smoother; 5¾″ H, 11½″ Dia (Private Coll.). (Lower left) **1126. DUTCH DELFT CHARGER, c.1740–1750:** The Dutch often used religious themes, per this ''Sampson and the gates'' illustration; it has purple (from manganese) and yellow (antimony) coloring; 13½″ Dia (Private Coll.).

(Next page, Upper left) **1127. DUTCH DELFT CHARGER, c.1700–1760:** An intricate design as favored in Holland; note the early diagonal/dot blue border; 13¾″ Dia. (Upper right) **1128. DUTCH DELFT CHARGER, c.1750:** Polychrome, in brown, yellow, purple, green, and blue; 13½″ Dia. (Center row left) **1129. FRENCH FAIENCE PLATE, c.1750–1760:** A typical thick French delftlike faience plate using underglaze yellow, blue, green, orange, and magenta; 9⅝″ Dia. (Center row right) **1130. FRENCH FAIENCE PLATE, c.1760:** Polychrome floral decoration; 9⅞″ Dia. (Lower left) **1131. FRENCH FAIENCE BOWL, c.1750—1780:** A design from eastern France in blue, black, yellow, and red; 1⅜″ H, 9″ Dia. (Lower right) **1132. FRENCH FAIENCE PLATE, c.1760:** Busy blue, green, orange pattern; 12″ Dia (Au.).

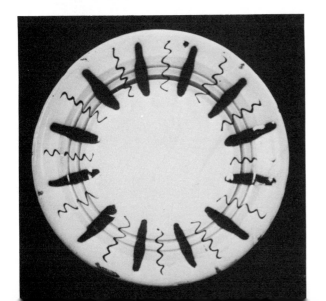

(Left) **1133. FRENCH FAIENCE PLATE, c.1760–1780:** A brown and white Rouen-area faience; its flower basket design is in blue; the plate's back is solid brown; 12 3/8" Dia. (Right) **1134. DUTCH DELFT STORAGE JAR, c.1740:** A vaselike jar in shades of blue; 7 1/2" H (Private Coll.). (Below left) **1135. DELFT SALTERS, c.1690–1760:** Polychrome ''salts'' for the dining table (see page 235); both are 5 3/4" W.

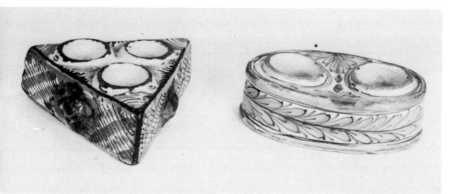

(Right) **1136. FRENCH FAIENCE PITCHER** (two views), **c.1750–1760:** A striking pattern using black and green vertical designs on a red backround; yellow interior; (see below) these bottom marks are from the potter's twisted wire used to free the vessel from his wheel (often smoothed off); from eastern France in a period of heavier tin glazing; 8 3/4" H, 7" Dia (Author).

(Left) **1137. FRENCH FAIENCE PITCHER, c.1750:** A simple design in red, green, black, and yellow, covered by a tin glaze; pewter lid (Private Coll.).

259

1138. LONDON DELFT POSSET POT, c.1660–1680: Notice these raised designs of the early period; the vessel has two side handles to grasp, and a strainer/spout through which to drink or pour hot spiced spirits (see **#1114**); 6¹⁄₈″ H (Lillian Blankley Cogan).

(Above) **1139. BRISTOL DELFT FLOWER HOLDER (BRICK), c.1760:** An English rectangular flower "brick" with the usual center opening—flanked by holes for the stems; it is decorated in an underglaze cobalt-blue oriental design; 3¹⁄₈″ H (Museum of Fine Arts, Boston).

(Above) **1140. FRENCH FAIENCE STORAGE JAR, c.1740–1750:** A form popular for storage in homes and commercial locations (it was often called an "apothecary" jar); the decoration is done in light and dark blues ("rapé" meant "snuff"); the jar is tin glazed inside and out; 8³⁄₈″ H.

(Above) **1141. DUTCH DELFT TILES, c.1680–1750:** These were widely used by Dutch settlers as wall or fireplace tiles; note the familiar central scenes, and "ox-head" corner designs in underglaze blue (more colors appeared in the later 1700s); 3″ and 5″ sq., ³⁄₈″ D (floor tiles were usually ³⁄₄″ thick).

(Upper left) **1142. SPANISH MAIOLICA (LISBONWARE) BOWLS, c.1660–1700:** The Spanish and Portuguese form of delft was "maiolica"; these everyday household tin-glazed bowls include crude green oriental-style figures; 11½″, 9″ Dia.

(Left) **1143. EUROPEAN DELFT BOWLS, c.1660–1700:** A lesser quality delftlike earthenware (poorer homes and trade goods) bearing blue rims and Chinese-like markings; note spots in the bottoms ("stilt marks") from the frames used to stack vessels in the kiln for firing (mostly eliminated by the 1700s); 7¾″–13¾″ Dia.

(Right) **1144. SPANISH MAIOLICA BOWL, c.1660–1700:** This bowl bears vague green-painted designs like **#1142**; note the excess tin glaze that ran down the bare outside face; 9⅝″ Dia.

(Below) **1145. SPANISH MAIOLICA SERVING BOWLS, c.1680–1780:** Tin-glazed-blue decorated bowls of a quality for lesser homes; this thick-sectioned form is glazed inside and out; 11″, 12½″ Dia.

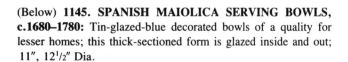

(Left) **1146. SPANISH MAIOLICA CHARGER, c.1760:** A large serving charger painted in rural freehand with a cobalt-blue decoration; 16″ Dia.

(Below) **1147. DELFT EWER & RENISH STONEWARE MUG:** A comparison of smooth vulnerable delft, and the hard, coarse stoneware. (*Left*) c.1650–1680, a blue-decorated delft "ewer" (i.e., a long-necked pitcher); its pewter lid and base were added c.1700–1780; the body is 8″ H; (*right*) c.1700–1780, a light-colored stoneware mug with applied handle, covered by the usual salt glaze; the body is 5³/4″ H (Author).

STONEWARE: A harder and less porous ceramic than earthenware, stoneware accompanied the earliest settlers as jugs and mugs (a gray form mostly from Germany and Flanders); the English soon imitated it, although New England potters found no suitable clay nearer than Long Island. An apparent association of illness with redware (actually its lead glaze reacting to acid foods) led many colonists to favor the harder stoneware.

(Lower right) **1148. GERMAN "BEARDED MAN" STONEWARE JUGS (BELLARMINES, GRAYBEARDS), c.1600–1650:** Such Germanic "bottles," with their impressed grotesque human faces and armorial medallions, developed c.1550 and lost appeal here by 1740; these are the early rotund forms; note the close-up of a Germanic type face (*lower left*); 15″, 16¹/2″ H (Private Coll.).

ENGLISH STONEWARE JUGS: (Left) **1149. c.1684:** A "graybeard" or "bearded-man" jug (English terms) attributed to Dwight of Fulham, 1684; note the early squat, rotund form; 6½" H. (Right) **1150. c.1670–1690:** This is the evolving pear shape; observe the man's flatter face in most English jugs vs. **#1148**; the iron-oxide slip became this brown mottle when fired in a salt-glaze kiln; 7½" H (Private Coll.).

(Above right) **1151. ENGLISH STONEWARE JUG, c.1725:** Note the jug's less bulbous bellarmine form that had developed by this later date; 18" H.

(Above left) **1152. AMERICAN STONEWARE JUGS, c.1780–1830:** Typical locally made tan-colored stoneware vessels with salt glaze; they now display an inverted pear shape vs. the earlier forms **#1049–#1051**; 11¼", 16⅝" H. (Left) **1153. AMERICAN STONEWARE BOWL, c.1750–1800:** This thick brown bowl has a heavy rim and pouring lip (see **#1098**); 13½" Dia.

(Upper left) **1154. STONEWARE MUG, c.1750–1770:** A stoneware mug with an incised checkerboard design (cobalt-blue coloring), and an impressed medallion marked "GR" ("Georgius Rex," i.e., King George); probably German-made for England; 6″ H (Private Coll.). (Upper right) **1155. STONEWARE JUGS, c.1730–1780:** Blue-colored incised designs; these are vessels also used as measures (per the numbers on their sides); 9¼″–11½″ H (Private Coll.). (Right) **1156. RHENISH STONEWARE JUG, c.1740–1760:** A gray salt-glazed Germanic style made for the English market; note its lavish scribed decorations and "GR" medallion—colored with cobalt blue; the neck continues an earlier high-ringed neck form; 12″ H (Author).

WHITE SALT-GLAZED STONEWARE: By 1720, England developed this white tableware (stoneware coated in white salt-glazed slip) that would not flake or chip like the softer delft; it added molded-rim patterns by mid-century, and was popular here from c.1730–1770 (when supplanted by creamware).

(Lower left) **1157. WHITE SALT-GLAZED PLATE, c.1750–1760:** English molded stoneware in the "Queen's shape" (border) and the raised dot "barley" pattern (brim). (Lower right) **1158.** A close-up of three variations of the popular barley design; 9¼″–9½″ Dia.

(Above) **1159. "SCRATCH BLUE" SALT-GLAZED STONE-WARE, c.1750–1770:** An English variation of the white salt-glazed ware was this scratched design filled with cobalt blue; it was used in many country homes; 3″–4½″ Dia (Private Coll.).

CREAMWARE: A lead-glazed creamy-colored earthenware that established lightweight dinnerware as we know it today. Perfected by Wedgwood, it was moderately priced, and became common here c.1760–1800.

(Above) **1160. ENGLISH CREAMWARE PLATES, c.1760–1790:** Light durable creamware soup and dinner plates in the "Royal" pattern outline; 9½″, 9⅝″ Dia. (Left) **1161. ENGLISH CREAMWARE PLATE, c.1760–1780:** A relief-molded octagonal form; 7½″ Dia. (Right) **1162. ENGLISH SAUCEBOAT, c.1750–1760:** A molded white salt-glazed sauce-boat; 7½″ L.

(Below) **1163. ENGLISH CREAMWARE SAUCEBOATS, c.1760:** These low, squat pitchers served gravy and sauces at the table; (*right*) note the brown mottled decoration; 6¾″, 7″ L.

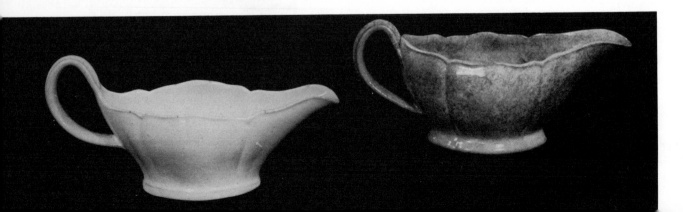

(Above) **1164. ENGLISH MOLDED CREAMWARE, c.1760–1790:** Such pierced-rim plate patterns were produced from block molds, a form more typical of the better country homes; 9¹/₄″, 9³/₄″ Dia (Author).

(Left) **1165. ENGLISH CREAMWARE, c.1765–1775:** The rounded teapot that was stylish in this period, plus a teacup and saucer (few handles were applied at this time); the teapot is 5³/₈″ H.

(Below) **1166. ENGLISH CREAMWARE, c.1760–1790:** Fashionable creamware forms—a mug, teapot, and pitcher—all mounting the period's entwined strap handles with foliated terminals (Au.).

266

(Right) **1167. ENGLISH ENAMELED CREAMWARE, c.1760–1770:** A further variation of creamware was to decorate it with enamel colors as seen in this selection of pieces bearing the hand-painted "King's rose" pattern (a coffeepot, teapot, bowl, teacup, and saucer); the tall pot is 8½" H (Private Coll.).

(Above) **1168. TRANSFER-PRINTED CREAMWARE, c.1760–1780:** Preprinted transfer designs were often applied to creamware; (left) a molded "feather-edged" plate decorated with black and yellow floral transfers; (right) the rim is molded in a "shell edge with combing"; the shell and sea forms were added as transfers; "Wedgwood" is marked on the bottom (notice his spelling omits the "e"); both are 7⅝" Dia.

(Left) **1169. ENGLISH CREAMWARE PLATE, c.1780–1790:** A more formal creamware dinner plate decorated in the Wedgwood style; the design is in brown, magenta, and green; 10⅛" Dia.

(Left) **1170. CREAMWARE TRANSFER PITCHERS (LIVERPOOL WARE), c.1785–1810:** These transfer designs were engraved on copper plates, printed on thin paper, and transferred to the body before applying the lead glaze; great numbers were exported to America; 8⁷/₈″, 5³/₈″ H (Author).

PEARLWARE: Developed in England during the 1770s as a transition from creamware, pearlware was whiter, brighter, and held the decoration better. Common here by the 1790s, it went on to dominate the early 1800s.

(Right) **1171. ENGLISH TEAPOTS, c.1785–1800:** This is a comparison of transfer designs on creamware (*left*), and the brighter pearlware (*right*). (Lower left) **1172. ENGLISH CREAMWARE CHARGER, c.1765–1780:** This charger has a molded "feather edge," plus obvious wear in its softer creamware surface; 14⁷/₈″ Dia. (Lower right) **1173. ENGLISH PEARLWARE PLATTER, c.1790–1830:** The more durable pearlware in platter form (i.e., oval) includes the new "shell edge"—colored in blue (green and red were also favored); 15³/₈″ x 12³/₈″.

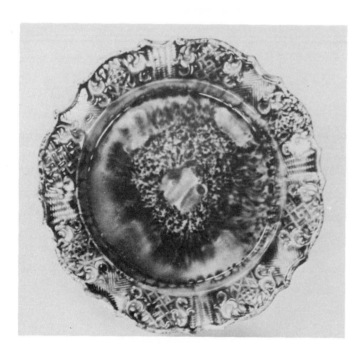

CHINOISERIE: The pseudo-oriental decoration that was used to imitate China's export porcelain. (Upper left) **1174. c.1780:** An English plate decorated with blue chinoiserie transfers; 8¼″ Dia. (Upper right) **1175. c.1780–1800:** This English pearlware example has a blue transfer, plus brushed blue color over a combed-shell edge; 9⅝″ Dia (Author).

(Left) **1176. ENGLISH "WHIELDON" PLATE, c.1755–1775:** Whieldon's distinctive mottled coloring came from clouded lead glazes usually in brown, yellow, and green on a cream-colored body; note its molded rim of the period, in this case the "dot-diaper-and-basket" pattern (see **#1158**); 9¼″ Dia. (Lower left) **1177. ENGLISH JACKFIELD WARE, c.1760–1770:** A lustrous black lead-glazed earthenware attributed to Jackfield in Shropshire (pitcher, coffeepot, salt, tea caddy) (Private Coll.).

(Below) **1178. CHINESE EXPORT BOWL, c.1760–1780:** A hand-decorated bowl; this porcelain surface has the frequent cold white-grayish tone of export porcelain; 10″ Dia.

(Right) **1179. "TOBY" JUGS:** Their production began c.1750 and has never ceased; these two earthenware figures have early translucent coloring (heavier, more opaque enamels appeared after 1790); (*left*) c.1770–1790; (*right*) c.1790–1810; note that the hat and base have sponge-applied decorations; 11″, 9³/₄″ H.

CHINESE EXPORT PORCELAIN: This porcelain is found on many early American sites (reshipped from England). The Europeans tried to imitate oriental "hard paste," and created an imitation "soft paste," before commercially developing a "true" porcelain by the 1750s. Although Europe often used transfer prints, Chinese porcelain was always hand painted.

(Above) **1180. CHINESE EXPORT PORCELAIN: SAUCERS, c.1760–1780:** Examples typically hand painted in underglaze blue (two sides); both are 6¹/₂″ Dia. (Lower right) **1181. BOWLS:** Early marginal quality export porcelain bowls; (*left*) c.1680–1700; (*right*) c.1720–1750: both 4⁵/₈″ Dia. (Lower left) **1181A. BOWL, c.1780–1820:** The popular "Canton" pattern of Chinese export porcelain; it is typically colored in underglaze blue; such patterns were usually identified by the border design; 5⁷/₈″ Dia.

(Left) **1182. CHINESE EXPORT POLYCHROME PORCELAIN, c.1770:** A chinese plate that was typically hand painted in multicolors and then glazed (one of a pair); 9″ Dia.

(Right) **1183. CHINESE EXPORT POLYCHROME PORCELAIN, c. 1760:** An underglaze design like #1182, but embellished by colors also applied over the glaze (adding deeper dimension); 8⅞″ Dia.

(Left) **1184. CHINESE EXPORT PUNCH BOWL, c.1750–1770:** A punch bowl was used to prepare and serve mulled cider, flip, punch, and other mixed spirits; note the high-quality polychrome hand decoration; a high-footed base ring is also included; 10″ Dia.

(Below) **1185. CHINESE EXPORT PUNCH BOWLS, c.1760–1780:** This comparison demonstrates the variances when matching hand-painted pairs; their colors include magenta, green, orange, blue, black, and red; 7½″ Dia (Author).

CHINESE EXPORT PORCELAIN, c.1760–1770: (Lower right) **1186.** A teapot in six colors; 4½″ H. (Lower left) **1187.** A polychrome bowl that includes figures and floral designs; 2¾″ H.

(Above) **1188. CHINESE EXPORT TEACUPS, c.1760–1780:** By 1740, tea drinking was deeply established in American homes—including the need for appropriate tableware; most early teacups lacked handles; (*above*) these were imported into Europe, where "baskets" were painted under the Chinese flower design (called "clobbering"), and then reshipped to America; red, green, black, and magenta were used; the saucer is $5^1/4''$ Dia.

(Below) **1189. ENGLISH TEAPOTS:** An interesting comparison between the c.1780 teapot (*left*) of hard paste, or "true" porcelain (i.e., like the Chinese), vs. (*right*) one in the less bright soft paste or "artificial" porcelain (c.1770–1790); $4^7/8''$, $5^1/8''$ H.

(Above) **1190. CHINESE EXPORT "CHOCOLATE" PATTERN, c.1740–1760:** A Chinese porcelain style known as the "chocolate" pattern (the outer surface is dark brown); this teapot measures $4^3/4''$ H (Author).

272

(Above) **1191. ENGLISH SUGAR BOWLS, c.1760–1790:** Another comparison (see **#1189**) between a hard-paste porcelain sugar bowl having a cleaner, brighter surface (*left*), and a duller soft-paste example (*right*); 5″, 3½″ H.

(Above) **1195. ENGLISH PUNCH BOWL, c.1780:** Such soft-paste porcelain included ground glass added to the clay, and a shiny lead glaze; this punch bowl has a simple design resembling modern tableware, and a high base; 8½″ Dia (Private Coll.).

(Below, left to right) (*1*) **1192. ENGLISH MUG, c.1780–1810:** This hand-painted soft-paste mug illustrates the period's strong oriental influence; 5¾″ H. (*2*) **1193. ENGLISH CREAM PITCHER, c.1760–1780:** Another soft-paste example; 4⅞″ H. (*3*) **1194. ENGLISH MOCHA-WARE CUP, c.1790–1810:** "Mocha ware" began near the end of our period and spawned during the 1800s; this early soft-paste cup has a typical strap handle, plus the distinctive "seaweed" pattern—achieved by dropping dots of a special color onto a still-moist background and letting them disperse; black on orange; 3½″ H.

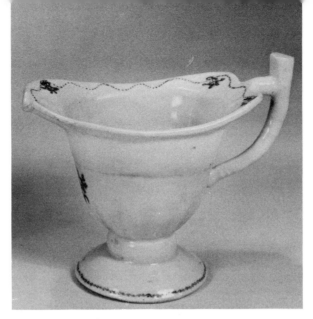

ENGLISH PORCELAIN: (Upper row, left to right) (*1*) **1196. CREAM PITCHER, c.1750–1780:** This hard-paste porcelain pitcher mounts a distinctive handle and floral medallion; 4³/₄″ H (Private Coll.). (*2*) **1197. CREAM PITCHER, c.1770–1800:** A distinctive "helmet" creamer in hard paste; 4⁵/₈″ H. (*3*) **1198. TEA CADDY, c.1785–1820:** A hard-paste porcelain English tea holder (or "caddy"); 5⁵/₈″ H.

(Center row) **1199. WEDGWOOD SETTING, c.1760–1780:** English sets of light tableware gained favor at this time; here are a covered tureen, vegetable dish, platter, and plate from a Wedgwood setting of soft-paste porcelain (plain design with combed-shell edges) (Author).

(Right) **1200. ENGLISH SETTING, c.1780–1790:** These later soft-paste examples bear a classical scene transfer design in their center; upper plate is 9³/₄″ Dia.

(Left) **1201. ENGLISH TEA-POT, c.1760** A hard-paste porcelain teapot decorated in blue; 5″ H (Private Coll.).

(Right) **1202. ENGLISH SUGAR BOWL, c.1790–1815:** Such "silhouette" porcelain relief designs began in the late 18th century; this is brown on white; 3⅝″ H to rim.

(Above) **1203. "ARMORIAL" PORCELAIN, c.1780–1820:** As affluence grew, some families ordered monogramed or initialed tableware from Europe or China. (*Left*) This plate has a griffin figure; 10″ Dia; (*right*) a Chinese polychrome plate with a locally painted armorial symbol added to its rim; 10″ Dia.

(Lower left) **1204. ENGLISH PUNCH BOWL, c.1760–1780:** This hard-paste porcelain bowl has added a brass ring to protect the rim; 3⅞″ H, 9⅛″ Dia. (Lower right) **1205. ARMORIAL PORCELAIN, c.1780–1790:** Examples from a British-made setting bearing an initialed monogram in blue and gold.

(Above) **1206. TEACUPS, SAUCERS, c.1760–1780:** These are typical of the hard-paste porcelain polychrome cups and saucers shipped to America in large numbers; (*left*) Chinese export; (*two right*) English; the cups are 2″ H.

(Below) **1207. ENGLISH TEA SERVICE, c.1770–1800:** Black-decorated elements that include a teapot and its diamond-shaped tray, a waste bowl (for emptying residue before refills), and cups (saucers are missing).

(Bottom) **1208. ENGLISH TEA SERVICE, c.1770–1800:** A handsome porcelain set with a helmet cream pitcher, sugar bowl, cups, and saucers; the design is in red, orange, and gold (Au.).

Pewter Tableware

In keeping with the prevailing 18th-century mercantile system (whereby colonies existed as a source of raw materials for the Mother Country, and then as a market for the finished goods), manufacturing in America was actively discouraged. England was acknowledged to be the source of the finest pewter, and completely dominated our market (e.g., one early source estimates finding 125 English plates here for every American one). Even when pewterers began to establish themselves in the colonies during the 1700s, most had been trained in Britain and brought molds with them to duplicate the Old World forms.

The quality of the metal varied from that of the finer vessels (as much as 96 percent tin and only 4 percent lead) to *trifle,* the common pewter which was softer and darker (up to 82 percent lead and 18 percent antimony). Although the housewife took pride in keeping her pewter shined, its vulnerability to damage and wear led to the practice of returning old pieces for remelting into new. The frugal pewterer also found multiple uses for his molds, so that the same form would reappear as different components of his product line.

1209. EARLY PLATE BRIMS, c.1676–1725: English pewter plates of the late 1600s usually had a "multiple-reeded" brim (the upper three here are "triple reeded"); (*from top*) (*1*) John Russel, London, c.1676; (*2*) George Scott, London, 1680/81; (*3*) John Shorley, London, c.1708–1725; (*4*) an alternate wide smooth-brim style (narrow reed on back); pewter plates were not in general use here until c.1700; 8^1/$_2$″–9^3/$_4$″ Dia (Author).

1210. 18th-CENTURY BRIMS: In the early 1700s, the multiple brim changed to a single reed that lasted into the 1800s (*top two*); (*from top*) (*1*) Samuel Ellis, London, 1721–1764; (*2*) Stephen Barnes, Middletown/Wallingford, Conn., c.1791–1800; (*3*) a smooth face with a single reeding underneath that coexisted with the upper face reed design c.1740–1790; "LONDON" marking; (*4*) a small unmarked plate; 3^1/$_2$″–8^3/$_4$″ Dia.

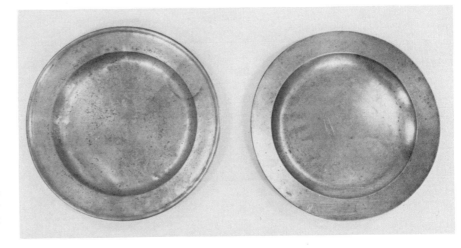

(Left) **1211. BROAD-BRIM FORM, c.1640–1690:** Prior to the multiple-reeded pattern (see **#1209**), this broad smooth brim was the common form; note the practice of striking the maker's touchmarks and owner's initials on the upper face; pewter vessels were either cast, or beaten into a mold; this charger and platter still bear their original hammer marks; 16³/₄", 12" Dia (Author).

(Right) **1212. ENGLISH CHARGERS, c.1720–1800:** These "chargers" (large serving plates) repeat the two basic patterns of contemporary smaller plates–the single reeded, and the smooth brims (see **#1210**); both are 13¹/₂" Dia.

(Lower left) **1213. ENGLISH CHARGER, c.1770–1780:** A wavy-edged variation that follows that period's ceramic "Queen's" pattern; by Bush & Perkins, Bristol; 14⁵/₈" Dia.

(Above) **1214. SERVING BOWL, c.1750–1790:** A single-reeded-brim form with its early hammer marks still visible; 11⁷/₈" Dia.

(Below) **1215. SOUP BOWLS, c.1750–1800:** (*Right*) This tinned-copper bowl was copied from the common pewter form at its left; 9", 8⁵/₈" Dia.

(Left) **1216. PEWTER BASINS** (two views): These English pewter basins illustrate their 18th-century evolution. (*Left*) c. 1750–1790, note the earlier extended brim and rounded sides that slope gradually into a flat bottom (see the lower illustration); (*right*) c.1780–1820, the lip remains, but the sides are now straighter and create an abrupt angle with the base (a form carried into the 1800s); 9″, 8″ Dia.

(Above) **1217. HOT-WATER PLATES, c.1760–1800:** Such hollow plates held about a quart of hot water to keep food warm (a top and bottom are shown); note their typical handles, and the brim's hinged opening for the water; English; both are $1^5/8″$ H, $9^1/8″$ Dia.

(Left) **1218. ENGLISH DOMED TANKARD, c.1695–1715:** The pewter tankard was a cylindrical drinking vessel usually dated by the design of its hinged cover, handle, and thumbpiece; the flat-topped form (see **#1221**) predominated from c.1675–1720, but by 1690 the domed cover was also established; notice this early domed style and its wide lobe-shaped thumbpiece; 7″ H. (Au.)

ENGLISH DOMED TANKARDS: (Left) **1219. c.1735–1755:** This English tankard is now more squat (vs. **#1218**), and has a lower domed lid, plainer thumbpiece, raised midrib ring around the body, and a "hooded-ball" terminal on the handle; 6½" H. (Right) **1220. c.1775:** By this date, notice the new "tulip" (pear shape) profile (introduced in England c.1720), open thumbpiece, footed base, and "bud" handle terminal; by Bush & Perkins; tankards were cast in several pieces and soldered together; 7⅝" H.

(Above left) **1221. TANKARD:** A flat-lidded quart with a typical projecting lip; by Frederick Bassett, N.Y.C., 1761–1800; 7" H. (Above center) **1222. MUG:** The mug was a coverless tankard (also a "pot" or "can"); note this mid-ringed tulip body and bud terminal; Robert Bonnynge, Boston, 1731–1736; 5" H. (Above right) **1223. MUG:** A slope-sided pint form; by William Will, Philadelphia, 1780–1790; ball terminal; 4⅛" H. (Lower left) **1224. TEAPOT:** The pear-shaped Queen Anne style (wooden handle); Frederick Bassett, N.Y.C., 1761–1800; 7½" H. (Lower right) **1225. TEAPOT:** By Johann Phillip Alberti, Philadelphia, 1754–1780; 7½" H (this group, Dr. & Mrs. Melvyn D. Wolf).

(Left) **1226. EUROPEAN MUGS, c.1780–1820:** Pewter mugs were favored by rural Americans over the more expensive tankards, and they continued to use them into the 1800s; these late-century forms include the "double-C scroll" handle with a lower strut that appeared in England c.1750, and is found on some American-made mugs; 4³/₄"–6¹/₈" H.

AMERICAN PEWTER FORMS: (Above left) **1227. BABY'S NURSING BOTTLE, c.1750–1800:** 6¹/₄" H (Smithsonian Institution). (Above center) **1228. COVERED SUGAR BOWL:** Attributed to William Will, Philadelphia, 1764–1798; 5" H (Dr. & Mrs. Melvyn D. Wolf). (Above right) **1229. PEDESTAL "CUP SALT":** Also by William Will; 2¹/₂" H (Dr. & Mrs. Melvyn D. Wolf). (Lower right) **1230. CREAM PITCHER (CREAMER):** Note the unique circular base; it is attributed to Philadelphia; 4¹/₂" H (Dr. & Mrs. Melvyn D. Wolf).

(Above) **1231. PEWTER BEAKERS:** Such cylindrical drinking vessels usually had a flaring lip and molded base; (*left*) c.1750–1800, 3³/₄" H; (*right*) c.1790–1830; this later beaker has now lost its height, flared rim, and projecting base; 3¹/₈" H.

(Above) **1232. PEWTER TEAPOT:** A late-century oval teapot by William Will, Philadelphia, 1764–1798 (Metropolitan Museum of Art). (Upper right) **1233. PEWTER MEASURES:** Sets of graduated measures were used in the better homes; (*left*) c.1750–1810, the "French" (continental European) cylindrical style with a broad brim and base; 3³/₈″ H; (*right*) c.1750–1810, the English baluster shape; handles were optional in both forms; 3¹/₈″ H (Private Coll.).

(Near right) **1234. PEWTER FLAGON, c.1750:** Originally for sacramental use, the flagon was accepted for table service (usually wine), or as a measure by the 1700s; note this popular "twin-acorn" thumbpiece; a "French" form; 7″ H (Private Coll.). (Far right) **1235. PEWTER FLASK, c.1785–1810:** Made of two soldered halves, plus a threaded cap; 7″ H. Note: At the end of the 1700s, England developed a superfine pewter called "Britannia" (harder and lighter; usually spun instead of cast); most "pewter" of the 1800s is Britannia.

(Left) **1236. SHAKERS ("CASTERS," or "DREDGERS"):** "Shaking" vessels (for pepper, flour, spices) varied in shape, size, and name. (*Left to right*) (*1*) c.1750–1850, a tinned-iron dredger; (*2*) c.1760–1820, a baluster-style brass caster; (*3*) c.1770–1820, a silver-plated brass "shaker"; (*4*) c.1770–1790, a silver-plated pewter caster (see **#1237, #1238**); 2″–5¹/₄″ H.

(Left) **1237. SHAKERS, c.1760:** English baluster-shape footed shakers in creamware; they are of single-piece construction, and are filled through a corked hole in the base; 4³/₈″, 5″ H (Au.).

(Right) **1238. SHAKER, c.1760–1770:** A high-domed English soft-paste porcelain shaker; it bears the name "J E Choate" (an owner); the cylindrical body omits a base; 5¹/₄″ H (Private Coll.).

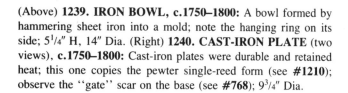

(Above) **1239. IRON BOWL, c.1750–1800:** A bowl formed by hammering sheet iron into a mold; note the hanging ring on its side; 5¹/₄″ H, 14″ Dia. (Right) **1240. CAST-IRON PLATE** (two views), **c.1750–1800:** Cast-iron plates were durable and retained heat; this one copies the pewter single-reed form (see **#1210**); observe the "gate" scar on the base (see **#768**); 9³/₄″ Dia.

(Lower left) **1241. PEWTER CANTEEN, c.1755–1790:** The pewterer apparently reused the base mold for a porringer to create these sides; 4³/₈″ Dia (Neumann Coll.; Valley Forge National Historical Park).

(Lower right) **1242. TINNED-IRON PANS, c.1750–1800:** Coating thin sheet iron with tin ("toleware") was common in the 1700s (by the "whitesmith"); it was mostly done in Europe (tin was scarce here); these are typical "milk" or utility pans; the sloping sides straightened in the 1800s; 15¹/₄″, 12¹/₂″ Dia.

(Upper left) **1243. TINNED-IRON CAN-TEEN, c.1755–1780:** A tall crescent shape that was employed for civilian and military use; note soldered seams, shoulder cord loops; 9¹/₂″ H (Au.). (Upper center) **1244. TINNED-IRON CUP, c.1760–1800:** This lip is typically rolled down over an iron wire; 5″ H. (Upper right) **1245. TINNED-COPPER MUG, c.1750–1800:** A simple form with a riveted strap handle; 4³/₄″ H.

(Right) **1246. CHOCOLATE POT, c.1750:** Warmed chocolate was a popular beverage; this tinned-iron pot has the usual cover hole for a stick to break up and agitate the chocolate chunks; body 6″ H (Private Coll.).

(Above) **1247. PAINTED CANNISTER, c.1760–1820:** A tinned-iron cannister covered by locally painted familiar scenes and initials; 7³/₈″ H.

(Far right) **1248. TINNED-IRON MUG, c.1700–1750:** A bulbous form popular among Dutch settlers; 6″ H (Private Coll.). (Near right) **1249. TINNED-IRON CUP, c.1760–1870:** This civilian cylindrical type is also found on military sites of both the Revolution and Civil War; 3¹/₈″ H.

(Left) **1250. TINNED-IRON MUGS/MEASURES, c.1760–1800:** Utility mugs with riveted strap handles and rolled rims; they would normally be kept by the hearth for drinking or measuring; 8⅝″, 5½″ H.

(Upper right) **1251. TINNED-IRON SUGAR BOWL, c.1780–1820:** A popular cylindrical bowl with soldered seams; note its applied 3-roll handle; painted brown; 3⅞″ H.

(Above) **1252. TINNED-IRON "COFFIN" TRAY, c.1750–1810:** A common 8-sided coffin-shaped tray; it was originally painted black; 12¾″ L. (Above right) **1253. TINNED-IRON CHIPPENDALE TRAY, c.1740–1780:** This "Chippendale" form usually had a scrolled rim and painted decorations on its shiny black ("japanned") finish; 17¼″ L.

(Lower left) **1254. BRASS TRAY, c.1750–1800:** A heavy round brass tray with incised rings and fleur-de-lis stamps; 10⅜″ Dia. (Lower right) **1255. BRASS "MONTEITH", c.1750–1780:** Developed c.1720, such notched monteith bowls were used to suspend wineglasses in water (as shown) to cool and rinse them between fills; 4¼″ H (Au.).

(Left) **1256. BRASS CUP, c.1750–1800:** A small gobletlike cup (not for drinking—per the serrated rim); probably for an egg, condiments, or seasonings; 3¹/₈″ H. (Right) **1257. COPPER COFFEEPOT, c.1750–1780:** Note the practical wooden side handle, flared base, and notched spout; 7¹/₂″ H (Conn. Historical Society).

(Right) **1258. COPPER "ALE SHOE," c.1750–1800:** This vessel was filled by ale or wine and placed at the hearth with its long "toe" in or near the embers to warm the spirits; it has a hinged top and flat handle; 14³/₈″ L.

(Lower left) **1259. SHEFFIELD PLATE TEAPOT, c.1790–1810:** England developed a substitute for solid silver c.1742 called "Sheffield plate"; a sheet of copper was sandwiched between two layers of silver, then rolled and beaten until they were bonded; it appeared in many of the better country homes; this Hepplewhite (Federal) period teapot (i.e., a bowed-panel body, reeded spout, and wooden handle) shows wear from continued polishing that has exposed areas of copper (common); 6″ H.

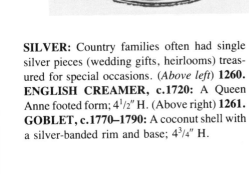

SILVER: Country families often had single silver pieces (wedding gifts, heirlooms) treasured for special occasions. (*Above left*) **1260. ENGLISH CREAMER, c.1720:** A Queen Anne footed form; 4¹/₂″ H. (Above right) **1261. GOBLET, c.1770–1790:** A coconut shell with a silver-banded rim and base; 4³/₄″ H.

(Above) **1262. SOAPSTONE TABLEWARE, c.1780–1820:** Rural homes sometimes carved soft soapstone into usable forms; (*left to right*) (*1*) A sunken plate, $9^3/8''$ L; (*2*) condiment dish with a salt hole, $6^7/8''$ L; (*3*) a covered salt, $3''$ L.

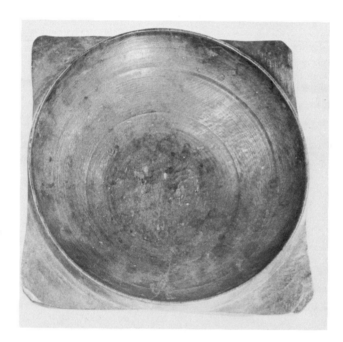

PORRINGERS: These shallow bowls with flat handles were used for eating (stew, porridge, pudding), drinking (beer, wine, cider), and measuring. Obsolete in England by 1750, they continued in America until c.1825. (Above) **1263. ENGLISH DELFT PORRINGER, c.1660–1700:** Its tin glaze was stained, and splashed with a white tin pigment (a French technique) (Metropolitan Museum of Art). (Above right) **1264. WOODEN PORRINGER, c.1700–1750:** A turned wooden version having four flat handles; $8^3/4''$ Dia. (Right) **1265. WOODEN PORRINGER, c.1700–1800:** This crude example was hand carved from a block of wood; $3^1/2''$ Dia.

CAST-IRON PORRINGERS, c.1690–1720: Early cast-iron forms. (Far left) **1266.** A flat base and heart-pierced handle (later copied in pewter, see **#1269**) with no lip on the rim; $3''$ Dia. (Near left) **1267.** This is cast in the usual single piece; it includes two tab handles; $3^1/2''$ Dia.

(Above) **1268. CAST-IRON PORRINGERS, c.1770–1825:** Cast-iron porringers usually copied the pewter form; note that the edges now have lips (vs. **#1266**), and the use of a ceramic liner (*right*); 6″, 4³/₈″, 4⁵/₈″ Dia.

(Above) **1269. PEWTER PORRINGERS (believed American):** (*Left to right*) (*1*) c.1690–1720, early high sides and two lobelike pierced handles; 5¹/₄″ Dia; (*2*) c.1750–1780, a double-handled open ''crown'' design; 4¹/₄″ Dia; (*3*) c.1780–1800, the popular ''heart'' handle; 3¹/₂″ Dia; (*4*) c.1760–1790, a scrolled ''flower''-style handle—favored by many of the prolific Providence, R.I.–area pewterers; it is marked ''LL''; also note the common domed bottom; 5¹/₂″ Dia (Author).

(Left) **1270. SILVER PORRINGER, c.1760–1780:** A more affluent flower pattern crafted in silver; it is unsigned; 5¹/₂″ Dia.

(Above) **1271. ENGLISH WINE BOTTLE, c.1630–1685:** This early "onion" or "shaft & globe" form was used for storing or serving spirits as a semidecanter. Note its "string rim" set below the lip to hold the packthread that secured its cork in place; olive green color; the shallow kick-up has a rough pontil scar; 8^3/$_4$" H (Au.).

Glass Bottles

Few bottles were made in America during the 1600s, and even 18th-century glass production here was a minor industry, as England and Holland supplied most needs. Although a few bottles bear dated glass seals, most are identified by shape, pontil treatment, and lip form.

In the mid-1700s, molds were already in use, but earlier bottles (and many up until 1800) were "free blown" as a pliable bubble at the end of a blowing rod. After being flattened on the marver (a flat surface) and a pontil (an iron rod attached to a flat base), the neck and rim were worked. Then the pontil was pushed up to create a semiconical indentation ("kick-up") in the base. Snapping off the pontil rod left a scarred apex which is characteristic of early glass (usually ground smooth by the later 1700s).

The earlier formulation was "soda glass" (sand, limestone, soda; tinted green from iron oxide in the sand). About 1676, clear, bright "lead glass" developed in England (sand, lead, and potash) for higher-quality ware.

(Left) **1272. SQUAT (ONION) BOTTLES, c.1680–1720:** By 1680, the neck had shortened, the kick-up was deeper, and the string rim closer to a defined lip. (*Two left*) These are English. The Dutch favored the taller neck with a sloped body that appeared about 1700; (*two right*) c.1700–1720; olive green; 6^1/$_2$"–7^1/$_2$" H.

(Right) **1273. BELL BOTTLES, c.1720–1750:** During the 1700s, bodies grew higher, reflecting a new popularity of wines needing to be laid on their sides for aging. The transition began with these "bell" forms which retained the high kick-up; olive green; 6"–7^3/$_4$" H (Author).

(Right) 1274. PORTER LIQUOR BOTTLES, c.1740–1770: This taller "porter" style evolved as binning wines increased. (*Three left*) The English form followed a straight-sided profile. (*Two right*) The Dutch favored a heart or flowerpot shape to the body. Most early spirits bottles have thick walls and dark glass to preserve the contents and protect color; olive green; 8³/₄"–11" H.

(Below) 1276. "FRENCH" WINE BOTTLES: (*Three left*) A form also made by the English and Dutch—with a sloping body, tapering neck, high kick, and scarred pontil; (*two left*) c.1740–1770; the other is c.1750–1770 because of its straighter base. (*Far right*) An English sack bottle, c.1730–1750, that shows a cylindrical base sloping up into a long neck; moderate kick-up; 10"–11³/₄" H.

(Above) 1275. CYLINDER BOTTLES, c.1760–1810: The evolution of today's liquor-bottle form is now apparent. (*Left*) Two transitional shapes, c.1750–1760; (the others) typically c.1775–1800; their kick-up is lower, and the pontil scar is usually ground smooth—while the lip and string rim are blending as corks are now driven flush with the lip; olive green to black; 7¹/₂"–10" H.

(Left) **1277. CASE (GIN) BOT-TLES, c.1740–1780:** These common squared bottles had flat tapering sides and broad brims; they were blown into a mold and could easily be stored in a rectangular case (see **#1297**); $8^{7}/_{8}''$–$10^{3}/_{8}''$ H.

(Above) **1278. BOTTLE BOTTOMS:** (*Left to right*) (*1*) A rough unimproved pontil (scar left intact); (*2*) a high kick-up with the pontil scar now ground smooth; (*3*) the four marks from a mold's quadrafoil pontil iron are visible; (*4*) a case bottle blown into a mold that retains marks from the mold's air-release slots.

(Lower left) **1279. FACETED BOTTLES, c.1735–1800:** A molded design having faceted corners and a tall neck; $9^{1}/_{2}''$, $6^{1}/_{4}''$ H. (Lower center) **1280. UTILITY BOTTLES, c.1730–1810:** These American ovoid utility forms were often taken to the fields covered in leather or wicker; they have a slight kick and rolled-over rims; $5''$, $4^{1}/_{4}''$ H. (Lower right) **1281. PINCHED BOTTLE, c.1730–1770:** A Dutch bottle adding a pinch in the neck to create a double orifice; $7^{1}/_{8}''$ H.

(Above) **1282. BOTTLE SEALS:** Glass seals were sometimes added as a drop of hot glass to a hot bottle (i.e., to cool and contract together) and then stamped with the desired marking; this excavated seal is dated "1732"; $1^5/_8''$ Dia.

(Above) **1283. POCKET BOTTLE, c.1750:** A flattened oval flask with a rolled-over rim; it is light green in color; $4^1/_8''$ H.

(Above) **1284. GLASS CANTEEN, c.1750–1780:** A thick-walled ($^1/_4''$) canteen—a style often leather covered; $10^7/_8''$ H. (Left) **1285. MEDICINE BOTTLES, c.1750–1820:** Glass vials for medicines and oils; $2^3/_4''$–$4^1/_2''$ H. (Below) **1286. UTILITY BOTTLES, c.1730–1810:** Originally for snuff, shoe blacking, medicines, etc.—such bottles were reused for years; $4^1/_2''$–$6^1/_2''$ H (Author).

292

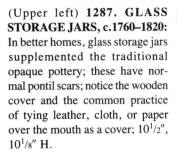

(Upper left) **1287. GLASS STORAGE JARS, c.1760–1820:** In better homes, glass storage jars supplemented the traditional opaque pottery; these have normal pontil scars; notice the wooden cover and the common practice of tying leather, cloth, or paper over the mouth as a cover; 10$\frac{1}{2}$″, 10$\frac{1}{8}$″ H.

(Upper right) **1288. ENAMELED FLASKS, c.1770:** The clear glass bottles are decorated with foliate designs in colored enamels (blue, white, yellow, red); a form made by "Baron" Wm. Henry Stiegel (Penn.), but most found here are from Holland and the Rhineland; tinned caps; 6$\frac{1}{4}$″ H (Private Coll.).

(Left) **1289. CORKSCREW, c.1750–1820:** A typical 18th-century corkscrew form; 6$\frac{1}{8}$″ H.

(Lower right) **1290. "AIR TWIST" WINEGLASS, c.1740–1760:** This innovation inserted air traps into the glass stem and "drew" them up in a spiraled pattern; 8$\frac{3}{4}$″ H (Author).

(Above) **1291. WINEGLASSES:** By 1730, American homes were using imported stemmed wineglasses for social occasions, as well as heavy tumblers for cider and flip (see **#1300**); (*left to right*) (*1*) c.1740–1750; 6″ H; (*2*) c.1765–1780; 5$\frac{7}{8}$″ H; (*3*) c.1780, a 1-piece drawn "trumpet" stem form (earlier versions were taller); 4$\frac{3}{8}$″ H; (*4*) c.1760–1790, a variation of the trumpet shape; 4$\frac{5}{8}$″ H; (*5*) c.1790–1820, a design in style for many years; this early example is hand blown; 4$\frac{1}{8}$″ H.

(Upper left) **1292. GLASS DE-CANTERS, c.1770–1830:** Most country homes served spirits from bottles or jugs, but by this date these conical wide-rimmed decanter forms were beginning to appear; notice the "spirit" label and the dark amethyst decanter; $7^1/2"$–$9^1/2"$ H.

(Upper right) **1293. DECAN-TER & PLATE, c.1785–1810:** A similar tapering decanter ($10^1/2"$ H) and glass stopper on a broad-brimmed glass plate that has a pontil scar (9" Dia).

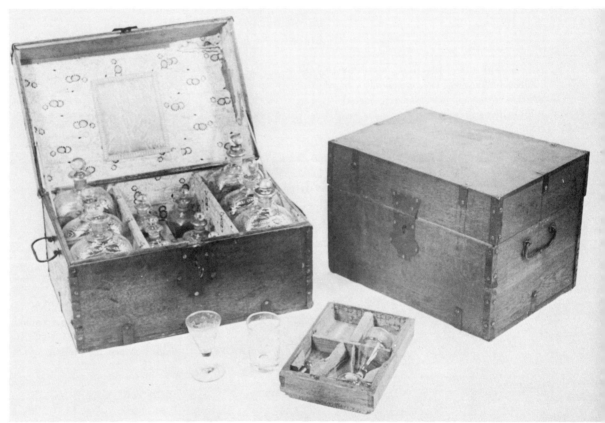

(Above right) **1294. LIQUOR CHESTS, c.1760–1820:** These typical iron-bound liquor chests are equipped with compartmented decanterlike "coach" bottles (see **#1295**), and a removable tray for glasses; the chest is 11" H, $17^1/4"$ W, $11^1/4"$ D (Author).

(Right) **1295. COACH (CASE) BOTTLES, c.1760–1820:** Sets of such bottles were blown to size for a given chest or case (see **#1294**); (left) an undecorated bottle; (right) a matching gold-wash design was added to the bottle, wineglass, and tumbler (same set); these bottles are $9^1/2"$ H.

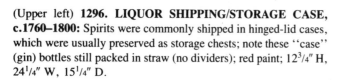

(Upper left) **1296. LIQUOR SHIPPING/STORAGE CASE, c.1760–1800:** Spirits were commonly shipped in hinged-lid cases, which were usually preserved as storage chests; note these ''case'' (gin) bottles still packed in straw (no dividers); red paint; $12^{3}/4''$ H, $24^{1}/4''$ W, $15^{1}/4''$ D.

(Upper right) **1297. LIQUOR CHEST, c.1760–1800:** A simple lidded chest with compartments for twelve bottles; it includes nailed butted joints, crude end handles, and is painted blue; $11^{1}/4''$ H, $17^{1}/2''$ W, $13''$ D (Author).

(Above) **1298. GLASS WINE RINSERS, c.1740–1800:** Stemmed wineglasses would be inverted in these water filled vessels, leaving their bases outside the spoutlike openings; this cooled and rinsed them between the various wines being consumed (see **#1255**); $4^{1}/4''$ H.

(Left) **1299. GLASS TUMBLERS, c.1770–1800:** Such fluted-base tumblers were blown into a mold; their pontils are ground out; a gray tone in the glass suggests an American maker (it was cleared by c.1800); $3''$ H.

(Right) **1300. GLASS TUMBLERS:** (*Two left*) c.1750–1800, a broad-base form; (*two right*) c.1760–1810, a mold-blown design with a raised lip; $3^{1}/8''$–$4''$ H.

(Upper left) **1301. TUMBLER (FLIP GLASS), c.1740–1800:** Tall tumblers were used to mix "flip" (liquor, spirits, and sugar—heated by a "toddy iron"); 6″ H. (Upper right) **1302. TODDY (SWIZZLE) STICKS (MUDDLERS):** These turned sticks stirred mixed spirits; 6³/4″–8″ L.

(Left) **1303. TODDY IRONS (LOGGERHEADS):** Such iron forms were plunged red hot into a drink to "mull" it; 18″, 27¹/4″ L. (Left) **1304. BRANDY WARMER, c.1720–1800:** The unique copper spoon warmed beverage portions over a candle or embers. (Lower right) **1305. TUMBLER, c.1750–1790:** A flip glass engraved from a copper wheel; Dutch or American; 8″ H. (Lower left) **1306. TUMBLERS, c.1780–1830:** A pair with etched designs and fluted bases; 6¹/2″ H (Private Coll.).

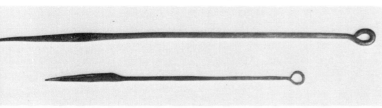

(Left) **1307. GLASS MUGS, c.1760–1790:** Clear glass mugs decorated by "copper-wheel" floral engravings; they were also called "beer" or "cider" mugs; notice the flat applied glass handles, slight kick-up, and pontil scar—plus the projecting bases; a form made by the Dutch, Germans, and Americans; 4⁷/₈″– 6³/₈″ H (Author).

(Above) **1308. GLASS SALT, c.1780–1800:** A blown-glass salt that still retains its pontil scar on the bottom; 2³/₄″ H.

(Above) **1309. GLASS SALT, c.1780–1820:** A boat-shaped salt holder, molded in the raised-diamond pattern of the famed Irish "Waterford" glassware of this period; 3¹/₈″ H.

(Center row, left) **1310. OPAQUE-WHITE GLASS MUG, c.1750–1780:** This smooth "milk," "Bristol," or "enamel" glass was decorated with enamel or oil painting; probably Dutch or English; a slight kick-up and pontil scar remain; 6³/₄″ H. (Left) **1310A. OPAQUE-WHITE GLASS TABLEWARE, c.1760:** As with the milky glass mug, this teacup and saucer were hand decorated with bright enamel colors and fired; probably from Bristol (England); the saucer is 4³/₄″ Dia (Private Coll.).

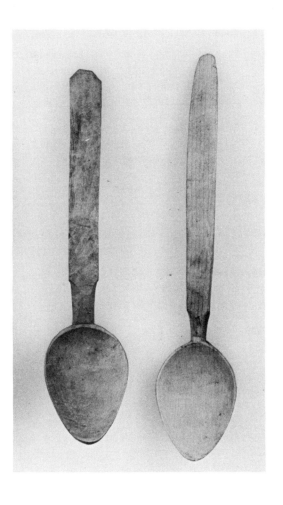

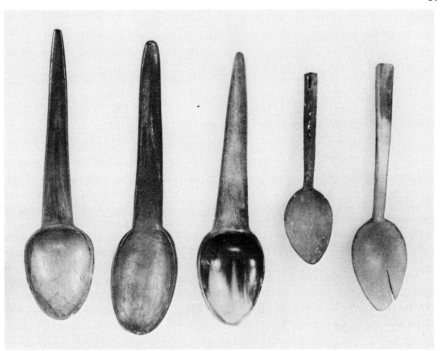

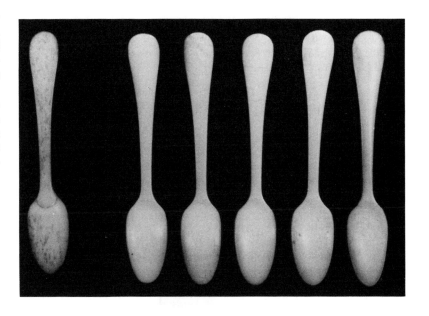

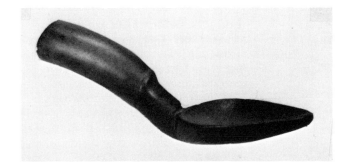

(Upper left) **1311. WOODEN TABLESPOONS, c.1700–1800:** Simple carved wooden eating spoons with plain handles; 9″, 9³/8″ L.

(Upper right) **1312. HORN TABLESPOONS:** (*Three left*) c.1680–1750, an early form using oval bowls and wide, tapering flat handles; (*two right*) c.1750–1800, these straight handles resemble the 17th-century slipped-end style (see **#1317**); 5⁷/8″–9³/4″ L.

(Left) **1313. BONE "TASTING" SPOON, c.1600–1660:** A delicately carved short-handled tasting spoon of bone that includes the fig-shaped bowl of the early 1600s (see **#1316**); 5¹/4″ L.
(Below) **1314. WOODEN TABLESPOON, c.1700–1800:** A sturdy angled form carved from a single piece of wood (Neumann Coll.; Valley Forge National Historical Park).

(Above) **1315. BONE TEASPOONS. c.1750–1820:** About 1730, smaller specialized spoon sizes became accepted; this set of carved-bone teaspoons has the flat bulbous end developed in the early 1700s, and the U-shaped "drop" (where handle meets the bowl; see spoon at left) which was popular c.1750–1800; 5¹/4″ L.

298

(Below) **1317. PEWTER SPOONS:** (*Left to right*) (*1*) "Slipped-End," c.1650–1680—Another 16th–17th–century design was this straight rectangular shaft cut off at a slant; the mid-1600s oval bowl continued in America until c.1790; (*2*) "Trifid" (Wavy-End) (two views), c.1680–1710—a 3-pointed end that evolved in the late 1600s and early 1700s; note the now-established oval bowl's new "rattail" formed by extending the handle along the bowl's back; spoons were normally laid face down on the table; 7⁵/₈″ L; (*3*) "Round-Tipped" (two views), c.1715–1800—this bulbous outline evolved from the trifid shape; it had a median ridge, and the end curved up—until c.1760 when it turned down; 7¹/₂″ L.

(Right) **1318. PEWTER "SHELL" DESIGN, c.1750:** At mid-century, it was also popular to mark a shell form into the rounded "drop" (handle-bowl junction) that was replacing the rattail (see **#1315**).

(Upper left) **1316. SEAL-TOP LATTEN SPOON:** This 17th-century (and earlier) "seal-top" form ends in a flat disc over a baluster shape; "latten" spoons were those made of cast brass, and by the mid-1600s were being coated with tin. (*Left*) c.1620–1660, note the "fig-shaped" bowl of the 17th-century's first half; 6³/₈″ L; (*right*) c.1660–1690, this later bowl has now assumed the newer oval shape; 6⁷/₈″ L (Conn. Historical Society).

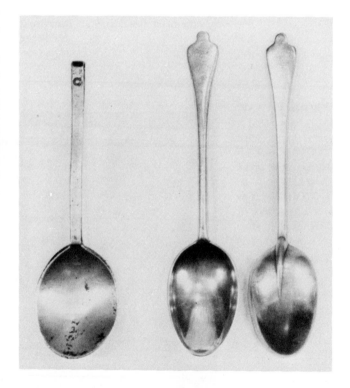

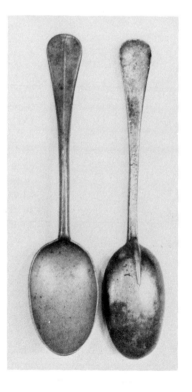

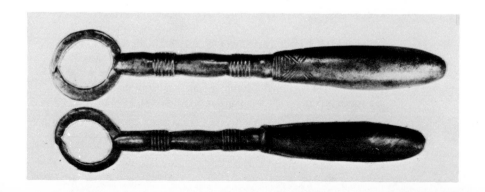

(Left) **1319. IRON MARROW SPOON** (two views), **c.1680–1740:** Bone marrow was considered a delicacy; this special form used its long scoop for digging inside the bone to remove the marrow; note the early turnings, plus a ring for a strap or chain; 6″ L (Author).

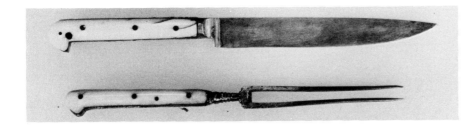

(Left) **1320. TABLE KNIFE & FORK (pair), c.1680–1700:** These "pistol-grip" ivory-paneled handles were too costly for most country homes, but the matched knife and fork are typical of the late 1600s' form; 8″, 6⅞″ L.

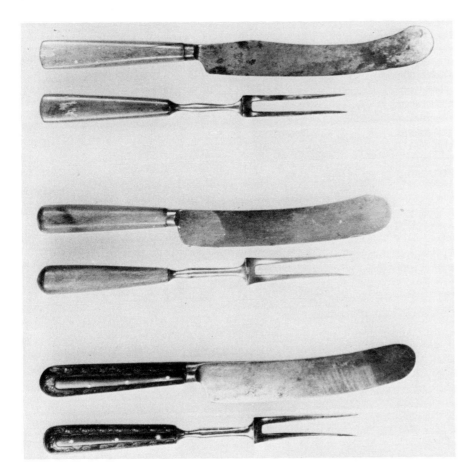

(Left) **1321. TABLE KNIVES & FORKS (pairs):** (*Top*) c.1700–1770, as the fork found acceptance at the table (in the late 1600s), the knife's pointed tip was not needed to lift food, and evolved to the rounded profile. Its humpback upper edge and bulbous tip are normal for this period; the bone handles are dyed green; knife 8½″ L; (*center*) c.1775–1820, by the last quarter, the straight-backed shorter blade was favored; notice the discolored steel from the heat used to apply its soft iron tang that extended into the horn handle; knife 7⅝″ L; (*bottom*) c.1780–1820, a similar form with a less bloated tip; the more formal horn handles now have designs pressed into them—reflecting increased well-being among the middle class; knife blade 8¼″ L.

(Right) **1322. TABLE FORKS:** The 2-tined fork predominated through the 18th century; (*top*) c.1685–1710, an early "pistol grip" form with that period's slouched shoulders; the other forks shown are typical of the 1700s (note their abrupt shoulders). The 3- and 4-tined examples appeared in the last quarter, and became popular during the 1800s. Forks were usually placed to the left of the plate (knife at the right) with the tines turned down; wood, bone, horn, and antler handles saw use; 6½″–7¾″ L.

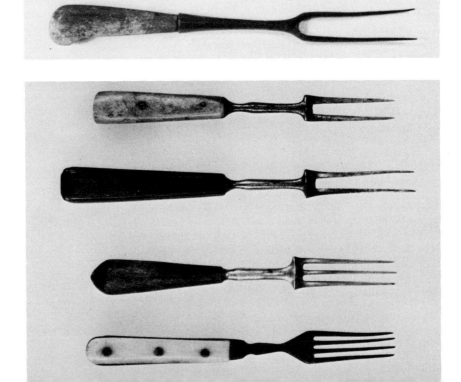

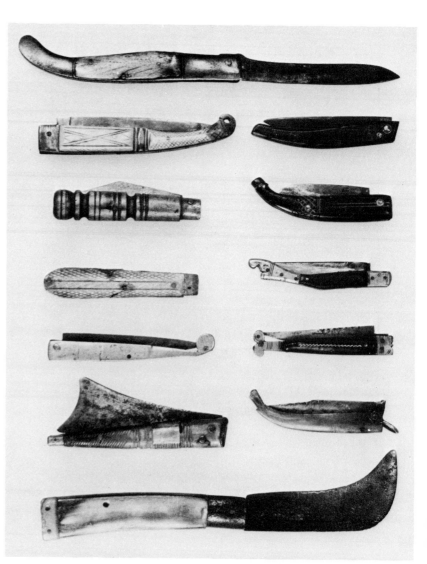

(Below) **1323. UTILITY (BELT) KNIVES, c.1690–1820:** The colonist's working knife was not the long wide-bladed "Bowie" fighting form of the 1800s, but normally a plain "butcher style" mounting a single-edged blade plus a simple handle (wood, bone, antler, or horn); its blade length was the practical 5″ to 9″—often made from an old file or sword.

(Right) **1324. JACKKNIVES (POCKET, FOLDING), c.1750–1840:** Many in settled areas preferred jackknives to the belt type. (*Top*) the popular English form mounting horn panels between long iron bolsters; most had single blades and often omitted a spring; their handles were of iron, brass, wood, bone, and horn; 3¾″–6⅛″ L (closed).

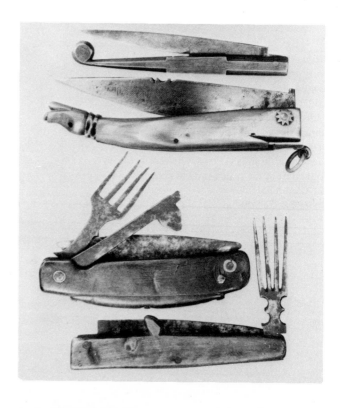

(Right) **1325. JACKKNIVES:** (*Top to bottom*) (*1*) c.1740–1790, the cut-steel design with a scrolled end; 8¾″ (blade open); (*2*) c.1760–1850, a French-Spanish form, the extended spring's slot locks the blade stud when opened; (*3*) c.1730–1790, a rare multi-blade knife that includes a fork and medical lancet; horn handle; (*4*) c.1740–1780, a fork and blade; 8¼″ L (Neumann Coll.; Valley Forge National Historical Park).

⚞ VOLUME III ⚟

PERSONAL CARE & INDULGENCES

The country people of our colonial past were strong in their convictions, but not necessarily the drab, prudish, or self-righteous individuals often portrayed in textbooks. The core of their lives was a prodigious workday. It required a firm discipline within the home, yet like most obligations commonly shared, led to closely knit families bound by mutual respect and common pleasures. Beneath it all, however, laced with the drive for a better life, was a rockbound spirit of personal independence kindled by Herculean efforts to clear and work their own land with their own hands.

A LIFE OF ESSENTIALS: The 18th-century man averaged 5′4″ to 5′6″ in height and, judging by surviving clothing, was slight of build. He appeared clean shaven, kept his hair at neck length in its natural color, and tied it at the back. Wigs were normally used by the more well-to-do in the city or on formal occasions. The woman appears to have been even smaller in size and usually wore a simple top and skirt with a large linen work apron.

Although about a third of these settlers could neither read nor write, they were extremely practical and very much in tune with their environment. Creativity found outlets for expression through a variety of available media, including primitive paintings, unusual iron forgings, wood carving, delicate sewing projects, innovative weaving, or even daily chores such as the shaping and laying of stones to achieve a tight-fitting dry wall. It is also interesting to note that the colors of their clothing and furniture were far brighter and more varied than is generally recognized today.

SIMPLE PLEASURES: The limited periods after chores were usually consumed by readings from the Bible, indulging in board games such as checkers, backgammon, or fox and geese, and—in the man's case—smoking his clay pipe. Country music typically found expression through singing hymns or familiar ballads; folk dancing; playing simple flutes, jews harps, traditional instruments from Europe, or fifes and drums of the local militia.

For a full understanding of these disciplined lives, a great deal of study is still required to separate three centuries of intermingled fact and fancy. The succeeding pages, illustrating many of these colonists' intimate possessions, are intended as a contribution in this direction.

(Lower left) **1326. CARVED CANTEEN, c.1750–1790:** Notice the rural carving of a familar house, animals, and fish; Mohawk Valley; 7¼″ Dia. (Lower right) **1327. CARVED POWDER HORN, c.1750–1800:** A town scene of churches and buildings (Author).

Art

There was little formal art associated with the lesser homes during this period. Creative outlets were normally satisfied through opportunities available in home chores and domestic skills.

As the middle class grew in size and resources during the 1700s, however, the upper segment of our country population began to indulge in more conventional artwork—especially family portraiture. Unlike the professionally trained artist retained by the wealthy, the usual painter for the average man was referred to as a *limner*, a name originally associated with the painter of miniatures. He began as an itinerant artisan who traveled from town to town painting everything from furniture and fire buckets to tavern signs and floorcloths. Local portraits were also attempted, and eventually became popular.

There was little professional artistry in most of these works. The sharply outlined figures usually appear two dimensional in a flat design where all of the elements receive equal emphasis. Pastels, as well as oils, became accepted toward the latter part of our period, and regional preferences were evident—such as the symbolic religious paintings in the Dutch homes of the Hudson Valley.

By 1800, there had been a substantial improvement in the quality of available artwork, reflecting the continual striving by these Americans for an elegance well beyond their humble beginnings.

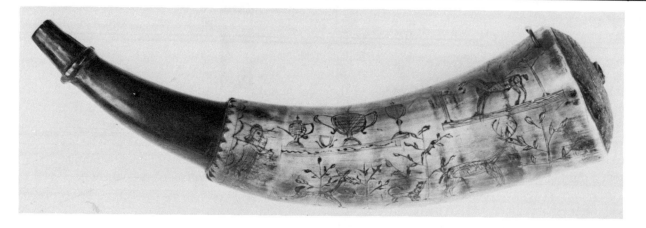

(Above) **1328. CARVED POWDER HORN,** Marked **"1758":** Notice the everyday sights recorded here—a man, tableware, animals, plants, and trees; its shaved end was a typical 18th-century form; 9¹/₂" L. (Lower left) **1329. SILHOUETTE, c.1780–1800:** A woman's head in its original black frame; from upper N.Y.; 4⁷/₈" H (Private Coll.).

(Lower right) **1330. SILHOUETTE COMPONENTS:** Many were center cutouts of white paper mounted over black paper or cloth. (Right) **1331. CARVED BUSK, c.1740–1780:** Women wore wooden busks to keep their bodices straight; they were often carved, as shown, by their "intended"; mahogany; 13" L.

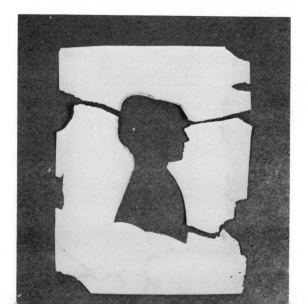

(Left) **1332. MEZZOTINT PRINTS, c.1750–1700:** These are mezzotints of country life in their original frames (black with gilded borders); this popular engraving method roughed and burred the copperplate to achieve soft, delicate tonal effects. Both of the pictures are colored by hand in watercolors, and were printed in London—using English and French captions (i.e., for export); 12⅜″ x 16½″.

MINIATURES: Small personal portraits of loved ones or important people were created for the more affluent; most of them were done in oils or watercolors on ivory, tin, parchment, or vellum. (Two, near right) **1333. c.1760–1780:** Typical miniatures. (Far right) **1334. c.1785–1800:** Painted on ivory and mounted in a brass frame; 2½″ Dia.

(Above) **1335. REVERSE GLASS ("BACK") PAINTINGS, c.1760–1790:** An ancient method revived in the 1700s; this painting was done on the back of glass. (*Left*) English; an artisan is shown carrying his fabrics (in its original frame); 12½″ x 10¼″; (*right*) a Germanic example titled "Hirsch" (stag); 6⅝″ x 9″ (Private Coll.). (Upper right) **1336. OIL PORTRAIT, c.1760–1775:** An oil painting (paperboard mounted on canvas) of Guy Johnson (from N.Y.'s Mohawk Valley), who later led Loyalist raids during the Revolutionary War; 13¾″ H (Author).

(Above) **1337. PAINTED OVERMANTEL WALL PANEL:** A hunting scene painted on the wall panel of a home in Conn. (not uncommon) (Metropolitan Museum of Art). (Above) **1338. OIL PORTRAITS, c.1760–1790:** A pair that reflects upper middle-class success in the later 1700s; they retain their original gilded frames; 24³/₈″ x 19¹/₂″ (Author).

Fabrics

Most of the well-to-do colonists relied primarily upon textiles imported from Europe, but the majority produced what they needed for themselves. The typical farm raised its own flax for linen and maintained sheep for the wool. Since only a poor grade of cotton in sparse amounts was raised here, cotton cloth had to be purchased abroad (mostly after 1760).

The flax produced a coarse "tow" needed in rough use, or a finely hetcheled linen for clothing and domestic fabrics. Wool, in turn, was usually reserved for homespun blankets and outer garments. Although spinning and weaving were practiced in virtually every household, professional weavers also worked in settled localities, or traveled with a portable loom to do special work during short stays with a family.

Prowess with a needle and thread also began early. By the age of three, girls were usually assigned patchwork. Between five and twelve, it was customary to produce a "sampler" (see **#1366**) that aided in learning their numbers and alphabet—as well as demonstrating various stitches.

As might be expected, women took great pride in their sewing capabilities, which included canvas work (i.e., needlepoint), mending, tailoring, quilting, patchwork, knitting, embroidery, lace making, and weaving.

LINEN HETCHELS (HACKLES): The flax plant's fibers (lying between the bark and core) were separated by soaking, pounding, scraping—and then drawing them through the spikes of these "hetchels" (using up to five in descending opening widths) until the long broken fibers were ready to spin. (Upper left) **1339. c.1780–1810:** A heart-decorated Penn. hetchel, and a handle form; 26″, 18¼″ L. (Upper right) **1340. c.1770–1800:** A small "wig" hetchel, plus a larger one dated "1775"; boxlike wooden covers fitted over the nail points; 6¾″, 13½″ L.

FLAX SPINNING WHEELS: The hetcheled linen was spun into thread on these foot-operated spinning wheels. (Lower left) **1341. UPRIGHT WHEEL, c. 1700–1760:** The early European style with its "flyer" above the driving wheel; note its bold post turnings and flat "distaff" (see **#1349**); 49¾″ H. (Lower right) **1342. FLAX WHEEL, c.1750–1820:** This was the popular form here by 1750; its distaff was cut from a tree crotch and bent (while green) to hold unspun flax; the cup held water to wet the fibers; 40¾″ H (Private Coll.).

(Right) **1343. WOOL CARDS (CARDERS), c. 1750–1850:** Each face has short wire teeth; the raw wool (*upper left*) was placed on one card and the other repeatedly drawn across it to produce a fluffy cylindrical roll of wool fibers (a ''rolag'') ready for spinning (Private Coll.).

(Above) **1344. WOOL SPINNING WHEEL, c.1750–1800:** Unlike the foot-treadled flax wheel (see **#1342**), this high wool wheel was operated by hand while standing; its large driving wheel turned the spindle which twisted the fibers into yarn (Smithsonian Institution). (Right) **1345. BATTEN (BAT) HEAD, c.1770–1810:** This is the single-post 18th-century spindle form; it was replaced after 1800 by the double-post ''miner's'' head style (Private Coll.).

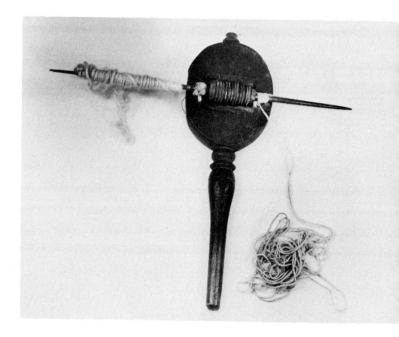

(Left) **1346. FIBERS:** (*Left to right*) (*1*) A heavy tow linen; (*2*) finely hetcheled linen; (*3*) dyed 2-ply wool yarn. (Below) **1347. ''WHEEL BOYS'':** These were used to turn the large wool spinning wheel; note the wear below their heads (Private Coll.).

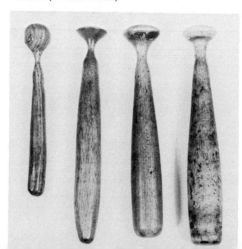

(Left) **1348. TREADLE LOOM, c.1700–1800:** A large bed-size "gunstock" loom for weaving fabric; it was usually kept in the attic, shed, or loom room, and could be disassembled for storage; because the weaving width seldom exceeded 32″, most blankets and bed coverings were woven in strips and sewn together (Smithsonian Institution).

(Right) **1349. DISTAFFS, c.1680–1730:** The early European form (see **#1341**); raw flax was wound around the broad top; its base was then set into the spinning wheel for the flax to be drawn into thread—or held under the arm and used with a drop spindle (see **#1351**); 35$^1/2$″–41″ H.

(Far left) **1350. PORTABLE YARN WINDER, c.1700–1850:** A handy notched holder for small amounts of yarn (e.g., darning, embroidery); 9″ L (Private Coll.).

(Near left) **1351. DROP SPINDLES:** A form used since ancient times; the wool yarn was wound as shown, and drawn from for small work; (*right*) an early carved drop spindle, c.1680 (Private Coll.).

(Right) **1352. NIDDY NODDY, c.1750–1800:** A frame with its arms at right angles; yarn from the spinning wheel's spindle was wound onto it as a supply for small hand work (crewel, knitting, etc.) (Private Coll.).

(Below) **1353. NIDDY NODDIES:** Interesting variations of niddy-noddy end forms in ash, cherry, and maple.

308

(Upper left) **1354. WINDER (YARN WINDER, SWIFT) c.1720–1820:** A rotary frame to wind yarn or linen from the spinning wheel (measured in ''skeins'') before unwinding to weave on the loom; 42³/4″ H (Private Coll.). (Upper center) **1355. CLICK REEL, c.1750–1770:** A winder with a toothed wheel that counted yarn or thread length by its ''clicks''; T-base footing (Merle E. Bouchard). (Upper right) **1356. SQUIRREL-CAGE WINDER, c.1720–1780:** These adjustable cages wound yarn or linen between them; 42″ H (Author).

(Lower left) **1357. WINDER, c.1730–1780:** A horizontal axle on a 4-legged base (Merle E. Bouchard). (Lower center) **1358. WINDER, c.1740–1820:** A T-base form. (Lower right) **1359. KNITTING NEEDLE, CROCHET HOOKS:** England's machines furnished most of the knitted goods, but country homes still produced woolen stockings, mittens, etc.; 6″–10″ L (Private Coll.).

TAPE (BRAID) LOOMS: Small slotted looms for weaving tapes, ribbons, belts, etc. (Above, left to right) (*1*) **1360. c.1680–1720:** Tape loom with an X base; butternut and cherry; 35″ H (Author). (*2*) **1361. c.1730–1790:** A vertical board nailed to a recessed pine block; 33$\frac{1}{2}$″ H. (*3*) **1362. c.1770–1800:** A 3-legged base like the "candle stand"; pine; 38$\frac{1}{2}$″ H (Conn. Historical Society). (*4*) **1363. c.1750–1800:** Hand loom made from a reused pine "feath-eredge" wall board; 18$\frac{5}{8}$″ H.

(Lower left) **1364. SCISSORS (SHEARS):** (*Left to right*) (*1 & 2*) c.1650–1700, the early narrow concave blades; (*3*) c.1770, note these later closed loops and decorated shanks; (*4 & 5*) c.1700–1770, this period's broad blades taper near the ends; 6$\frac{3}{4}$″–10$\frac{3}{8}$″ L. (Lower right) **1365. WEAVER'S SHEARS & BUCK-SKIN CASE:** 4$\frac{1}{2}$″ L.

SAMPLERS: This needlework recorded one's sewing progress; samplers were long and narrow during the 1600s and shorter in the 1700s; most were done by girls aged five to twelve. (Upper left) **1366.** Dated **"1739":** A formal sampler by Ann Wing that displays silk on a linen base (Museum of Fine Arts, Boston). (Upper right) **1367. c.1775–1810:** A plainer sampler; notice that "J" was commonly written as "I."

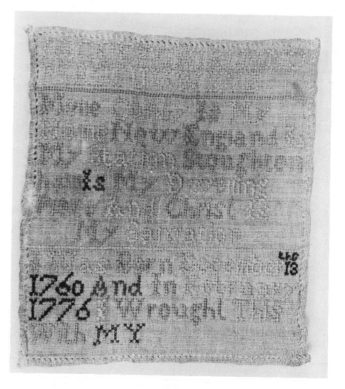

(Above) **1368. FRAMED NEEDLEWORK (CANVAS WORK),** Dated **"1745":** Fine needlework was often framed for display in parlors and chambers; this is a floral design in wool on linen canvas (19th-century frame); 9³/₄″ H (Private Coll.).

(Above) **1369. SAMPLER:** Its message reads, "Melle Coney is My/ Name New England Is/ My station Stoughten/ ham Is My Dwelling/ Place And Christ is/ My Salvation/ I Was Born December the 13/ 1760 And In February/ 1776 I Wrought This/ With My . . ." (unfinished) (Author).

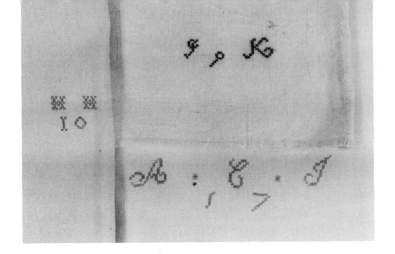

(Upper left) **1370. LINEN MARKINGS:** This common marking on a woman's dowry fabrics was her initials and the piece's sequence number (not the year or her age) (Private Coll.). (Right) **1371. IMPORT PRINTS, c.1770:** The illustrated "pocket" or "bag" was made from squares of English linen and cotton prints available to the colonists (Private Coll.). (Row below) **1372. LINEN:** A comparison of textures from heavy tow (*left*) to fine clothing linen (*right*).

(Row above) **1373. LINEN TABLE-CLOTHS, c.1720–1840:** Typical weights and patterns. (Right) **1374. LINEN CLOTHS, c.1720–1800:** Colorful linen pieces (blues, reds, browns) used as handkerchieves, food or table covers, lunch wrappings for the fields, etc. (Private Coll.).

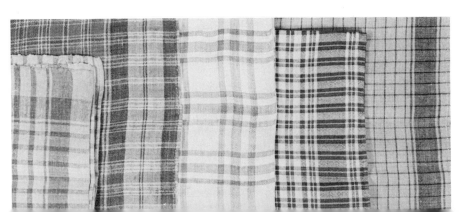

(Upper left) **1375. CREWELWORK EMBROIDERY, c.1750:**
A crewel design (woolen yarn on a linen base) as favored for bed hangings, chair seats, pocketbooks, and clothing; it includes blue, green, brown, red, and yellow (vegetable dyes) (Private Coll.).
(Upper right) **1376. COUNTRY CREWEL COVERLET, c.1750–1800:** A simple wool pattern with blue overstitches on a white wool base; it joins two 37″-wide strips (typical; limited by loom width); 94″ x 74″. (Below) **1377. COUNTRY CREWEL BLANKET, c.1750–1800:** A common 6-point pattern (Private Coll.).
(Left) **1378. WOOL BED HANGING, c.1700–1750:** The popular blue-and-white wool check design; 1⅝″ squares (Private Coll.).

(Left) **1379. BED RUG, c.1778:** An 18th-century "rug" went on the bed as a coverlet—while a "carpet" covered furniture or the floor; this rug is attributed to Elizabeth Foot of Colchester, Conn. (married in 1778); it uses three natural shades of blue, one of brown; 83″ × 78″ (Conn. Historical Society).

(First & second row, left) **1380, 1381. BLANKET PATTERNS, c.1750–1830:** Most blankets were two strips sewn together (limited by loom's width; length was optional); these homespun woolen patterns persisted into the early 1800s, usually in 2-ply thread of 1- or 2-ply weft and warp; these colors include blue, brown, orange, red, green, and white; typical width 64″ (Au.).

(Third row, left) **1382. HEAVY BLANKETS, c.1750–1800:** (*Left to right*) (*1*) The linen and wool ''Canadian'' style; (*2*) a ''fisheye'' wool pattern; (*3*) a ''snowflake'' coverlet in ''double weave'' (i.e., double thickness); both its weft and warp are wool and woven together (not applied); red, white, blue; (*4*) ''quilting'' with its raised stitched designs. (Lower left) **1383. WOOLEN SHAWL, c.1700–1800:** Folded square of a woolen check pattern with a fringe; 67″ sq. (Lower right) **1384. WOOLEN COVERLET, c.1760–1790:** Another double weave with its pattern typically reversed on the underside; this type was usually by a professional weaver who visited homes.

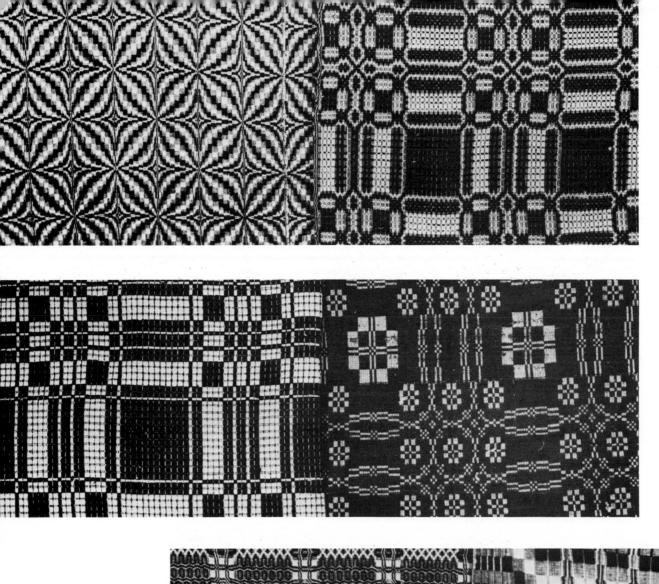

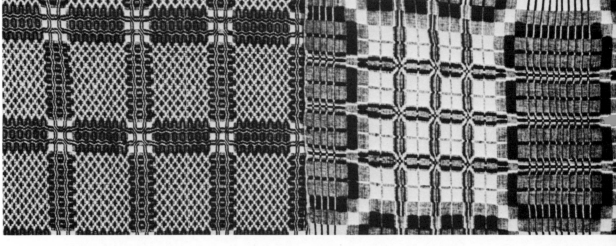

(Opposite page) **1385. WOVEN BED COVERLETS (COUN-TERPANES), c.1780–1840:** These are typical "overshot" patterns, i.e., formed by long threads that skip, or "overshoot," the foundation; they were mostly spun, dyed, and woven at home in designs passed down from prior generations; most are of wool, with linen or cotton for the warp (Author).

QUILTS: (Upper left) **1386. c.1700–1800:** The quilt was a bed coverlet formed by two outer fabrics and a soft center filler, usually raw wool (cotton was also popular by 1780); the designs were stitched through the quilt. (Upper right) **1387. c.1700–1800:** A homespun quilt (later term, "patchwork") made from remnants of clothing and used fabrics; the squares are 4″ W (Private Coll.).

(Above) **1388. PRESSING IRONS, c.1740–1800:** Called "sad irons" ("sad" meant "heavy"), they were preheated to press fabrics. (Right) **1389. PRESSING IRON STANDS, c.1775–1820:** These are late-century holders for the irons; 10″, 11¼″ L.

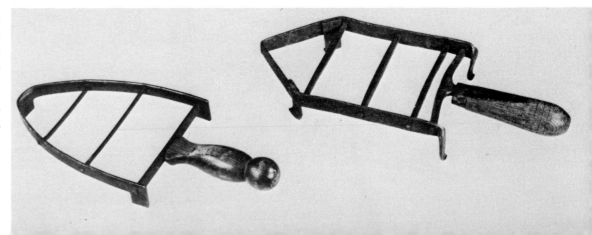

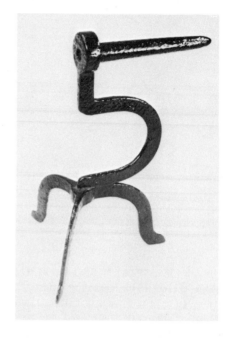

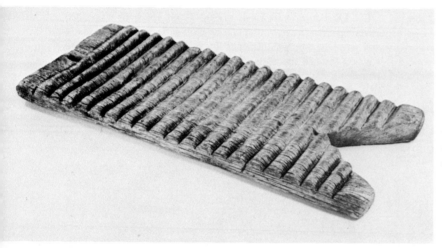

(Upper left) **1390. GOFFERING (TALLY) IRON, c.1690–1720:** The removable iron rod was heated in embers and thrust red hot into the horizontal cylinder; as the cylinder heated, small or delicate fabrics to be ironed were drawn over it; New England; 6¹/₂″ H (Lillian Blankley Cogan). (Above) **1391. GOFFERING IRON, c.1710–1730:** An alternate flat-frame form; 7″ H.

(Left) **1392. SCRUB BOARD, c.1700–1850:** The earliest laundry was done on rocks at the stream, but when large tubs became available, the scrub board gained acceptance; 25″ L. (Below left) **1393. SCRUBBING STICK, c.1700–1800:** A narrower variation with a handle; 20″ L.

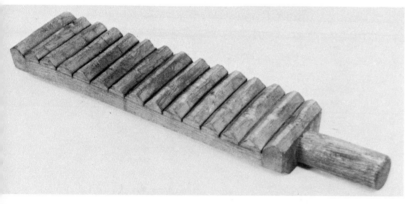

(Right) **1394. SOFT SOAP SCOOP, c.1700–1850:** Families made soap by boiling animal fats and lye (leeched wood ashes); it was stored (soft) in a barrel, and scooped out as needed; this scoop is typical; 12″ L. (Below) **1395. WASHING PADDLE, c.1700–1850:** Notice the wood damage from the soap's lye; 17″ L.

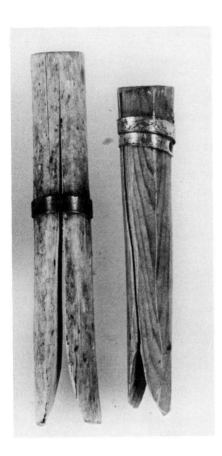  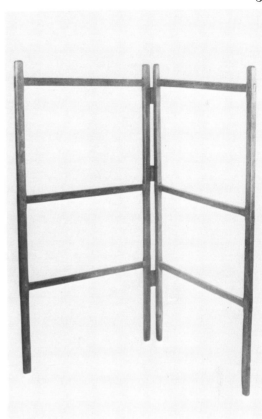

(Upper left) **1396. CLOTHESPINS, c.1760–1830:** Laundry was normally dried on branches or bushes, but hemp clotheslines were also used; these whittled clothespins have bands to limit splitting; 5³/₄", 5" L. (Upper center) **1397. DRYING RACK (AIRING HORSE), c.1740–1820:** A pine drying frame for various needs from herbs to laundry; it includes trestle feet plus mortised and pinned joints; 36" H (Private Coll.). (Upper right) **1398. DRYING RACK, c.1750–1850:** These two sections are joined by leather hinges; 40³/₄" H.

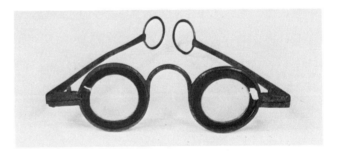

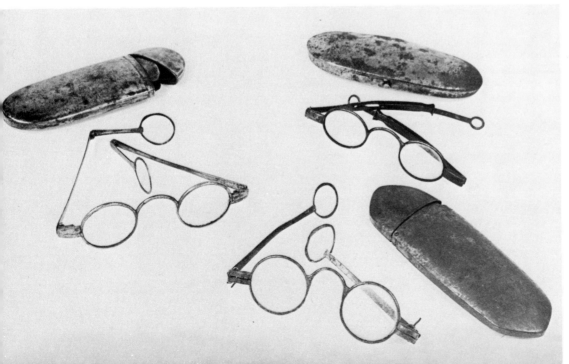

SPECTACLES: Lenses were preground and chosen by trial. The earlier round frames were supplemented by the oval form c.1760; they were held against the head by a cord or ribbon that was tied between their rear loops. (Left) **1399. c.1740–1820:** (*Upper right*) These telescoping frames were introduced c.1770; also note the iron cases. (Above) **1400. c.1750–1800:** Horn inserts inside the iron frames were probably to adjust for eye differences.

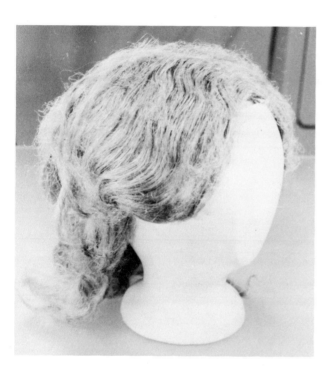

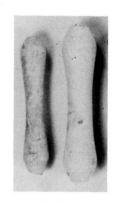

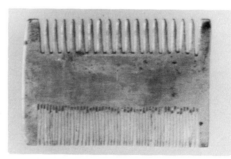

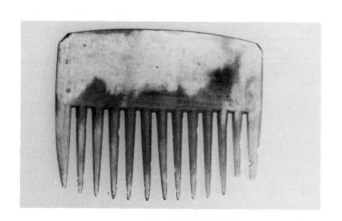

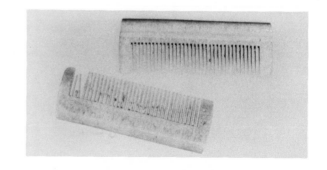

(Left) **1401. MAGNIFYING GLASSES, c.1760–1800:** Poor lighting and impaired eyesight encouraged use of the magnifying glass; (*left*) a frame with neck-cord loops; (*right*) a brass frame on a wooden handle; both cases are pressed pasteboard; 4″, 6¼″ L (Private Coll.). (Below) **1402. PRISM MAGNIFIER, c.1740–1770:** This variation uses a prismlike glassed center plus turned handles; water filled the center (the plug is visible) to provide its refraction density; 10″ L (Author).

HEAD COMBS: (Below) **1403. c.1740–1800:** A double-tooth form cut from sheet brass. (Wm. Richard Gordon Coll., Valley Forge Hist. Society). (Lower right corner) **1404. c.1750–1820:** Paired wooden combs. (Lower left) **1405. c.1750–1800:** A wide-tooth horn comb; 4³⁄₈″ W.

(Above) **1406. WIG, c.1750:** Wigs were mostly worn in urban areas or on formal occasions, as country people normally kept their hair natural and tied at the back; the wigs ranged from human hair to horsehair, wool, and even tow; this rural example is coarse linen sewn to a cloth and a linen head net (Private Coll.). (Far right) **1406A. PIPE CLAY CURLERS:** The hair was wrapped around them in strips of damp paper and heated.

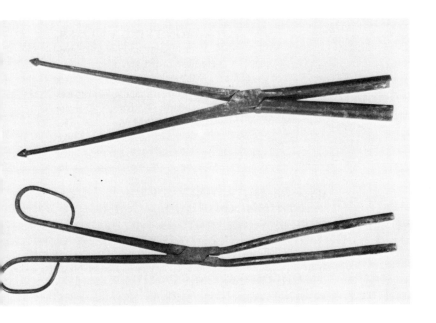

(Upper left) **1407. CURLING IRONS, c.1750–1840:** Such scissors-type irons were heated and pressed over moist hair ends to form curls in wigs or natural hair; (*top*) one blade is a solid rod, the other a concave half sleeve; (*bottom*) both of these blades are solid rods; 10⅝″, 10¼″ L.

(Upper right) **1409. DUTCH DELFT SHAVING BASIN (BARBER'S BOWL), c.1700–1740:** The brim's concave "cutout" fitted under the chin when shaving, or against an arm while being bled; it is decorated in blues; 10¼″ Dia (Lillian Blankley Cogan).

(Below) **1408. WOODEN SHAVING BASIN c.1700–1740:** This turned wooden shaving bowl includes the typical chin opening and hanging ring (Author).

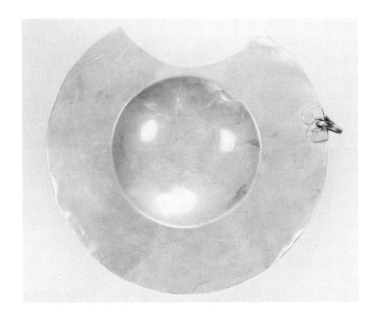

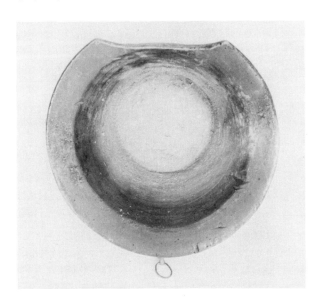

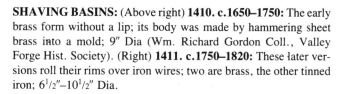

SHAVING BASINS: (Above right) **1410. c.1650–1750:** The early brass form without a lip; its body was made by hammering sheet brass into a mold; 9″ Dia (Wm. Richard Gordon Coll., Valley Forge Hist. Society). (Right) **1411. c.1750–1820:** These later versions roll their rims over iron wires; two are brass, the other tinned iron; 6½″–10½″ Dia.

(Upper left) **1412. RAZOR, c.1650–1700:** Straight razors arrived during the 1600s (previous shaving favored a sharp knife or pumice stone); note the steel blade's continuous cutting edge, without the thin neck of the 1800s; its horn handle adds an applied stamped-brass shell finial. (Upper right) **1413. RAZOR c.1750–1810:** A typical period horn handle with rivets; 6″ L. (Second left) **1414. SOAP HOLDER/BRUSH, c.1750–1780:** A carved wooden soap holder and shaving brush (Ft. Ticonderoga Museum). (Third left) **1415. SHAVING BRUSH, c.1750–1800:** A more elegant brush; the cap unscrews to store the bristles inside the handle; 5″ L (Joan W. Friedland).

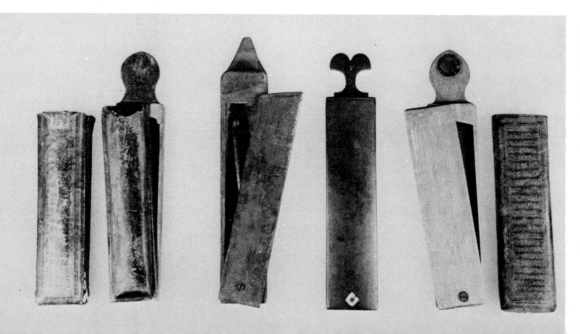

(Above left) **1416. HONING STONE, c.1750–1800:** The stone is mounted on a wooden base (Valley Forge Hist. Society). (Above) **1417. TOILET KIT, c.1760–1800:** A brass container with two hinged covers—revealing the mirror and a soap compartment; 3½″ L. (Left) **1418. RAZOR BOXES, c.1740–1820:** Hollowed wooden boxes (pivoting tops) for razors; two pasteboard covers are shown at the ends; 10″–10⅝″ L.

MEDICAL: Country people put more trust in botanicals and home remedies than physicians, who practiced induced bleeding and primitive surgery. (Upper left) **1419. FLEAM (LANCET), c.1700–1850:** A bloodletting tool; its brass handle holds two pivoting blades to open veins, plus a short scalpel; $3^1/_2''$ L. (Upper right) **1420. CUPPING GLASSES, c.1740–1770:** These were placed over an opened vein to create a semivacuum and induce bleeding, or to draw out infection; $2^3/_8''-3''$ H. (Right) **1421. APOTHE-CARY MEASURE, c.1700–1800:** Nested cast-brass measures; $1^3/_4''$ H. (Below) **1422. TOOTH EXTRACTOR, c.1750–1850:** It pulled a tooth free by a turn of the handle.

INFUSION POTS: (Far right) **1423. c.1750–1800:** This was filled with botanicals or medication and heated to release vapors for purifying a patient's room, easing congestion, etc.; tinned iron; $11^3/_8''$ H. (Near right) **1424. c.1785:** A pewter version by Joseph Danforth, Middletown, Conn.; note the spout and steam holes; $4^1/_2''$ H (Conn. Historical Society).

322

(Right) 1425. COINS: Families satisfied most of their needs from the land, barter, or shared work with neighbors; yet many coins circulated, such as these low-value examples: (*Top, left to right*) a Spanish silver cob (cut from a bar); an English shilling, c.1695–1697; the English Rosa Americana penny, 1722; a Spanish real, 1723; (*bottom left to right*) English half-pennies—the reversed one is dated "1732," the other "1746"; a French ecu, 1756.

(Left) 1426. PAPER CURRENCY: England discouraged minting, and usually paid for imports with exports to retain hard money; the colonies, however, printed currency as early as the 1600s; most surviving examples are from the Revolutionary War period, e.g., (*top, left to right*) Penn., 1773; N.Y., 1776; (*bottom, left to right*) the Continental Congress, 1776; Conn., 1776; Rhode Island, 1780.

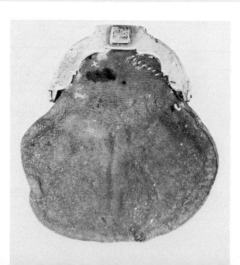
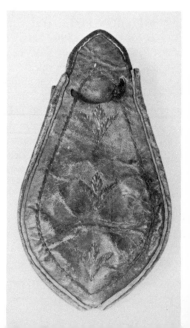

(Far right) 1427. PURSE (POCKET), c.1680–1720: A tall European purse of green leather (accordion side pleats) and a paper liner; 8″ H (Private Coll.).

(Near right) 1428. PURSE, c.1730–1760: From a Dutch area in the Hudson Valley; note its heavy brass clasp (over an interior iron frame) plus the stitched-leather body; 6½″ H (Private Coll.).

(Right) **1429. LEATHER POCKET-BOOKS:** These rectangular forms normally held diaries, records, personal papers, and currencies; (*left*) c.1760, the front folds down to reveal two vertical pockets faced with heavy paper; 5³/₈″ W; (*right*) c.1750, an embossed "single-fold" type; 5¹/₂″ W; (*lower left*) c.1780–1840, the wraparound-strap form with one inside pocket; 6¹/₂″ W; (*lower right*) c.1750, a single-fold pocketbook interior (embossed names); 5¹/₂″ W (Author).

(Lower left) **1430. "WORKED" POCKET-BOOK ("POCKET")** (two views), **c.1740–1810:** Needlework ("canvas work") pocketbooks were usually made at home—often in this "flame stitch," which displays bright crewel yarns; its inside pocket is divided (accordion pleats); note the common 3-branch tie-tape; 7¹/₄″ W (Author).

(Right) **1431. WORKED POCKETBOOK** (two views), Dated **"1768":** This is a fold-down form (one pocket above the other); the polychrome needlework design includes "NR" and "1768," while the clasp on the flap is initialed; linen lining; 6¹/₄″ W (Private Coll.).

324

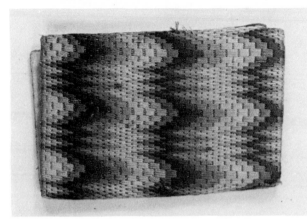

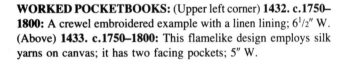

WORKED POCKETBOOKS: (Upper left corner) **1432. c.1750–1800:** A crewel embroidered example with a linen lining; $6^{1}/_{2}''$ W. (Above) **1433. c.1750–1800:** This flamelike design employs silk yarns on canvas; it has two facing pockets; 5″ W.

(Lower left) **1434. POCKET, c.1770–1790:** A flat parchment "pocket"—folded on all sides; $5^{1}/_{4}''$ W (Neumann Coll., Valley Forge National Historical Park). (Lower center) **1435. DOCUMENT CONTAINER, c.1750–1810:** A tinned-iron document holder with a friction-fitted cover; $5^{5}/_{8}''$ H. (Lower right) **1436. WORKED POCKETBOOK, c.1750–1800:** Crewel embroidery appears on all faces; $6^{1}/_{2}''$ W.

(Upper right corner) **1437. LEATHER POCKETBOOK, c.1785:** This is made from leather squares stitched together (brown, red, tan, green); inside are double pockets and a linen lining; $6^{1}/_{4}''$ W (Private Coll.). (Above) **1438. WORKED POCKETBOOK, c.1750–1780:** Polychrome crewel; the edges are typically bound in linen tape; its lining is glazed linen; $6^{3}/_{4}''$ W (Private Coll.).

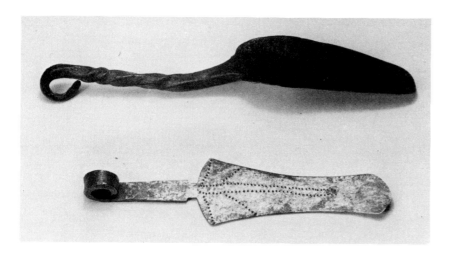

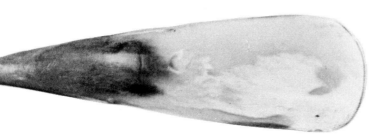

(Left) 1439. SHOE (SHOEING) HORNS: Known throughout our period, shoehorns are found in many forms. (*From top*) (*1*) c.1750, this wrought-iron "horn" has a twisted handle; (*2*) c.1720, a punched-dot iron version; (*3*) c.1760, a concave triangular shape in cow's horn; $5^{1}/4''$–$8^{3}/8''$ L.

(Below) 1440. WARMING PAN COVER: A close-up of the engraved decoration on a lid.

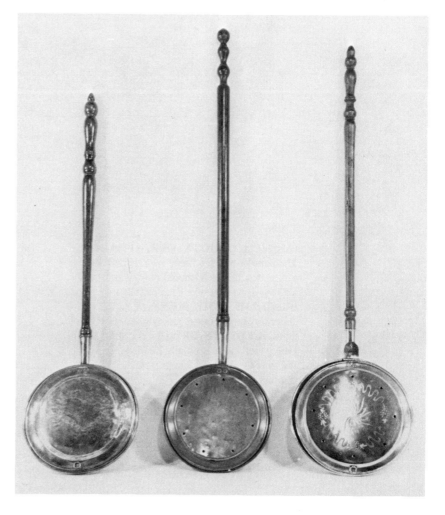

(Lower right) 1441. WARMING PANS, c.1750–1800: Holding hot charcoal or embers, these pans were placed between icy bedcovers before retiring; note their baluster-turned wooden handles; such pans at this time were usually of copper and/or brass—with dovetailed bottoms (i.e., like the tea kettles); pewter and tinned-iron forms were also used; $40^{1}/2''$–$45^{1}/2''$ L.

(Left) 1442. WARMING PAN: An earlier form that mounts a wrought-iron handle on a brass pan covered by a domed lid (etched with a star design); 44″ L (Roger Bacon; Robert W. Skinner, Inc.).

FOOT STOVES (FOOT WARMERS): Feet were often kept warm in winter by resting them on heated stones and bricks—or brass, tinned-iron, and wooden boxes that held a pan of hot coals. (Right) **1443. DUTCH BRASS FOOT STOVES:** (*Near right*) c.1690–1720, an octagonal pierced form; 5¼″ H; (*far right*) c.1730–1760, an oval body mounting curved wooden foot rests; 4⅜″ H (Author).

(Above) **1444. FOOT STOVE, c.1740–1830:** The popular wooden frame with its perforated tinned-iron center (charcoal pan inside); note also the usual iron wire handle; both are 6″ H. (Right) **1445. BOOTJACKS:** A simple necessity in every home for removing boots. (Left) **1446. CLOTHES BRUSH, c.1700–1720:** Heavy clothing was usually cleaned by brushing; note these sharp turnings from the William & Mary period; 8¼″ L.

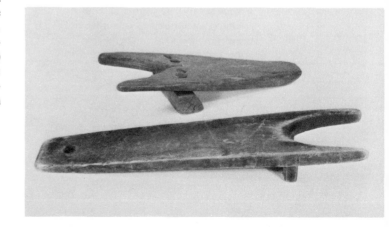

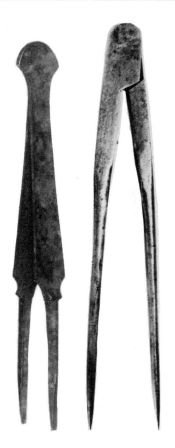

(Upper left) **1447. FOOT STOVE, Marked "1761":** This box is of oak instead of tin; perforations in its front create the date "1761"; New England; 6″ H (Conn. Historical Society).

(Upper right) **1448. FOOT STOVE, c.1790–1830:** A round combination of wood and tinned iron; it includes the usual interior pan to hold coals; 6½″ H (Deerfield Memorial Hall Museum, PVMA).

(Left) **1449. BABY RATTLE, c.1750–1850:** A country baby rattle from interlocking wooden panels, projecting ends, and a chamfered handle; 6″ L.

(Far right) **1450. DIVIDERS (SCRIBE), c.1740–1840:** Iron dividers were handy in the home for marking distances and scribing circular forms.

(Near right) **1451. TWEEZERS, c.1750–1820:** Early scalloped tweezers of iron; 5″ L.

(Left) **1452. TALLY BOARD, c.1750–1800:** The "tally" was a counting record for tabulating; this pine board has a handle, chamfered upper edges, and three rows of twenty evenly-spaced holes (plus three at the top for the counting pegs); it should not be confused with similar game scorers; 12⅝″ L.

(Above) **1453. BRANDING IRONS, c.1750–1850:** Heated brands were a common means of permanently identifying property ranging from furniture to cattle; 16″, 13″ L.

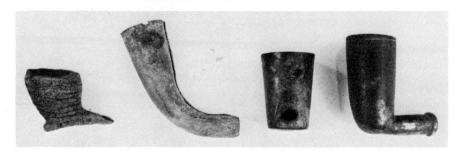

(Above) **1454. PIPE BOWL VARIATIONS:** (*Left to right*) (*1*) An excavated wooden bowl (stem gone); 7/8″ H; (*2*) lapped sheet brass (a reed or wooden stem was inserted in the end); 2″ H; (*3*) the cast-brass bowl has a removable stem hole; 1 1/4″ H; (*4*) a late-century right-angled iron bowl; 1 5/8″ H.

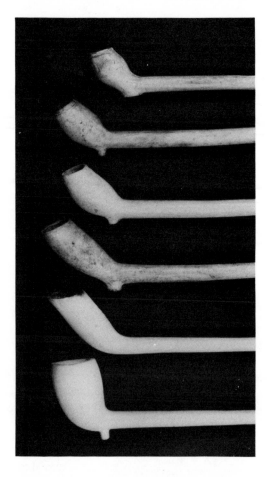

(Upper right) **1455. ENGLISH CLAY PIPE EVOLUTION:** During our period the bowls became larger, they pivoted up from an oblique angle (vs. the stem) to near 90° by 1800, and the stems lengthened—yet their hole diameter decreased (an important dating method). (*From top*) (*1*) c.1600–1640; (*2*) c.1620–1660; (*3*) c.1650–1680; (*4*) c.1680–1710; (*5*) c.1720–1820; (*6*) c.1770–1840 (Au.).
(Below) **1456. PIPE TAMPERS (STOPPERS), c.1750–1790:** These cast-brass pipe tampers used their disc to pack tobacco into the bowl (Private Coll.).

Smoking

The Indian practice of smoking tobacco had already achieved a fashionable status in Britain by the beginning of the 1600s. It was equally accepted by the American colonists, who imported most of their white clay pipes from England and Holland—supplemented with some domestic production by the mid-17th century.

Finding broken pipe stems and bowls in an archeological site is a welcome discovery because they are helpful in determing the age of that excavated level. Most pipes were used soon after being manufactured, which, in turn, can be reasonably dated by their bowl form, stem bore size (successively smaller in succeeding years), producer's marks, and decorative design.

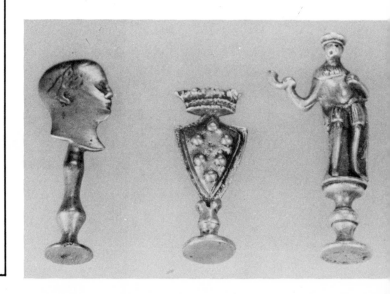

329

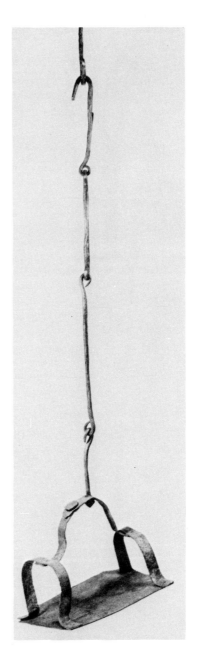

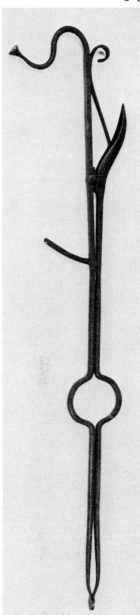

(Upper left) **1457. TOBACCO LEAVES:** Tobacco usually hung in the home; some considered the mellow aroma health giving—others that it discouraged house pests; it was also convenient for smokers to tear off a section when needed. (Upper center) **1458. TOBACCO TWIST:** Leaves were often twisted into a ropelike hank, which the smoker broke off and crumbled for smoking; these twists were sometimes mixed with vanilla, molasses, or licorice to enhance flavor; 5″ H.

(Near upper right) **1459. PIPE DRYING RACK, c.1640–1740:** Clay pipes were often washed and dried by the fire; this early drying rack (hung from a fireplace lug pole) would hold the pipes on its slope; legs were added to an open cylindrical frame in the later 1700s; base 7¼″ L.

(Far upper right) **1460. PIPE (EMBER) TONGS, c.1750–1800:** Such spring-tension tongs were made for lifting a small coal from the hearth to light a pipe (see **#1463**, **#1464**); 22″ L (Stanley-Whitman House, Farmington, Conn.).

TOBACCO BOXES: (Left) **1461. c.1750–1800:** This lead "coffin" shape includes a poorly defined head on its domed lid; 5″ H (Private Coll.). (Right) **1462. c.1760–1770:** A more precise iron box uses a beveled cover and brass handle; 4″ H.

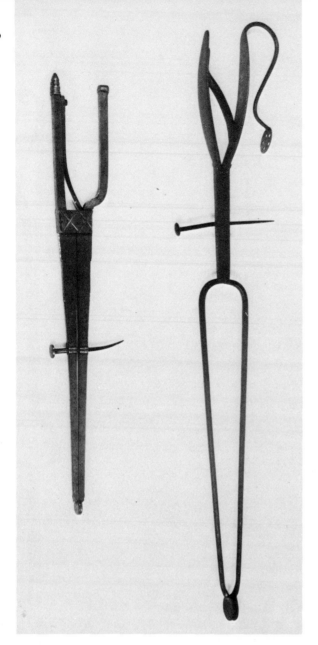

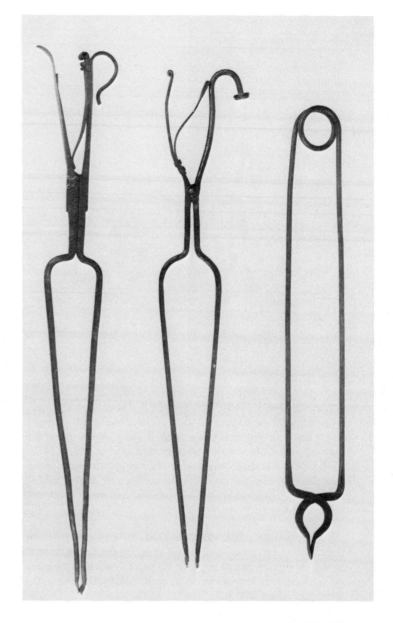

(Upper left) **1463. PIPE (EMBER) TONGS, c.1750–1800:** These long iron tongs were squeezed to grasp a live coal from the hearth for lighting a pipe; notice the disc on a curved extension to tamp tobacco into the pipe bowl, and the nail-like crosspiece ("rasp" or "rooter") that scraped residue from the bowl before relighting; 18″, 26″ L (Conn. Historical Society).

(Upper right) **1464. PIPE TONGS, c.1750–1800:** Three additional tongs which include a simple "safety-pin" form in wrought iron (*right*); 20″–23³/4″ L (Author).

(Right) **1465. DUTCH TOBACCO BOXES:** Typical Dutch hinged tobacco boxes in brass and copper (also see **#1466**); the upper decorated example dates **c.1700–1720,** the lower one is **c.1750–1760;** both are 6¹/2″ L.

331

(Above) **1466. TOBACCO CONTAINERS, c.1750–1760:** Smokers utilized a variety of small tobacco holders for easy access. (*Left to right*) (*1*) An oval tinned-iron box; (*2*) a buckskin pouch; (*3*) an elliptical horn box dated "1753"; (*4*) a Dutch brass/copper box with an embossed hinged cover (Neumann Coll., Valley Forge National Historical Park).

1467. TOBACCO/SNUFF BOXES: (*Right, going clockwise*) (*1*) c.1750–1780, an oval hinged-top brass box; (*2*) c.1770–1810, a Scottish "mull" (ram's horn with a silver-mounted lid) used to hold snuff; 2¹⁄₈″ H; (*3*) c.1760–1790, a black lacquered wooden container with a hinged lid; 2⁷⁄₈″ W; (*4*) c.1740–1810, a wooden base in a serrated leather wrap; pull-out cover; 2¹⁄₄″ H; (*5*) c.1750–1790, a popular wooden style with iron pin hinges; 3¹⁄₂″ L; (*6*) c.1750–1780, a brass snuff or tinderbox with engraved cover; 3⁷⁄₈″ W.

(Left) **1468. DUTCH TOBACCO BOX, c.1710–1730:** This Dutch brass tobacco holder was converted to a strongbox by adding the heavy iron clasp, hinges, and handle; 6¼″ Dia.

(Right) **1469. UTILITY CONTAINER, c.1720–1750:** A cast-brass octagonal storage box; 2⅝″ W.

(Below right) **1470. PAINTED CHECKER-BOARD, c.1750–1900.** (See #1474.) (Lower right) **1471. BONE DICE AND LEATHER SHAKERS, c.1780–1800;** 4¾″ H.

(Above) **1472. TOBACCO BOX, c.1750–1780:** A hinged-top brass tobacco box with two eyelets for attaching to a table or wall; 6⅜″ W.

Games and Playthings

Many of the 17th- and 18th-century playthings for children were small, locally made versions of familiar objects ranging from undersized furniture to miniature tableware (illustrated elsewhere under their appropriate classifications). These formal pieces were supplemented by more personal items from the family environment, i.e., dolls shaped from wood, corn husks or stuffed rags, carved whistles, wooden tops, clay marbles, whittled guns—or secret treasures such as a smooth rock, an abandoned bird's nest, or pressed field flower.

Adults often indulged their own spare moments with games that included dominoes, dice, cards, checkers, backgammon, or fox and geese. America was not a land given to idling, but such simple pleasures afforded them the luxury of precious well-earned moments of pause and geniality.

333

(Upper left) **1473. DOMINOES, c.1770–1820:** These were made of bone; their white and black halves are joined by brass pins.

(Upper right) **1474. FOX & GEESE BOARD:** A solitaire game still in use today; this incised board with applied sides is the reverse face of **#1470**.

(Left) **1475. PLAYING CARDS:** Typical playing cards of our period.

(Below) **1476. CLAY MARBLES:** A popular form in common use until the mid-1800s.

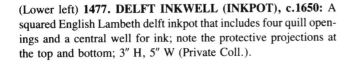

(Lower left) **1477. DELFT INKWELL (INKPOT), c.1650:** A squared English Lambeth delft inkpot that includes four quill openings and a central well for ink; note the protective projections at the top and bottom; 3″ H, 5″ W (Private Coll.).

(Lower center) **1478. DELFT INKWELL, c.1700–1740:** a European tin-glazed round form with sloping shoulders and a raised lip around the ink opening; its cracking surface is indicative of delft's vulnerability in use; 2$\frac{1}{2}$″ H (Author).

(Lower right) **1479. INK STORAGE BOTTLE, c.1790–1810:** Ink was kept as a powder and mixed with water when needed; this horn container held powder conveniently available; threaded cap; 1$\frac{7}{8}$″ H.

334

(Upper left) **1480. BRASS INKWELL, c.1680–1710:** An early cast-brass inkwell in a turned-baluster form; four holes for quill pens are visible, but the ceramic or glass insert is gone; 2⁷/₈″ H.

(Upper center) **1481. BRASS INKWELL, c.1700–1720:** A cylindrical form with the spread brim and base popular in the early 1700s; note its incised lines at midpoint; the typical bottom is soldered; 2³/₄″ H.

(Upper right) **1482. BRASS INKWELL, c.1690–1730:** An earlier version of the cylindrical body shape that adds a pivoting conical cover over its ink opening; holes for pens are omitted; body is 1¹/₂″ H (Author).

(Center row, left) **1483. PEWTER INKWELL, c.1780–1810:** The later pewter "capstan" form, which includes a decorative mid-ring and raised lip; its white ceramic inkpot is removable; 2″ H.

(Near left) **1484. BASALT INKWELL, c.1780–1810:** A drum-shaped design made of the black "basalt" stoneware that was perfected by Josiah Wedgwood; 2″ H.

(Left) **1485. PEWTER INKSTAND, c.1720–1760:** Two cylindrical holders are joined to a candle socket; the one (*left*) held the ink and pens, the other, sand or seals (the cover is missing); 5¹/₂″ H. **STONE INKWELLS:** Inkwells were also cut from soft stone. (Above right) **1486. c.1750–1810:** This includes four pen holes and a surplus ink ring; 1¹/₄″ H. (Right) **1487. c.1740–1800:** A higher-domed form without penholders; 2″ H (Au.).

(Below) **1490. SMALL WRITING SETS, c.1760–1820:** Such small combinations of writing instruments were useful in travel or a crowded home. (*Left to right*) (*1*) A brass case (cover at left) that held an ink bottle and two quills; 4¼″ H; (*2*) the papier-mâché cover is shown next to the separated inkpot, long pen-holder, and blade to sharpen the quills; 4¾″ H; (*3*) a turned horn holder in three sections for the sander, inkwell, and quill; 7″ H.

(Above) **INK SANDERS (CASTERS):** Early paper was made from linen that had its fibers separated to create a thick slurry in a liquid, and then was poured onto a fine screen which retained the solids that dried as a sheet of paper; being acid-free, it is more durable than today's product; most writing was done with ink and a quill pen; to help dry the ink, absorbent sand or ground pumice was sprinkled over it. (Above left) **1488. c.1720–1750:** A bulbous cast-brass sander that had no base openings—it was filled with sand through the top holes; 2¼″ H; (Above right) **1489. c.1740–1800:** A popular baluster-turned wooden sander with a dished top; 3½″ H.

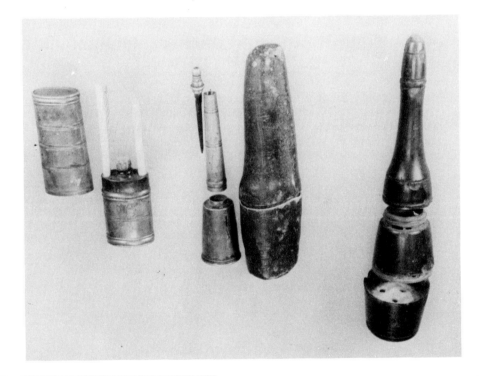

(Left) **1491. DESK STAND (STANDISH), c.1775–1795:** The "standish" was a stand containing writing materials; this brass Spanish example has three pots—(*left*) a sander; (*center*) holes for the quills or steel-nibbed pens, and ink; (*right*) a holder for sealing wax or "wafers" (thin discs to seal letters or receive seal impressions); 9″ W.

(Upper left) **1492. DESK STAND (STANDISH), c.1770–1790:** A Spanish brass stand more suited to the better country homes; note its handle and candle, as well as the usual pen and ink, sand, and sealing wax pots; 6³/4″ H (Private Coll.).

(Upper right) **1493. DESK STAND, c.1770–1790:** Another Spanish standish, but on a chamfered wooden platform; 8³/4″ H (Private Coll.).

(Center left) **1494. PORTABLE DESK, c.1770–1790:** An English wooden writing box covered in leather; it includes brass fittings and compartments (lined with wallpaper) that held writing materials (see **#181**) (Private Coll.).

(Right) **1495. PEWTER STANDISH, c.1760–1840:** A popular double-lidded form for writing accessories. (Below) **1496. PEN-KNIFE, c.1760–1790:** A folding knife with a blade designed to sharpen quill points.

337

DOCUMENT SEALS: Cut with appropriate designs, they were pressed into warm wax to seal or validate a document. (Upper left) **1497. c.1740–1800:** (*Left*) The fob seal that often hung on a watch chain or cord; (*right*) a brass ring seal with handle. (Upper right) **1498. c.1750–1820:** Disc seals mounted on baluster handles; 3″–4¼″ H (Author).

(Left) **1499. BRASS WAX JACK (TAPER JACK), c.1780:** An English stand that had a candlelike wax taper coiled around its post; when lighted, the end (some remains here) dripped the sealing wax (Smithsonian Institution). (Right) **1500. LEAD MARKER:** Soft lead was often hammered into a thin shape as a crude pencil.

(Lower left) **1501. ALMANACS, 1788, 1795:** These annual compendiums of facts, observations, wisdom, and predictions were widely used in country homes; 4″ x 7″ (Private Coll.). (Lower right) **1502. FARMER'S RECORD BOOK, 1789–1795:** A typical farm workbook from the Mohawk Valley (Private Coll.).

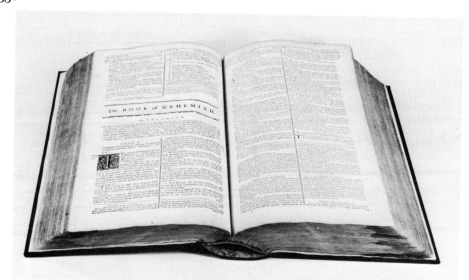

(Left) **1503. FAMILY BIBLE, 1775:** The Bible served as a constant reinforcement for the deep religious faith in most families—and often as a record of their genealogy; this large ''Universal Family Bible'' (London, 1775), still contains handwritten notes of births and deaths through several generations; 15¼" x 9½".

(Right) **1504. BOOKS:** A library was extremely rare, but selective books were not uncommon and generally shared; illustrated here is a bound volume of ''The Spectator'' (London, 1729), and ''The Duties of All Military Officers'' (Philadelphia, 1776).

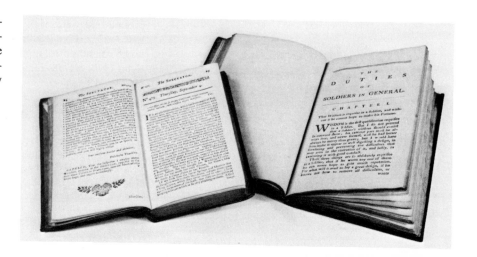

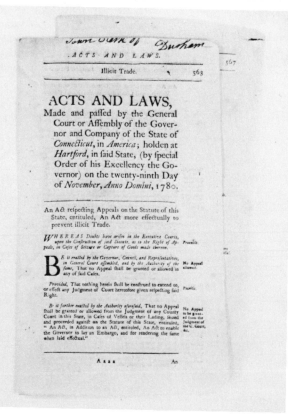

(Left) **1505. PAMPHLETS & POLITICAL CARTOONS:** These could be as vitriolic in those times as now, and reached new heights as America's Revolution began, as seen (*far left*) in this English example, ''News from America, or the Patriots in the Dumps'' (Nov. 1776; following Washington's evacuation of New York City); (*near left*) a reprint of ''Acts & Laws of the Connecticut Legislature'' (1780) as dispersed to the towns and rural areas.

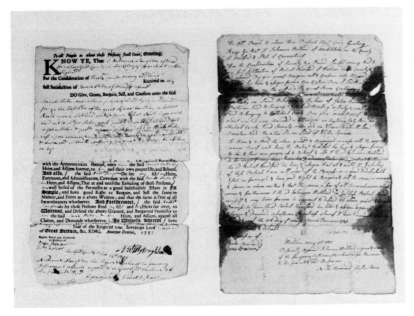

(Above) **1506. LAND DEEDS:** One of the critical documents in a country home was the land deed. (*Left*) A printed form with specifics added for property in Windsor, Conn. (1753); (*right*) a simple letter of transfer from Haddam, Conn., in 1781. (Upper right) **1507. NEWSPAPER:** This typical 4-page newspaper from Cambridge, Mass., (Aug. 3, 1775) is understandably dominated by the Revolution's outbreak; advertisements commonly appeared on the front page, and important news was often relegated to the inside; 15″ x 10″ (Author).

(Left) **1508. MAP:** An English engraved map of North America published in 1763 at the end of the French & Indian War; 15″ x 11″; it has been hand colored (not uncommon) in watercolors; note the line along the ridges of the Allegheny Mountains intended as a final limit in the colonists' westward migration—a vain effort to stem the vigor of a free people moving unceasingly toward creating a nation of world destiny.

NOMENCLATURE REFERENCE

TALL CLOCK

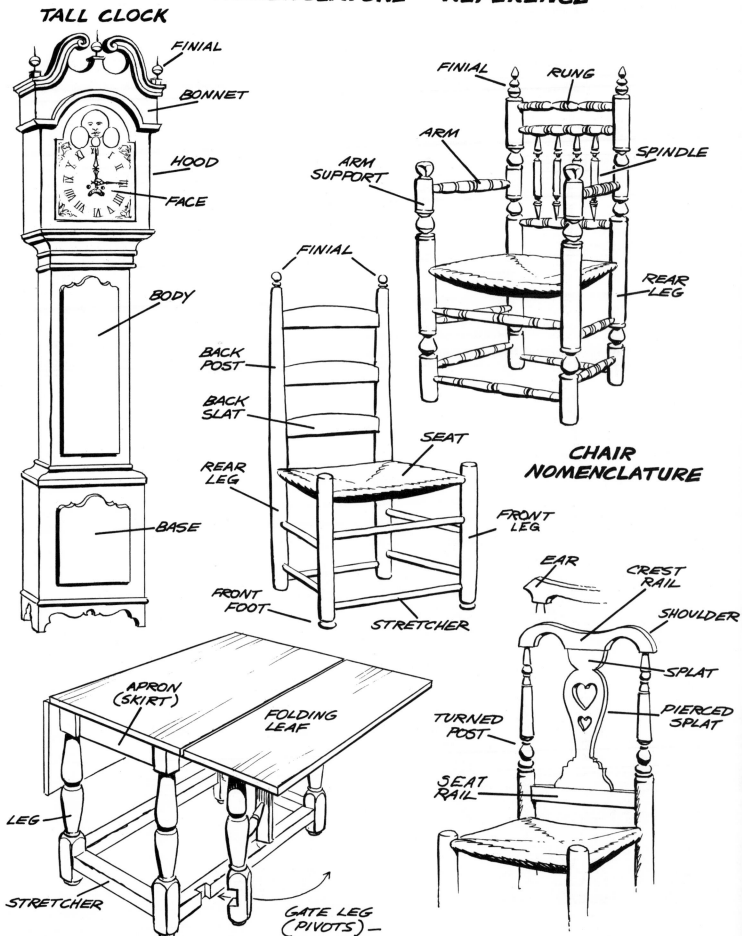

FINIAL

BONNET

HOOD

FACE

BODY

BASE

FINIAL

RUNG

ARM

ARM SUPPORT

SPINDLE

REAR LEG

FINIAL

BACK POST

BACK SLAT

REAR LEG

SEAT

CHAIR NOMENCLATURE

FRONT LEG

FRONT FOOT

STRETCHER

EAR

CREST RAIL

SHOULDER

SPLAT

PIERCED SPLAT

TURNED POST

SEAT RAIL

APRON (SKIRT)

FOLDING LEAF

LEG

STRETCHER

GATE LEG (PIVOTS)

341

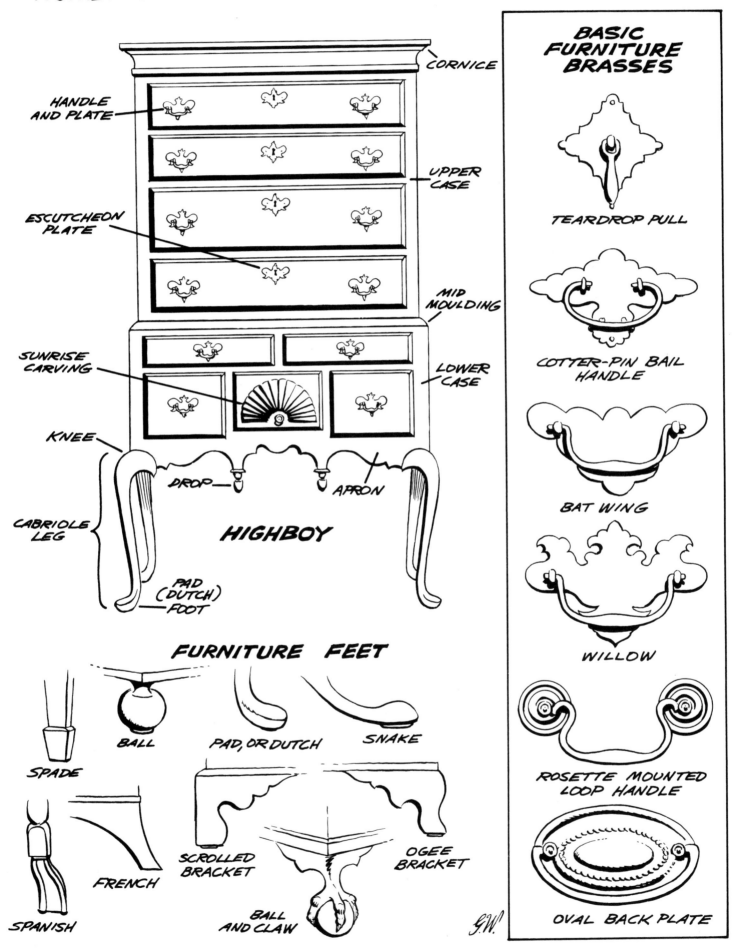

NOMENCLATURE REFERENCE

HANDLE AND PLATE

ESCUTCHEON PLATE

SUNRISE CARVING

KNEE

CABRIOLE LEG

PAD (DUTCH) FOOT

CORNICE

UPPER CASE

MID MOULDING

LOWER CASE

DROP

APRON

HIGHBOY

BASIC FURNITURE BRASSES

TEARDROP PULL

COTTER-PIN BAIL HANDLE

BAT WING

WILLOW

ROSETTE MOUNTED LOOP HANDLE

OVAL BACK PLATE

FURNITURE FEET

SPADE

BALL

PAD, OR DUTCH

SNAKE

FRENCH

SPANISH

SCROLLED BRACKET

OGEE BRACKET

BALL AND CLAW

G.W.

NOMENCLATURE REFERENCE

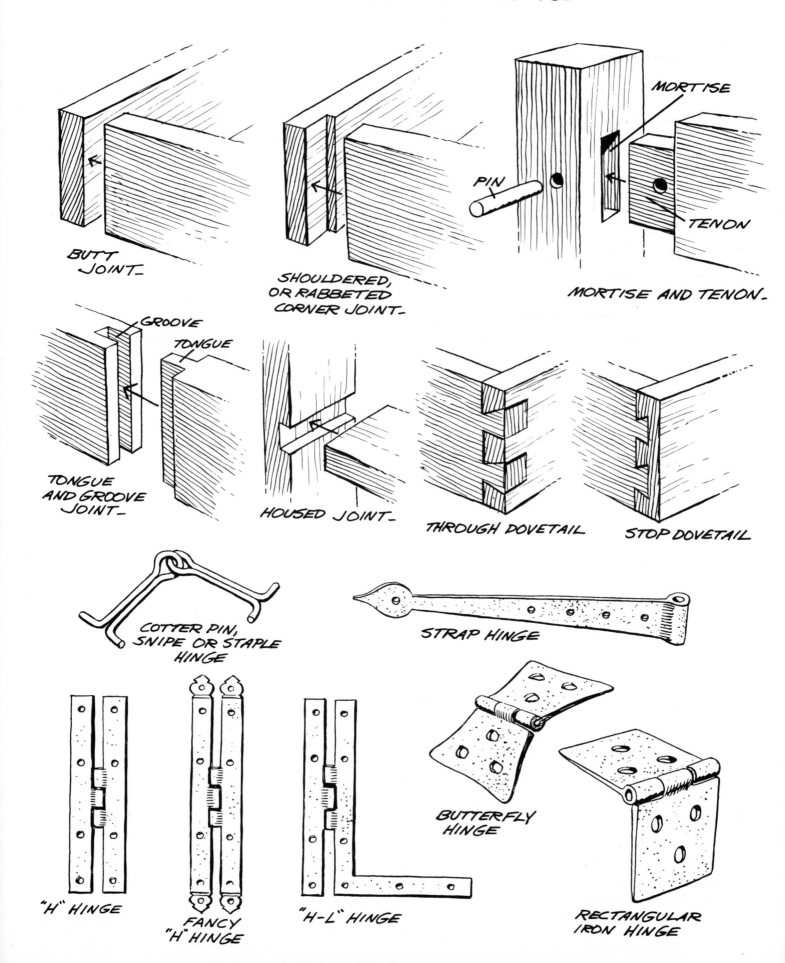

BUTT JOINT

SHOULDERED, OR RABBETED CORNER JOINT

MORTISE AND TENON

MORTISE

PIN

TENON

TONGUE AND GROOVE JOINT

GROOVE

TONGUE

HOUSED JOINT

THROUGH DOVETAIL

STOP DOVETAIL

COTTER PIN, SNIPE OR STAPLE HINGE

STRAP HINGE

"H" HINGE

FANCY "H" HINGE

"H-L" HINGE

BUTTERFLY HINGE

RECTANGULAR IRON HINGE

❦ GLOSSARY ❦

APPLIED: A piece attached to the basic surface of an item, e.g., applied moldings on furniture

APRON: The horizontal boards that link the legs, usually just below a tabletop, or at the base of a case piece

BALL FOOT: A ball-shaped foot popular on William & Mary–period furniture

BALUSTER TURNING: A turning that includes a narrow neck that flares out into a bulbous shape

BAMBOO TURNING: A form turned to resemble the joints found in bamboo

BATTEN: A strip of wood fastened across one or more boards as a cleat

BEADING: A narrow half-round molding cut into, or applied to an edge

BECKET: A rope handle

BEDSTEAD: The frame of a bed

BLANKET CHEST: A simple storage chest, usually with a lid and bottom drawer

BONNET TOP: A top on furniture having a cyma-curved arch form from each side that leads to an open center

BOSS: A convex ornament applied as decoration to early furniture

BRACED ARM: A chair arm set back from the seat front

BRACKET FOOT (or BRACKET BASE): A base of flat boards cut in various scrolled, molded, or plain designs

BRAZIER: A small, open-topped, portable stove

BREADBOARD END: A transverse piece of wood attached across the end of a tabletop or door to lessen warping and conceal the ends of the wood

BUN FOOT: A ''flattened'' ball foot

CABRIOLE LEG: A curving leg with a knee at the top and a narrow ankle, usually ending in a Dutch or pad-type foot

CARPET: An expensive covering mostly spread on furniture rather than the floor in colonial times

CARTOUCHE: An ornamental or identifying frame-like shape that was carved, inlaid, or stamped into a surface

CASE PIECE: Furniture whose basic structure is boxlike, e.g., a chest-of-drawers

CHAMFER: A beveled edge on a panel, leg, beam, etc.

CHARGER: A large plate for carrying and serving food

CHASING: An engraving technique which displaces the metal as against the usual ''engraving'' that cuts it out

CHIP-CARVING: Decorating by a series of low-relief patterns cut or chipped from a surface or edge

CLEAT: A strip attached to a flat surface to strengthen it or prevent warping

CLUB FOOT: A heavy pad foot

COMB PIECE: The shaped crest rail on a fanback or comb-back Windsor chair

CORNICE: The topmost horizontal molding on a tall piece of furniture

COVE MOLDING: A concave style of cornice molding

CREST RAIL: The upper crosspiece between the back posts of certain chairs

CYMA CURVE: A curved form of which one-half is concave in profile, and the other half is convex

DENTIL MOLDING: Furniture molding that resembles widely spaced teeth

DROP: A turned pendantlike attachment usually found on the base of highboys

DUTCH FOOT: See PAD FOOT.

EAR: The end of a crest rail or comb piece protruding beyond a chair's back post or spindles

EARTHENWARE: Pottery vessels made from common clay (earth)

ESCUTCHEON: A brass plate usually surrounding a keyhole

344

EWER: A large pitcher, traditionally combining a long neck with a bulbous body

FENDER: A fencelike form set before the fire to keep coals from the floor

FINIAL: An ornamental turning or terminal on exposed points of furniture

FIREBACK: A cast-iron plate set against the rear wall of a fireplace to help reflect heat and protect the masonry

FIRE PAN: A metal holder to carry live coals from one source to another

FLOORCLOTH: A canvas base painted in various designs to create a floor covering

FLUTING: A series of half-round parallel grooves cut into a surface (the opposite of REEDING)

FRETWORK: Ornamental carving that is often pierced to create a latticework

FRIESIAN CARVING: A style of geometric carving used in America and Europe—named for an area in Holland that favored it

GADROONING: A decorative series of fluted elements in a molding or raised surface

GRAIN PAINTING: Paint applied to imitate wood grain

GRIDIRON: A portable grate to hold meat for broiling

GRISSET: A container to collect dripping meat fats and juices during cooking

INCISED CARVING: Designs cut down into a surface

INLAY: The insertion of decorative wood, metal, ivory, or wax into a surface

LIP: The extension of an edge, as the expanded front of a drawer to cover its surrounding gap from the frame

LUNETTES: Carved designs of intersecting semicircles

MARLBOROUGH LEG: A squared block foot found on some Chippendale period furniture

MOLDING: A decorative projection added along an edge or between elements of furniture

MORTISE AND TENON: Joining two pieces by inserting an extension of one piece (tenon) into a socket hole (mortise) of the other; usually secured by a pin piercing both

OGEE BRACKET FOOT: A version of the bracket foot that curves outward in a modified S shape

PAD FOOT: A flattish semi-oval foot, usually projecting from the end of a tapering leg

PATINA: The color and age character of a surface

PEEL: A broad, thin wood or iron form with a long handle, used to enter and remove items from the oven

PIGGIN: A wooden vessel with one long stave extending upward to act as a handle

PIPKIN: A small earthenware pot

PLANK SEAT: A chair seat made from one piece of wood

PORRINGER: A small short-handled pan or basin for eating or mixing

POSNET: A small skillet, usually on three short legs

REEDING: A decorative series of parallel convex half-rounded moldings of equal width (the opposite of FLUTING)

RUG: A cover for the bed or table

RUNDLET: A small cylindrical canteen or barrel

RUNNER: The horizontal sidepiece on which a drawer slides

RUSH SEAT: A seat made of twisted and woven marsh grass

SADDLE SEAT: Usually a Windsor chair plank seat with a dished center and median ridge at the front

SALAMANDER: A long-handled browning iron for meat or pastry

SAUCEPAN: A small skillet with a long handle

SAUSAGE TURNINGS: Turnings that resemble sausage links; mostly as chair stretchers

SCONCE: A hanging light holder made of a back plate from which a candle holder extends

SCRUBBED TOP: A tabletop that has acquired a whitish bleached-out color from years of scrubbing with water and cleaning materials

SECONDARY WOODS: Wood used for the interior and less visible parts of furniture

SHADOW MOLDING: A reverse molding form cut into a surface

SHOE FOOT: A rail-like foot that projects out beyond the width of a piece of furniture

SINGLE-ARCH MOLDING: An applied half-round molding

SIX-BOARD CHEST: Any chest constructed of six boards

SKILLET: A small metal pot having a long handle; often on three legs

SKIMMER: A broad spoonlike implement perforated with holes for stirring or lifting solids from a liquid

SLICE: See PEEL.

SLIP SEAT: A rush or upholstered seat that can be removed from the seat rails

SLIPPER FOOT: Like a pad foot, but with a pointed toe that resembles a slipper

SNAKE FOOT: An elongated curving foot; mostly on candle stands and tilt tables

SPANISH FOOT: A scrolled, outward-curving foot usually found with a turned and blocked leg (popular with the English during the William & Mary and Queen Anne periods)

SPINDLES: Vertical turned or flattened uprights used in the backs of chairs

SPIT: A long rod on which meat is held before the fire

SPLAT: A flat vertical piece forming the center of a chair back

SPLAY: The outward angle of chair or table legs

SPLINT SEAT: A seat of thin interwoven strips of hickory or similar wood

STRETCHER: A horizontal support that joins and braces furniture legs

THUMB-NAIL MOLDING: Molding cut along the edge of a board similar to an inverted thumb in cross section; common on chest lids

TILL: A small storage compartment as found inside many blanket chests

TOLE: Tinware; sheet iron coated with tin

TRAMMEL: An adjustable hanging device; usually supporting pots, griddles, or lamps

TREEN: Small household items of wood

TRENCHER: A wooden plate

TRIVET: A metal stand to support a vessel, usually by the fire

TURNED: Shaped on a lathe

VENEER: A thin layer of wood glued over a base

WAINSCOT: Paneled construction in a chest, chair, settee, wall, etc.

BIBLIOGRAPHY

This list does not include all of the sources employed in preparing this book. It is a compilation of the major references, and an indication of the range of the material studied.

I. TEXTS

American Antiques from the Israel Sack Collection, Vols. I–V. Highland House, Inc., Washington, D.C.

The American Hearth. The Broome County Historical Society, New York.

American Woodenware and Other Primitives. E. G. Warman Publishing Co., Uniontown, Penn., 1974.

Aronson, Joseph. *The Encyclopedia of Furniture*. Crown Publishers, New York, 1979.

Avery, Amos G. *New England Clocks at Old Sturbridge Village*. Old Sturbridge, Inc., Sturbridge, Mass., 1966.

The Blacksmith Artisan Within the Early Community. Pennsylvania Historical and Museum Commission, Harrisburg, Penn., 1976.

Bolton, Ethel Stanwood, and Eva Johnston Coe. *American Samplers*. Weathervane Books, New York, 1973.

Bridenbaugh, Carl. *The Colonial Craftsman*. The University of Chicago Press, Chicago, Ill., 1964.

Brown, Margaret Kimball. "Glass from Fort Michilimackinac: A Classification for Eighteenth Century Glass." *The Michigan Archaeologist*, Sept.-Dec. 1971.

Butler, Joseph T. *American Furniture*. Triune Books, London, 1973.

Card, Devere A. *The Use of Burl in America*. Munson-Williams-Proctor Institute, Utica, N.Y., 1971.

Cooke, Lawrence S. *Lighting in America*. Universe Books, New York, 1975.

Cooper, Ronald G. *English Slipware Dishes 1650–1850*. New York/Transatlantic Arts, New York, 1968.

Cotterell, Howard Herschel. *Old Pewter, Its Makers and Marks*. Charles E. Tuttle Co., Rutland, Vt., 1963.

Cotterell, Howard Herschel, Adolphe Riff, and Robert M. Vetter. *National Types of Old Pewter*. Weathervane Books, New York, 1972.

Davidson, Marshall B. *The American Heritage History of Colonial Antiques*. American Heritage Publishing Co., New York, 1967.

The Decorative Arts of New Hampshire. The New Hampshire Historical Society, Concord, N.H., 1973.

DeJonge, Eric. *Country Things from the Pages of the Magazine, Antiques*. Weathervane Books, New York, 1973.

Diderot, Denis. *L'Encyclopedie ou Dictionnaire Raisonne des Sciences, des Arts et des Metiers*. 1763.

Downs, Joseph. *American Furniture, Queen Anne and Chippendale Periods*. Bonanza Books, New York, 1952.

Earle, Alice Morse. *Home Life in Colonial Days*. Macmillan Publishing Co., New York, 1969.

Ebert, Katherine. *Collecting American Pewter*. Charles Scribner's Sons, New York, 1973.

Edwards, Ralph, and L.G.G. Ramsey. *The Connoisseur's Complete Period Guides*. Bonanza Books, New York, 1968.

Fales, Dean A., Jr. *American Painted Furniture 1660–1880*. E. P. Dutton & Co., New York, 1972.

Fales, Martha Gandy. *American Silver in the Henry Francis DuPont Winterthur Museum*. Winterthur, Del., 1958.

Filbee, Marjorie. *Dictionary of Country Furniture*. Hearst Books, New York, 1977.

Fredrick K. and Margaret R. Barbour's Furniture Collection. The Connecticut Historical Society, Hartford, Conn., 1963.

G. Dallas Coons Candlestick Collection. Valentine Museum, 1975.

George Dudley Seymour's Furniture Collection. The Connecticut Historical Society, Hartford, Conn., 1958.

Godden, Geoffrey A. *An Illustrated Encyclopedia of British Pottery and Porcelain*. Bonanza Books, New York, 1965.

Gordon, Elinor. *Chinese Export Porcelain*. Universe Books, New York, 1975.

Gould, Mary Earle. *Antique Tin and Tole Ware*. Charles E. Tuttle Co., Rutland, Vt., 1974.

———. *Early American Wooden Ware*. Charles E. Tuttle Co., Rutland, Vt., 1962.

———. *The Early American House*. Charles E. Tuttle Co., Rutland, Vt., 1965.

Greenlaw, Barry A. *New England Furniture at Williamsburg*. Colonial Williamsburg Foundation, Wiiiamsburg, Va., 1975.

Grimm, Jacob L. *Archaeological Investigation of Fort Ligonier 1960–1965*. Annals of Carnegie Museum, Pittsburgh, Penn., 1970.

Hanson, Lee, and Dick Ping Hsu. *Casemates and Cannonballs*. U. S. Dept. of the Interior, National Park Service, Washington, 1975.

Hayden, Arthur. *Chats on Cottage and Farmhouse Furniture*. A. A. Wyn, Inc., New York, 1950.

Hayward, Arthur H. *Colonial Lighting*. Dover Publications, New York, 1962.

Hudson, J. Paul. *Treasures from Jamestown*. Archeological Society of Virginia, Richmond, Va., 1980.

Hudson, Norman. *American Antiques*. A. S. Barnes & Co., Cranbury, N.J., 1972.

Hume, Audrey Noël, *Food*. The Colonial Williamsburg Foundation, Williamsburg, Va., 1978.

Hume, Ivor Noel. *Archaeology and Wetherburn's Tavern*. Colonial Williamsburg, Williamsburg, Va., 1969.

———. *Glass in Colonial Williamsburg's Archaeological Collections*. Colonial Williamsburg, Williamsburg, Va., 1968.

———. *A Guide to Artifacts of Colonial America*. Alfred A. Knopf, New York, 1970.

———. *Pottery & Porcelain in Colonial Williamsburg's Archaeological Collections*. The Colonial Williamsburg Foundation, Williamsburg, Va., 1966.

Hummel, Charles F. *With Hammer in Hand: The Dominy Craftsmen of East Hampton, New York*. Winterthur Museum and University Press of Virginia, Charlottesville, Va., 1968.

Kane, Patricia E. *Furniture of the New Haven Colony: The Seventeenth-Century Style*. The New Haven Colony Historical Society, April 1973.

———. *300 Years of American Seating Furniture*. New York Graphic Society, Boston, Mass., 1976.

Kauffman, Henry J. *American Copper & Brass*. Bonanza Books, New York, 1979.

Kerfoot, J. B. *American Pewter*. Houghton Mifflin Co., Boston, Mass., 1924.

Kettell, Russell Hawes. *The Pine Furniture of Early New England*. Dover Publications, New York, 1949.

Kirk, John T. *Early American Furniture*. Alfred A. Knopf, New York, 1979.

Kovel, Ralph M. and Terry H. *American Country Furniture 1780–1875*. Crown Publishers, New York, 1979.

———. *Dictionary of Marks, Pottery and Porcelain*. Crown Publishers, New York, 1979.

———. *A Directory of American Silver, Pewter and Silver Plate*. Crown Publishers, New York, 1979.

Langdon, William Chauncy. *Everyday Things in American Life 1607–1776*. Charles Scribner's Sons, New York, 1937.

Linen-Making in New England 1640–1860. Merrimack Valley Textile Museum, North Andover, Mass., 1980.

Lindsay, J. Seymour. *Iron and Brass Implements of the English and American House*. Alec Tiranti, London, 1970.

Little, Nina Fletcher. *Country Arts in Early American Homes*. E. P. Dutton & Co., New York, 1975.

———. *Floor Coverings in New England Before 1850*. Old Sturbridge Village, Sturbridge, Mass., 1972.

Lockwood, Luke Vincent. *Colonial Furniture in America, Vols. I, II*. Charles Scribner's Sons, New York, 1957.

Lyon, Irving W. *The Colonial Furniture of New England*. E. P. Dutton, New York, 1977.

MacDonald-Taylor, Margaret. *A Dictionary of Marks, Metalwork, Furniture, Ceramics*. Hawthorn Books, New York, 1968.

McClinton, Katharine Morrison. *Antique Collecting for Everyone*. Bonanza Books, New York, 1951.

McKearin, Helen, and Kenneth M. Wilson. *American Bottles and Flasks and Their Ancestry*. Crown Publishers, New York, 1978.

Mankowitz, Wolf. *Wedgwood*. B. T. Batsford, Ltd., London, 1954.

Marsh, Moreton. *The Easy Expert in American Antiques*. J. B. Lippincott Co., New York, 1978.

Michaelis, Ronald F. *Old Domestic Base-Metal Candlesticks*. Baron Publishing Co., Woodbridge, Suffolk, England, 1978.

Miller, Edgar G., Jr. *American Antique Furniture, Vols. I, II*. Dover Publications, New York, 1966.

Miller, J. Jefferson II, and Lyle M. Stone. *Eighteenth-Century Ceramics from Fort Michilimackinac*. Smithsonian Institution Press, Washington, D.C., 1970.

Miller, John C. *The First Frontier: Life in Colonial America*. Dell Publishing Co., New York, 1968.

Montgomery, Charles F. *American Furniture: The Federal Period*. Bonanza Books, New York, 1978.

———. *A History of American Pewter*. Weathervane Books, New York, 1973.

Montgomery, Charles F., and Patricia E. Kane. *American Art: 1750–1800 Towards Independence*. New York Graphic Society, Boston, Mass., 1976.

Morse, John D., ed. *Country Cabinetwork & Simple City Furniture*. Winterthur Museum and University Press of Virginia, Charlottesville, Va., 1970.

Neumann, George C. *Swords and Blades of the American Revolution*. Stackpole Books, Harrisburg, Penn., 1973.

Neumann, George C., and Frank J. Kravic. *Collector's Illustrated Encyclopedia of the American Revolution*. Stackpole Books, Harrisburg, Penn., 1975.

New England Begins: The Seventeenth Century, Vols. I–III. Dept. of American Decorative Arts and Sculpture; Museum of Fine Arts, Boston, Mass., 1982.

Nutting, Wallace. *American Windsors*. Cracker Barrel Press, Southampton, N.Y., 1917.

———. *The Clock Book*. Modern Books and Crafts, Inc., Green Farms, Conn., 1975.

————. *Furniture of the Pilgrim Century, Vols. I, II.* Dover Publications, New York, 1964.

————. *Furniture Treasury.* Macmillan Publishing Co., New York, 1974.

Ormsbee, Thomas H. *Field Guide to Early American Furniture.* Little, Brown & Co., Boston, Mass., 1951.

————. *The Windsor Chair.* Deerfield Books, New York, 1962.

Pain, Howard. *The Heritage of Country Furniture.* Van Nostrand Reinhold, Toronto, 1978.

Palmer, Brooks. *The Book of American Clocks.* Macmillan Publishing Co., New York, 1977.

Peal, Christopher A. *British Pewter and Britannia Metal.* Peebles Press, New York, 1971.

Pennington, David A., and Michael B. Taylor. *American Spinning Wheels.* The Shaker Press, Sabbathday Lake, Me., 1975.

Pennington, Samuel, Thomas M. Voss, and Lita Solis-Cohen. *Americana at Auction.* E. P. Dutton, New York, 1979.

Phipps, Frances. *The Collector's Complete Dictionary of American Antiques.* Doubleday & Co., Garden City, N.Y., 1974.

————. *Colonial Kitchens, Their Furnishings, and Their Gardens.* Hawthorn Books, New York, 1972.

Pinto, Edward H. *Treen and Other Wooden Bygones.* Bell & Hyman, London, 1979.

Quimby, Ian M. G., ed. *Arts of the Anglo-American Community in the Seventeenth Century.* Winterthur Conference Report 1974, University Press of Virginia, Charlottesville, Va., 1975.

————. *Ceramics in America.* Winterthur Conference Report 1972, University Press of Virginia, Charlottesville, Va., 1973.

Ramsey, L.G.G. *The Complete Encyclopedia of Antiques.* Hawthorn Books, New York, 1962.

Ray, Anthony. *English Delftware Pottery in the Robert Hall Warren Collection, Ashmolean Museum, Oxford.* Boston Book & Art Shop, Boston, Mass., 1968.

Roth, Rodris. *Floor Coverings in 18th Century America.* Smithsonian Press, Washington, D.C., 1967.

The Rushlight Club. *Early Lighting.* The Rushlight Club, Hartford, Conn., 1979.

St. George, Robert Blair. *The Wrought Covenant.* Brockton Art Center, Fuller Memorial, Brockton, Mass., 1979.

Santore, Charles. *The Windsor Style in America 1730–1830.* Running Press, Philadelphia, Penn., 1981.

Schiffer, Herbert, Peter, and Nancy. *Antique Iron.* Schiffer Publishing, Ltd., Exton, Penn., 1979.

————. *The Brass Book.* Schiffer Publishing, Ltd., Exton, Penn., 1978.

Schiffer, Nancy and Herbert. *Woods We Live With.* Schiffer Publishing, Ltd., Exton, Penn., 1977.

Schorsch, Anita. *The Art of the Weaver.* Universe Books, New York, 1976.

Shea, John G. *Antique Country Furniture of North America.* Van Nostrand Reinhold Co., New York, 1975.

Smith, Helen Everton. *Colonial Days and Ways.* The Century Co., New York, 1900.

Smith, Nancy A. *Old Furniture, Understanding the Craftsman's Art.* Little, Brown & Co., Boston, Mass., 1975.

Sonn, Albert H. *Early American Wrought Iron.* Bonanza Books, New York, 1979.

Sprackling, Helen. *Customs on the Table Top.* Old Sturbridge Village, Sturbridge, Mass., 1958.

Stillinger, Elizabeth. *The Antique Guide to Decorative Arts in America 1600–1875.* E. P. Dutton, New York, 1973.

Stone, Lyle M. *Fort Michilimackinac 1715–1781.* Michigan State University, East Lansing, Mich.,1974.

Swan, Susan Burrows. *A Winterthur Guide to American Needlework.* Crown Publishers, New York, 1976.

Thomas, John Carl. *American and British Pewter.* Universe Books, New York, 1972.

Trent, Robert. *Pilgrim Century Furniture, An Historical Survey.* Universe Books, New York, 1976.

Tunis, Edwin. *Colonial Craftsmen.* The World Publishing Co., Cleveland, Oh., 1965.

————. *Colonial Living.* The World Publishing Co., Cleveland, Oh., 1957.

Voss, Thomas M. *Antique American Country Furniture, A Field Guide.* Bonanza Books, New York, 1981.

Warwick, Edward, Henry C. Pitz, and Alexander Wyckoff. *Early American Dress.* Bonanza Books, New York, 1965.

Watkins, Laura Woodside. *Early New England Pottery.* Old Sturbridge Village, Sturbridge, Mass., 1966.

Watson, Aldren A. *Country Furniture.* New American Library, New York, 1974.

Weeks, Jeanne G., and Donald Treganowan. *Rugs and Carpets of Europe and the Western World.* Weathervane Books, New York, 1969.

Wilson, Kenneth M. *Glass in New England.* Old Sturbridge Village, Sturbridge, Mass., 1969.

Winchester, Alice. *How to Know American Antiques.* New American Library, New York, 1951.

Wyler, Seymour B. *The Book of Old Silver.* Crown Publishers, New York, 1937.

II. PERIODICALS

Bartlett, Margaret M. "Light of the Wick Turned the Trick."

The Antiques Journal, Nov. 1970.

Blackburn, Roderic H. "Branded and Stamped New York Furniture." *The Magazine Antiques*, May 1981.

Daniels, Bruce C. "Probate Inventories as a Source for Economic History in 18th Century Connecticut." *The Connecticut Historical Society Bulletin*, Jan. 1972.

Faust, Patricia. "Collecting Old Baskets." *Early American Life*, Dec. 1977.

Ginsburg, Benjamin. "Dating English Brass Candlesticks." *The Magazine Antiques*, Dec. 1969.

Goyne, Nancy A. "American Windsor Chairs: A Style Survey." *The Magazine Antiques*, April 1969.

Handler, Mimi. "Tea." *Early American Life*, August 1980.

Harlow, Henry J. "Signed and Labeled New England Furniture." *The Magazine Antiques*, Oct. 1979.

Hosley, William N., Jr., and Philip Zea. "Decorated Board Chests of the Connecticut River Valley." *The Magazine Antiques*, May 1981.

Hume, Ivor Noël. "The Rise and Fall of English Salt-Glazed Stoneware." *The Magazine Antiques*, Feb.-March 1970.

———. "Rouen Faience in Eighteenth-Century America." *The Magazine Antiques*, Dec. 1960.

Kaye, Myrna. "Marked Portsmouth Furniture." *The Magazine Antiques*, May 1978.

Kirk, John T. "The Tradition of English Painted Furniture." *The Magazine Antiques*, May 1980.

Lasansky, Jeanette. "Unusual Pennsylvania Ironware." *The Magazine Antiques*, Feb. 1981.

Little, Nina Fletcher. "Neat and Tidy: Boxes and Their Contents Used in Early American Households." *Early American Life*, Oct. 1980.

Neff, Merry. "Waffles & Wafers." *Early American Life*, Feb. 1982.

Papert, Emma N. "Baron Stiegel, Early American Industrialist." *Early American Life*, Dec. 1979.

Shaffer, Sandra C. "Sewing Tools in the Collection of Colonial Williamsburg." *The Magazine Antiques*, Aug. 1973.

Swan, Susan Burrows. "Collecting American Silver Spoons." *Early American Life*, 1980.

———. "Worked Pocketbooks." *The Magazine Antiques*, Feb. 1975.

Trent, Robert E. "Sources for the Heart-and-Crown Chairs." *The Magazine Antiques*, Feb. 1978.

Tyler, John D. "18th- and 19th-Century Cast-Iron Cooking Utensils." *Early American Life*, April 1978.

Ward, Gerald W. R. "American Pewter, Brass, and Iron in the Yale University Art Gallery." *The Magazine Antiques*, June 1980.

Wardwell, Allen. "One Hundred Years of American Tankards." *The Magazine Antiques*, July 1966.

Wiggins, David Bradstreet. "New England Wall Painting." *Antique Collecting*, July 1979.

INDEX

Alberti, Johann Phillip, 279
Ale Shoe, 285
Almanacs, 337
Andirons, 156–164
Apothecary Measure, 321
Armorial Tableware, 274
Art, 302–304

Ballermine Jugs, 261, 262
Band Box, 45
Banister-Back Chair, 98–102
Barrels, 221
Basins, 278; SHAVING 319
Baskets, 219, 220
Bassett, Frederick, 279
Batten Head, 306
Beakers, 280
Beaters, 216, 217
Becket, 20
Bed Keys, 14
Bedding, 11, 12, 312; SMOOTHER 15
Bedstead, 11–14; COT 14; FIELD 13, 14; FOLDING 13; PENCIL-POST 12, 14; TRUNDLE 12, 14
Bellows, 165
Benches, 121
Bible, 301, 338
Black Jack, 237
Blankets, 304, 312, 313
Bonnynge, Robert, 279
Boot Jack, 326
Borer, 215
Bottles, 288–291, 293, 294; SEALS 291
Bowls, 224, 225, 227, 228, 233, 234, 236, 249, 250, 255, 256, 262, 266, 268, 299, 270, 272, 275, 277, 282, 284
Boxes: BAND 45; DESK 45–49; PIPE 40; ROUND 233; TABLE 40; WALL 38–40
Branding Iron, 328
Brandy Warmer, 295
Braziers, 197, 198
Broilers, 186, 187, 188, 190, 195
Brooms, 199
Brushes: HEARTH 199; SHAVING 320; CLOTHES 326
Bucket, 221–223
Burl, 212, 223–225, 230
Busk Board, 302
Butter Patters, 206

Caldron, 177
Candles, 78, 79, 191; DIPPING 78; MOLDS 79
Candlestands, 58–60
Candlesticks, 61–72
Cannister, 248, 283
Canteens, 206, 231, 232, 237, 244, 282, 283
Canvas Work, 310, 323
Carder, 306
Cards, Playing, 333
Carpet, 53, 312

Cartoon, 338
Casters, 281
Cat, 189
Caudle, 254
Ceramic Tableware, 197, 237–275
Chairs, BANISTER-BACK 98–102; "BREWSTER" 86, 87; "CARVER" 86, 87, 88; CHAIR-TABLE 111, 112; CHIPPENDALE 107–109; CORNER 109, 110; QUEEN ANNE 103–107; ROCKING 88, 92, 93; SLATBACK 88–96; SPINDLE 86–88, 97, 102; WAINSCOT 86, 96, 97; WINDSOR 112–119; WING 120
Chambersticks, 69, 70
Chandeliers, 75
Chapin, Eliphalet, 52, 147
Chargers, 226, 254, 256, 257, 267, 277
Checker Board, 332
Chests, 16–30; BLANKET 16, 24–27; BOARD 16–20; CHESTS-OF-DRAWERS 16, 27–29; CHESTS-ON-CHESTS 16, 32; CHESTS-ON-FRAME 29, 30; "HADLEY" 22, 23, 46; "HATFIELD" 23; JOINED 20–23; LIQUOR 293; SPICE 209; "SUNFLOWER" 22; TABLE CHESTS 42–44; TEA 44
Chinoiserie, 268
Chocolate Pot, 283
Choppers, Food, 209, 217
Churns, 218
Clobbering, 271
Clocks, 151, 153, 154; KEY 154
Clothespins, 317
Coconut, 208, 237, 285
Coffee Pot, 266, 285
Coins, 322
Combs, 318
Compass, 152
Cooper, 223
Corkscrew, 292
Corn Husker, 215
Cotter Pin Hinges, 17, 18, 19, 23, 38
Country Antiques (definition), 7, 9
Courting Mirrors, 81, 84
Coverlets, 312, 313, 315
Cradles, 15, 16
Crane, 156, 166, 175
Creamware, 155, 238, 264–267
Cresset, 75
Crewel, 12, 307, 312, 324
Crimpers, 214
Crochet, 308
Cupboards, 34–37; CORNER 34, 36; COURT 34; PRESS 34; SPICE 209, WALL 34, 37
Cupping Glasses, 321
Cups, 206, 229, 230, 236, 247, 275, 283, 285, 291, 301
Curlers, 318, 319
Currency, 322
Cutting Boards, 215

Danforth, Joseph, 321
Decanters, 288, 293
Deeds, 339
Deerfield Chests, 23

Delftware, 155, 237, 254–261, 286, 319, 333
Dennis, Thomas, 20
Desk, 45–51; BOX 45–49; ON-FRAME 45, 50; PORTABLE 49, 336; SLANT TOP 45, 50, 51, 52; TABLE 51
Desk Stand, 335, 336
Dippers, 206, 207
Distaff, 305, 307
Dividers, 327
Dominoes, 333
Dough Box, 218
Dough Scraper, 215
Drawer Construction, 23, 136
Dredger, 281
Dressing Glasses, 85
Drop Spindle, 307
Drying Rack, 317
Dunlap Family, 32
Dutch Crown, 167
Dutch Oven, 183

Earthenware, 237–261, 264–269, 282, 286
Ewer, 261
Extinguisher, Candle, 76

Fabrics, 304–315
Faience, 237, 256–259
False Graining, 20
Fenders, 165
Fire Dogs (see Andirons)
Fire Pans, 169
Fireback, 164, 165
Firkin, 222
Flagon, 281
Flask, 248, 281, 292
Fleam, 321
Flip, 292, 295
Floor Coverings, 53; FLOOR CLOTH 53
Flower Brick, 259
Foot Stoves, 326, 327
Forks, 198, 203, 205, 299; TOASTING 204
Form, 86, 121
Fox & Geese, 301, 332, 333
Friesian Carving, 46
Funnels, 206, 216

Games, 301, 332, 333
Gerrish, B., 59
Glasses, Wine, 292, 293
Glassware, 288–296
Goblet, 285
Goffering Iron, 316
Gourds, 206
Grater, Food, 214
Grease Lamps, 54–58
Griddle, 189, 190
Gridiron, 190–193
Grinder, Coffee, 179
Grisset, 191, 192

"Hadley" Chest, 22, 23, 46
Hangings, Bed, 12
"Hatfield" Chest, 23
Heart & Crown Chairs, 101
Hearth, 155, 156, 175
Herbs, 208–211, 235
Hetchels, 305
Highboy, 16, 31, 32
Highdaddy, 30
Honing Stone, 320
Horn, 236, 301, 325, 333
Hot Water Plates, 278
Hubert, James, 153

Infusion Pots, 321
Ink, 333, 335
Inkwells, 333, 334

Jack Plane, 25, 49, 116
Jackfield Ware, 268
Jars, 244, 245, 258, 259, 292
Jigger, Pastry, 214
Joint Stool, 86, 122
Johnson, Guy, 303
Joined Chests, 20–23
Jugs, 240–245, 247, 261, 262, 263

Kas, 34
Keg, 221
Kettle, Iron, 176–179; TILTER 174, 182
Knife Case, 45
Knitting, 307, 308
Knives: 216; BELT 300; JACKKNIVES 300; PEN 336; TABLE 299

Ladles, 207, 208
Lamps: GREASE 54–58; HOLDERS 56; OIL 56, 73
Lantern Clock, 151, 153
Lanterns, 77, 78
Latten Spoon, 298
Lighting, 53–79; CANDLES 78, 79, 191; CANDLESTANDS 58–60; CANDLESTICKS 61–72; CHANDELIERS 75; CRESSETS 75; GREASE 54–58; HANGERS 60; HOLDERS 71, 72, 74; LANTERNS 77, 78; RUSH, SPLINT 57–60; SCONCES 73, 74; SNUFFERS 76, 77; TINDER BOXES 167, 168
Limner, 304
Linen, 11, 53, 304–308, 310, 311, 313–315, 318
Liquor Chests, 293, 294
Looking Glass, 80–86; COURTING MIRROR 81, 84
Loom, 304, 307; TAPE 309
Lowboy, 30, 31
Lug Pole, 156, 166

Magnifying Glass, 318
Maiolica, 237, 260, 261
Map, 339
Marbles, 333
Marrow Spoon, 298
Measures, 263, 281, 284, 286, 321

352

Medical, 321
Medicine, 211, 291
Mercantile System, 276
Mezzotint, 303
Miniature Portraits, 303
Mirrors (see Looking Glass)
Mocaware, 272
Molds, Candle, 79
Money, 322
Monteith, 284
Mortar & Pestle, 155, 211, 212
Mug, 247, 248, 261, 263, 265, 280, 283, 284, 296
Mulling Iron, 198
Music, 301

Nails, 53
Newspaper, 339
Niddy Noddy, 307
Nursing Bottle, 280

Oil Lamps, 56, 73
Opaque-White Glass Tableware, 296
Oven, 171, 175: DUTCH 183; REFLECTOR 188; WARMING 188

Paddles: BUTTER 217; WASHING 316
Pamphlet, 338
Pans, 180–184, 251, 252, 282; FRYING 180, 183; SAUCEPAN 181; HANGING 184
Paper, 335
Peacock, F., 152
Pearlware, 238; 267, 268
Peel, 171, 206
Periods (Furniture), 10
Pestle, 211, 212
Pewterware, 155, 276–282, 287, 334
Piecrust Table, 150
Piggen, 222
Pintle Hinge, 17
Pipe Bowls, 328
Pipe Boxes, 40
Pipe Drying Rack, 329
Pipe Tampers, 328
Pitchers, 230, 246, 247, 258, 265, 273, 275
Platters, 228, 229, 253, 267, 273, 277
Plates, 251–258, 263–268, 270, 278, 282, 286, 293
Pocketbooks, 323, 324
Poker, 170, 198
Porcelain: CHINESE 155, 237, 239, 268–271, 274, 275; EURO-PEAN HARD PASTE 155, 239, 269, 271–275; SOFT PASTE 155, 239, 269, 271–273
Porringer, 286, 287; TABLE TOP 135
Porter, Daniel, 154
Portraits, 303, 304
Posset Cup, 254, 259
Pot, 175–178, 243, 246, 252; CHOCOLATE 283; COVERS 177; LIFTERS 178; MARKINGS 175; PUSHERS 185; WARMERS 187
Pot Hooks, 166
Pottery, 237–269, 273
Powder Horns, 301, 302
Press, Cheese, 219

Pressing Irons, 315, 316
Prints (Butter, Cookie), 215
Prints, Fabric, 311
Pudding Molds, 249
Punch Bowls, 256, 270, 272, 274
Purse, 322, 323

Quilts, 315

Racks: SPOON 40, 41; HOOK 199
Rattle, 206, 327
Razors, 320
Record Book, 337
Redware, 155, 237, 238, 240–254
Reverse Glass Painting, 303
Rinsers, Wine, 294
Roasters: APPLE 187; BIRD 188; CHESTNUT 179; COFFEE 179
Roberts, Gideon, 154
Rocking Chair, 88, 92, 93
Rolling Pin, 214
Rug, Bed (see Coverlet)
Rundlet, 232, 248
Rushlights, 57–60

Sad Irons, 315
Salamander, 206
Salt, 211, 226, 232, 235
Salter, 235, 236, 258, 286, 296
Sampler, 304, 310
Sander, 335
Sand Glass, 151, 152
Sauce Boat, 264
Saucepan, 181
Saucer, 265, 266, 269, 275
Scales, 213
Scissors, 309
Sconce, 73, 74
Scoop, 217
Scrub Board, 316
Seals, Document, 337
Seats, Woven Types, 90
Secretary, 45, 52
Settees, 119
Settle-Table, 112
Settles, 124, 125
Sewing, 304
Sgraffito, 237, 241, 244, 247, 252
Shakers, 281, 282
Shaving, 301, 319
Sheffield Plating, 69, 155, 285
Shelf: FLOOR 42; WALL 42; WARMING 187
Shoe Feet, 16, 18, 35
Shoe Horns, 325
Shovels, Hearth, 170, 171
Sibley, S., 154
Sieve, 220
Silhouette, 302
Silver, 155, 285, 287
Simpson, Ralph, 254
Skewer, 172, 173; HOLDERS 172

Skewer Rests, 155, 156, 158
Skillet, 181, 182
Skimmer, 202
Slat Back (*see* Chairs)
Slice, 171
Slipware, 155, 237, 240–244, 246–254
Smoking, 328–332
Snuff, 291 (*see* Tobacco)
Snuffer, Candle, 76
Soap, 191
Soap Scoop, 316
Soapstone, 286, 334
Sofa, 125
Spectacles, 317
Spider, 183
Spinning Wheel, 304–306; FLAX 305; WOOL 306
Spit, 172, 173, 177, 188, 189
Spit Dog, 156
Splint Holder, 57
Spoon Rack, 40, 41
Spoons, 200, 201, 203, 206, 297, 298; MARKINGS 203
Standish, 335, 336
Stands, 143–151, 184, 186, 198
Stiegel, Wm. Henry, 292
Stirrers, 202, 216
Stoneware, 155, 237–240, 261–264, 334
Stool, 86, 122, 123
Strikers, 168
Sugar, 211, 232, 235; BOWL 234, 272, 275, 280, 284; CUTTERS 233, 234; LOAF 233
Sundial, 151, 152
Sunflower Chest, 22
Swift (*see* Winder)
Swigler (*see* Rundlet)

Table Boxes, 40, 42
Table-Chair, 92
Table Chest, 42–44
Table Cloth, 311
Table Desk, 51
Tables, 127–143; BUTTERFLY 130; CARD 141; DROP-LEAF 128, 139, 140; GATE-LEG 128–130; PEMBROKE 141, 142; SAW-BUCK 131; SIDE TABLE 133–135, 142; STANDS 143–151; SWING LEG 139–141; TAVERN 132–134; TEA TABLE 135, 149–151; TRESTLE 127, 128; WINDSOR 134
Tall Clock, 151, 153, 154
Tally Board, 327
Tankard, 229, 278, 279
Tea, 235
Tea Caddy, 44, 248, 273
Tea Cups, 265, 266, 271, 275
Tea Kettle, 174
Teapots, 265, 266, 267, 270, 271, 274, 275, 279, 281, 285

Tick, 11
Tiles, 259
Till, 18, 19
Tinder Box, 72, 167, 168
Toasters, 193–195
Toasting Forks, 204
Tobacco, 328, 329; BOXES 167, 329–332
Toby Jugs, 269
Toddy Iron, 198, 295
Toft, Thomas, 254
Toleware, 282–284
Tongs, 169, 170, 329, 330
Tooth Extractor, 321
Tracy, 119
Trammel, 166
Transfer-Printed Ceramics, 238, 266, 267, 273
Tray, 229, 284
Tree Trunk Chair, 95
Treen, 223
Trenchers, 226, 227
Trivets, 184–186
Trunk, 33
Tuck Table, 129
Tumblers, 292–295
Tureen, 273
Turkey Carpet, 53
Turners, 205, 206, 223
Tweezers, 327

Wafer Iron, 195, 196
Waffle Iron, 196
Wagon Seat, 126
Wainscot: CHEST 20; CHAIR 96, 97
Walker, Child's, 126
Wall Boxes, 38–40
Warming Pans, 325
Watch Box, 152
Watch, Pocket, 152
Wax Jack, 337
Wedgwood, 238, 264, 266, 273
Wheel Boys, 306
Whieldon, 238, 268
Whitesmith, 201, 203, 282
Wig, 318
Will, William, 279, 280
Winder, 307, 308
Windsor Chairs, 112–119
Wing Chairs, 120
Wool, 53, 304, 306–308, 310, 312–315, 318
Writing Sets, 335, 336

Yoke, 223